ANALYTICAL READING INVENTORY

Eighth Edition

*Comprehensive Standards-Based Assessment
for All Students
Including Gifted and Remedial*

Mary Lynn Woods
University of Indianapolis

Alden J. Moe
Rollins College

PEARSON

Merrill
Prentice Hall

Upper Saddle River, New Jersey
Columbus, Ohio

Vice President and Executive Publisher: Jeffery W. Johnston
Senior Editor: Linda Ashe Bishop
Senior Production Editor: Mary M. Irvin
Design Coordinator: Diane C. Lorenzo
Senior Editorial Assistant: Laura Weaver
Project Coordination and Text Design: Lea Baranowski, Carlisle Editorial Services
Cover Designer: Candace Rowley
Cover Image: SuperStock
Production Manager: Pamela D. Bennett
Director of Marketing: David Gesell
Marketing Manager: Darcy Betts Prybella
Marketing Coordinator: Brian Mounts

This book was set in Palatino by Carlisle Publishing Services. It was printed and bound by Banta. The cover was printed by Phoenix Color Corp.

Pearson Prentice Hall™ is a trademark of Pearson Education, Inc.
Pearson® is a registered trademark of Pearson plc
Prentice Hall® is a registered trademark of Pearson Education, Inc.
Merrill® is a registered trademark of Pearson Education, Inc.

Pearson Education Ltd.
Pearson Education Singapore Pte. Ltd.
Pearson Education Canada, Ltd.
Pearson Education—Japan

Pearson Education Australia Pty. Limited
Pearson Education North Asia Ltd.
Pearson Educación de Mexico, S.A. de C.V.
Pearson Education Malaysia Pte. Ltd.

10 9 8 7 6 5 4 3
ISBN 0-13-172343-X

Dedicated in memory of

my dad,
A. Edson Smith,
who taught me the value of an education,

and
Shirley Steele and Martha Zetzl,
committed educators devoted to literacy education,
who set high standards for excellence
and who, because they extended friendship
and compassion to colleagues and students,
inspired others to reach for new understandings
and to never give up.

TEACHER PREP

MERRILL
PRENTICE HALL

TEACHER PREPARATION CLASSROOM

YOUR CLASS. THEIR CAREERS. OUR FUTURE. WILL YOUR STUDENTS BE PREPARED?

We invite you to explore our new, innovative and engaging website and all that it has to offer you, your course, and tomorrow's educators! Organized around the major courses pre-service teachers take, the Teacher Preparation site provides media, student/teacher artifacts, strategies, research articles, and other resources to equip your students with the quality tools needed to excel in their courses and prepare them for their first classroom.

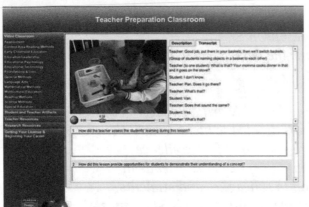

This ultimate on-line education resource is available at no cost, when packaged with a Merrill text, and will provide you and your students access to:

On-line Video Library. More than 150 video clips—each tied to a course topic and framed by learning goals and Praxis-type questions—capture real teachers and students working in real classrooms, as well as in-depth interviews with both students and educators.

Student and Teacher Artifacts. More than 200 student and teacher classroom artifacts—each tied to a course topic and framed by learning goals and application questions—provide a wealth of materials and experiences to help make your study to become a professional teacher more concrete and hands-on.

Research Articles. Over 500 articles from ASCD's renowned journal *Educational Leadership*. The site also includes Research Navigator, a searchable database of additional educational journals.

Teaching Strategies. Over 500 strategies and lesson plans for you to use when you become a practicing professional.

Licensure and Career Tools. Resources devoted to helping you pass your licensure exam; learn standards, law, and public policies; plan a teaching portfolio; and succeed in your first year of teaching.

How to ORDER *Teacher Prep* for you and your students:

For students to receive a *Teacher Prep* Access Code with this text, instructors **must** provide a special value pack ISBN number on their textbook order form. To receive this special ISBN, please email **Merrill.marketing@pearsoned.com** and provide the following information:

- Name and Affiliation
- Author/Title/Edition of Merrill text

Upon ordering *Teacher Prep* for their students, instructors will be given a lifetime *Teacher Prep* Access Code.

Acknowledgments

Sometimes words don't adequately convey the depth of gratitude felt toward the many individuals involved in the development of the *Analytical Reading Inventory (ARI)*. Yet, without making acknowledgments, the gratitude would go unrecorded.

First and foremost, to Katherine, John, and Ken Woods, family of the first author, a thank you for a memory that holds forever in mind—support, through thick and thin, from first to eighth edition—through laborious writing, revising, and editing, and more writing, revising, and editing—you always gave encouragement and fostered confidence.

The eighth edition is committed to supporting those who teach others to use the *ARI*. University professors, staff developers, and self-taught learners now have easy-to-use study packets for ready-made lectures and study sessions. Learning how to use the *ARI* has never before been so thorough and so convenient. Thank you to Ken Woods for providing support throughout the whole process. Thank you to Linda Bishop, Editor, Merrill/Prentice Hall, who provided perceptive, outstanding editorial advice. Thank you to Jeff Johnston, Mary Irvin, and other Merrill editorial staff for their continued support. Finally, thank you to the reviewers of the manuscript for their insights and thoughtful comments: Judith Calhoon, University of New Mexico; Porfirio Loeza, California State University, Sacramento; Alexa Parker, University of Oregon; Margaret Pope, Mississippi State University; and Timothy Shanahan, University of Illinois at Chicago.

Many people supported the development of the seventh edition. Kaaren Allen, Supervisor of Curriculum and Student Assessment, Research, Development and Accountability, Albuquerque Public Schools whose hard work with informal assessment and whose perceptive staff development questions created a focus for the revision; and to all of the Albuquerque second grade and special education teachers who participated in the benchmark assessment project. Thank you to Jenny Stapp, second-third grade teacher at Fishback Creek Public Academy; Indianapolis, Indiana who listened, reflected, and edited; Jennifer and Darren Wall, second-third grade teachers at Fishback Creek Public Academy, Indianapolis, Indiana, who participated in the remake of the audio CD; Darren Wall who illustrated the preprimer, primer, and level one passages; Stephani Johnes-Remetta, University of Indianapolis WICR 88.7 FM who served as the technical engineer producing and editing the seventh edition CD; Molly Seward, University of Indianapolis who piloted the seventh edition; Beth Berghoff, Indiana-University-Purdue-University at Indianapolis, who read and critiqued; to Lebanon Community Schools Summer Academy teachers and administrators who provided revision feedback.

The following people contributed to the sixth edition. Jenny Stapp, second grade teacher, Central Elementary School, Lebanon, Indiana, worked tirelessly and with dedicated spirit through the process. From editing, to laborious layout, to providing readers for the audiotape, Jenny hung in there. Nanci Vargus, primary multi-age teacher, Lynwood Elementary School, Indianapolis, Indiana, assisted in providing readers for the audiotape and kindly agreed to read and provide editorial advice. Thank you to Nancy Steffel, University of Indianapolis, who continues to provide trusted advice. Shannon Lohrmann and Tony Hamilton, journalism students from Butler University, Indianapolis, Indiana, served as proofreaders.

Students from Central Elementary School in Lebanon, Indiana (John Ashmore, Lillian Ashmore, Amanda Haney, Kala Haney, Patrick Miller, Andrew Shaw, and Chris Shaw), and children from Lynwood Elementary School, Indianapolis, Indiana (Freddie Dixson, Lindsey Garriott, Caitlin González, Erin González, Abigail Pinkston, and Rachel Pinkston), volunteered to read for the audiotape. A thank you also goes to the parents of the students for granting permission and for transporting the students to the University of Indianapolis radio station. Jason Collins and Christa Burkholder, University of Indianapolis, WICR 88.7 FM, were the technical engineers for the audiotape. Matt Rademacher, sixth grade special education teacher, served as the narrator on the audiotape (sixth edition).

For the fifth edition, Nancy Steffel from the University of Indianapolis, and Janet Groomer, Reading Specialist from Brownsburg Public Schools, Brownsburg, Indiana, provided important feedback; a special thank you is given for their friendship and caring expertise. Thank you to Joanna Uhry and Margaret Jo Shepherd, Columbia University Teachers College, for allowing the first author to speak with their graduate assessment classes. Their valuable feedback helped the authors to make meaningful and useful revisions.

Many people provided valuable feedback and support during the preparation of the fourth edition. Susan Robinson, Harcourt Elementary School, and Debbie Corpus, Washington Township Public Schools, both in Indianapolis, Indiana, provided invaluable feedback for decisions related to the content area material; the first author holds the highest regard for their professional opinions and personal friendships. To the teachers and students of Orchard School, Indianapolis—specifically Mrs. Colip's second grade, Mrs. Ayres' third grade, Mrs. Ator's fourth grade, Mrs. Yates' fourth grade, Miss White's seventh and eighth grades, Shirley Steele, and the first author's fifth and sixth graders—a hearty thank you for their candid feedback about narrative and expository text. Thank you to Marcia Allington and her sixth graders, also from Orchard, who provided recommendations related to gifted students.

As far back as the first and second editions, a sincere thank you goes to Helen Felsenthal who encouraged the first author to undertake this project in 1975. Thank you to Michael Igo and Anna Sanford for field testing the first edition of the *ARI* with undergraduates, for use of the inventory in the clinic, and for constructive suggestions for changes. Gratitude is extended to Gloria Brown and Cynthia Pulver for the time and energy expended in analyzing the passages. Thank you to Joan Gipe for field testing the *ARI* with undergraduates and for assistance in determining the readability levels of the narrative passages.

Mary Lynn Woods
Alden J. Moe

Contents

SECTION III ▣ INTERVIEWS AND PROFILE RECORDS 91

SECTION IV ▣ EXAMINER'S RECORDS 97

SECTION V ▣ DEVELOPMENT AND VALIDATION OF THE *ARI* 255

SECTION VI ▣ APPENDIX 263

READER'S PASSAGES

Contents

ANALYTICAL
READING
INVENTORY

SECTION I

Introduction

DESCRIPTION OF AN INFORMAL READING INVENTORY

An informal reading inventory is an authentic assessment instrument used to record, analyze, and summarize data about how a reader processes text. It is composed of a series of reading passages that begin at preprimer level and progressively become more difficult. The information rendered from an informal reading inventory is very specific. For example, it shows how a reader processes text at the independent, instructional, frustration, and listening levels, the strategies used to decode/problem solve the pronunciation of words, and the strategies used to comprehend the meaning of the passage. Knowing this specific standards-based data, classroom teachers, reading specialists, and school psychologists can focus instructional decisions and report progress.

DESCRIPTION OF THE *ANALYTICAL READING INVENTORY (ARI)*

What Is the *Analytical Reading Inventory (ARI)?*

The *Analytical Reading Inventory (ARI)* is an informal, individualized reading inventory that provides a convenient passage layout enabling an examiner to collect comprehensive data about a reader's specific strengths and needs in direct relationship to the standards and indicators that describe reading competency.

Who Uses the *Analytical Reading Inventory (ARI)?*

Classroom teachers use the *ARI* as a means of establishing standards-based data and for monitoring and reporting students' progress. **Reading specialists** and **school psychologists** use it in the clinical setting. **Undergraduate students** enrolled in teacher preparation courses use it during course study and student teaching experiences. Graduate students in language education and psychometry use the *ARI* in both classroom and clinical settings. **University professors** and **staff developers** use the *ARI's* audio training CDs and study packets to train pre-service and in-service teachers.

Which Students Should Be Given the *ARI?*

It is important that teachers collect standards-based data and monitor and report the progress of all students: **gifted, remedial,** and **all readers in between!** Students—**kindergarten through high school**—can be given the *ARI*.

Regardless of their ages or grade levels, all types of readers are sitting in today's classrooms. They include talented children who are reading far ahead of their peers, talented children who are experiencing difficulties, children who have been experiencing reading problems since the beginning of school, children who are encountering difficulties as the assignments become more complex, and children who are reading consistently in the average range. Teachers are held accountable for collecting standards-based data and monitoring the progress of **all readers** in their classrooms. Beyond the assessment information, teachers are also held accountable for making standards-based instructional recommendations. Because students' success in school depends on their ability to read, teachers need to know as much as possible about how the students in their classrooms, reading labs, and gifted programs process text. Traditional assessment does not provide such detailed, instructionally linked data.

When Can the *ARI* Be Administered?

Three forms (Forms A, B, and C) of narrative passages are included, so you—the examiner—can collect data at the beginning of the school year and then periodically reevaluate a reader's progress.

How Is the *ARI* Data Reported?

The data is reported during student and parent conferences, passed along to a student's forthcoming teachers, and shared with specialists and other educators. The *ARI* profile summary records are so logically organized, they are but a staple away from portfolio ready. Most teachers include *ARI* profiles in a student's literacy portfolio.

What Is Included in Section II: Learning How to Use the *ARI*?

> Section II
> Learning How to Use
> the *ARI*

This eighth edition provides **university professors, staff developers,** and **self-taught learners** with unparalleled support for learning how to use the *ARI*. For example, Section II provides study packets and CDs that are designed to create ready-made lectures and study session assignments. Section II of the *ARI* manual is divided into four subsections: "Acquiring Background Knowledge"; "Practicing 10 *ARI* Assessment Components Using Audio Training CD 2 and Study Packets"; "Practicing a Case Study Using Audio Training CD 1 and Study Packet"; and "Administering the *ARI*: Step-by-Step Instructions."

CD 2

> ▪ **Acquiring Background Knowledge**
> This subsection includes brief discussions about important issues related to informal assessment. For example, information is included about the differences between examiner behaviors during assessment and teacher behaviors during instruction. With knowledge about these differences and other issues included in this subsection, you can administer the *ARI* and interpret results with deeper understanding and consistency.

> ▪ **Practicing 10 *ARI* Assessment Components Using Audio Training CD 2 and Study Packets**
> An assessment component is one essential element of a comprehensive assessment session. The data from all 10 components constitute a reader's multidimensional profile because each component represents a comprehensive analysis of the standards and indicators that describe reading competency.

> For detailed information see the 10 *ARI* Assessment Components, Standards, and Indicators chart located inside the front cover of this *ARI* manual.

10 *ARI* Assessment Components

1. Reading Interviews
2. Word Lists/ Initial Placement
3. Prior Knowledge/Prediction
4. Oral Reading Miscue Analysis
5. Fluency Analysis

6. Retelling/Summary Analysis
7. Comprehension Questions/RTR Analysis
8. Cueing System Analysis
9. Quantitative and Qualitative Analysis
10. Summary of Results

> In this subsection each assessment component is presented in the format of a study packet. For your learning convenience, a study packet includes a list of component standards and indicators, an explanation of the component, study packet directions, study charts, sample passages, and CD tracks of schoolchildren reading *ARI* passages. Study packet answer keys are provided in the Appendix.

CD 1

▣ **Practicing a Case Study Using Audio Training CD 1 and Study Packet**
The case study offers you the opportunity to study the written documentation and listen as a student reads narrative and expository passages from the independent to the frustration levels. This case study provides the chance to gain a thorough understanding of a reader's multidimensional profile, consequently helping you acquire the competence and confidence to adminster the *ARI*. **University professors, staff developers,** and **self-taught learners** use this subsection for training.

▣ **Administering the *ARI*: Step-by-Step Instructions**
This subsection provides detailed directions for administering the *ARI*.

Section III
Interviews and
Profile Records

What Is Included in Section III: Interviews and Profile Records?

This section contains reading interviews that reveal information about the student's reading habits, interests, and perceptions of reading strategies.

The profile records offer a user-friendly system for summarizing the results. A time-saving grid called Student Profile Summary is included. This checklist-style grid corresponds, component by component, with the organization of the passages in the Examiner's Records, allowing the summary of data to flow smoothly and succinctly. A Class Profile Summary and *ARI* Profile Card are also included.

Section IV
Examiner's Records

What Is Included in Section IV: Examiner's Records?

The Examiner's Records are the passages the examiner uses to record all data. Each passage in the Examiner's Records is organized in a logical, convenient manner enabling you to efficiently record, analyze, and summarize the data. The Examiner's Records section contains five forms. Each form includes passages that begin at the preprimer level and continue with increasing difficulty to level nine.

▣ Form A (narrative) preprimer through level nine
▣ Form B (narrative) preprimer through level nine
▣ Form C (narrative) preprimer through level nine
▣ Form S (expository science) level one through level nine
▣ Form SS (expository social studies) level one through level nine

For detailed information about the standards and indicators assessed by the *ARI* see the 10 *ARI* Assessment Components, Standards, and Indicators chart located inside the front cover of this manual.

Section V
Development and
Validation

What Is Included in Section V: Development and Validation of the *ARI*?

Considerable effort was devoted to establishing the content validity of the *ARI*. For example, this section provides the data charts concerning the development and validation of the *ARI* passages, information related to the field studies done during the revision process from edition to edition, information about the matching of national and state standards and indicators to each *ARI* assessment component, and a description of an inter-scorer reliability study. Section V is divided into the following subsections:

▣ Matching *ARI* Components to National and State Standards and Indicators
▣ Passage Content: Narrative and Expository
▣ Readability and Vocabulary Diversity Results

- Field Testing
- Illustrations at Preprimer, Primer, and Level 1
- Inter-Scorer Reliability Study

Section VI Appendix

What Is Included in Section VI: Appendix?

- **Answer Keys**
  This section includes the answer keys that correspond to each study packet.

- **References**
  References for research and instruction and references for the content of the narrative and expository passages are provided.

• Inside Front Cover
• Inside Back Cover

What Is Inside Front and Back Covers of the *ARI*?

Inside the front cover is the 10 *ARI* Assessment Components, Standards, and Indicators chart.

Inside the back cover are audio training CD 1 and CD 2. Adjacent to the CDs is a written explanation of each CD track and directions for starting and stopping a CD player while you code and document data.

Reader's Passages (thin spiral book)

What Is Included in the *Reader's Passages* (thin spiral book)?

The *Reader's Passages* book is the separately bound book from which the student reads. It includes word lists and all narrative and expository passages. This book is ready to use; no copying is required. It includes:

- Form A (narrative) preprimer through level nine
- Form B (narrative) preprimer through level nine
- Form C (narrative) preprimer through level nine
- Form S (expository science) level one through level nine
- Form SS (expository social studies) level one through level nine

SECTION II

Learning How to Use the ARI

ACQUIRING BACKGROUND KNOWLEDGE ⸻

As an examiner, you are called upon to make decisions during the process of giving an informal reading inventory, so you must have some background knowledge related to informal assessment. With an understanding of the information included in this subsection, you will learn to make decisions with confidence and consistency.

Quantitative and Qualitative Analysis: Developing a Reader's Multidimensional Profile

In the past, users of informal reading inventories relied on a system for reporting results where all deviations from the text were tabulated. This procedure was referred to as a *quantitative analysis* (Pikulski, 1974) because deviations were simply counted and a score was computed with no regard for the quality of the miscue.

Since the 1970s, the word *miscue* has been widely used in informal assessment (Cecil, 1999; Goodman, 1973; Goodman & Burke, 1976). A miscue is defined as a deviation from the text. Miscue analysis implies that an analysis of the quality of the miscue can reveal important information about the reader's use of strategy. For example, if a student substitutes the word *the* for *a*, indicating no change in the meaning of the text, the miscue is not as severe as the substitution of the word *thought* for *through*. From this perspective the examiner analyzes miscues to find patterns within a single passage and across passages, offering a qualitative dimension to the assessment.

To obtain a multidimensional profile, it is necessary to analyze both quantitative and qualitative data, which includes miscue analysis among other factors. Thus, determining the results of an informal assessment involves more than just counting miscues and comprehension errors. Instead, when interpreting the data you will be asking yourself substantive questions such as these:

■ What motivates a reader? On what strategies does the reader presently rely?
■ How does prior knowledge affect the reader's performance?
■ At what level of performance is the reader fluent and confident?
■ What types of miscues occur consistently within a passage and across passages?
■ Do the miscues change the meaning of the text? If not, why not? If so, why?
■ Over a series of passages of increasing difficulty, how does performance change in relationship to both quantitative and qualitative factors?

Examiner or Teacher Behaviors: Assessment or Instruction

Because informal assessment is conducted in a personalized, relaxed manner, examiner behaviors have the potential to alter the outcome of a session. An examiner who is calm and relaxed, who waits patiently for the reader to respond, will achieve more accurate results. You should self-monitor oral and body language responses that might reveal personal feelings. Your reactions could influence the reader in a nonproductive way. Explain to the reader what is expected and how the session will be carried out. For example, you should explain such things as the procedure for reading the passage. Tell the reader that you will be writing during the session and that the results will reveal strengths as well as needs.

Examiner assessment behaviors differ from teacher instructional behaviors. The purpose of assessment is to *collect, observe, record, analyze,* and *summarize* data, while the purpose of instruction is to *facilitate* the reader's development. In essence, you must always keep in mind that assessment is not instruction. Making the distinction between the purpose of assessment and the purpose of instruction helps you to know what examiner behaviors are appropriate during an informal assessment session. When administering an informal reading inventory you must always keep this question in mind: "If I were not here to facilitate the reading of this passage, what strategies would the reader use?" When you take this stance, you will behave in a manner that causes the reader to respond without your support. This means that during assessment, you will provide little or no assistance. Aiding words should be kept to a minimum. A rule in most instances is to aid the reader only when he or she is at the frustration level.

Oral and Silent Reading

During assessment you need to hear the student read aloud to learn what strategies he or she uses to recognize words and process the meaning of the text; therefore, the *ARI* is an oral reading assessment. However, in certain situations a student may process the text more efficiently while reading silently. For example, a very competent student may read more rapidly and efficiently while reading silently, or a student experiencing excessive stress while reading orally may be more efficient while reading silently.

An analysis of the qualitative factors, such as emotional status or fluency, tells you whether you need to ask the student to read silently. You will be able to sense when a competent reader becomes impatient and bogged down by the oral reading. You will know if a reader is overly stressed during oral reading. In such a circumstance, select a passage from an alternate form and ask the student to read it silently. You will then follow the same procedures as with the oral reading.

Oral reading serves an important function during assessment. If the reader didn't read aloud, you would not be able to hear and observe the strategies a reader uses to process the text. Oral reading is done during instruction as well; however, the teacher may use it to serve a different instructional function (Hasbrouck & Tindal, 1992).

Comprehensive and Modified Assessment Sessions

A comprehensive *ARI* assessment session includes assessing a reader at all four levels (independent, instructional, frustration, and listening). Without a doubt, a comprehensive assessment session renders the most substantive data. However, a shorter, modified version of the assessment session can be administered, and it still produces meaningful information that can be used for instructional decisions and selection of appropriately leveled materials. Listed below are some recommendations for selecting passages for a modified assessment:

- For students who are functioning successfully with grade level material and for students experiencing reading problems:

  - a narrative passage one level below grade level
  - a narrative passage at grade level
  - an expository passage at grade level

- For an accelerated reader:

  - a narrative passage at grade level
  - a narrative passage above grade level
  - an expository passage at or above grade level

Teachers often add passages to this modified assessment depending upon the student's needs. For example, sometimes teachers find it important to assess a reader's listening level; therefore, they will add the necessary passages to the modified version. To administer the modified version passages, follow the directions found in the subsection, "Administering the *ARI*: Step-by-Step Instructions," beginning with step 4 (page 82).

Portfolio and the *ARI*

The essence of informal assessment is authenticity; thus, the relationship between the *Analytical Reading Inventory* and a student portfolio is like hand in glove. Many teachers include the documentation from an *ARI* assessment session in the student's literacy portfolio. The Student Profile Summary is designed to summarize all components of an *ARI* assessment session, and it works conveniently as a synopsis that can be included in a portfolio. Some teachers, however, include all of the documentation from a comprehensive or modified *ARI* assessment. Documentation obtained at the beginning of the year can be analyzed side-by-side with documentation obtained later in the year and then used to show student progress. Teachers who audiotape the assessment session can select a passage or series of passages from the tape to include in the portfolio. Some teachers conduct a reflective conference with the student, engaging the reader in an analysis of her or his reading development. Some teachers focus a reflective conference on two passages obtained at different periods in time. Another suggestion is to compare two narrative passages and/or compare a narrative and an expository passage. A reflective conference can be audiotaped or done as a writing assignment and used during a parent/student conference, and then placed in the portfolio.

Narrative and Expository Passages

Both narrative and expository passages are included in the *ARI*. The narrative passages are like stories found in reading or literature textbooks. The expository passages are like text found in science or social studies textbooks.

Because narrative and expository text are structured differently, some researchers (McGee & Richgels, 1985; Meyer & Rice, 1984; Piccolo, 1987; Vacca & Vacca, 2004) assume that most students enter kindergarten with a basic understanding of story structure, causing narrative text to be more comprehensible than expository text. On the other hand, others, including Pappas (1993), found that expository text for primary students is, in fact, as understandable and therefore suggest that the difficulty students encounter with expository text is caused when the instructional emphasis is placed mostly on narrative text.

During the preparation of the fourth edition of the *ARI*, some field testing was done focusing on the differences between narrative and expository text. The purpose of the study was to find out from among three *ARI* passages—a narrative, a science, or a social studies—which passage the students felt was the most difficult to comprehend and the reasons for the difficulty. Eighty-six students from grades two through eight (Orchard School, Indianapolis, Indiana) participated in the study. Each student selected for the study could read the passages at the instructional level.

In the study a fourth grader, for example, was given three unmarked Level 4 passages—a narrative, a science, and a social studies passage. He was asked to read all three passages and write a summary statement for each one. To ensure he comprehended the passages, the examiner interviewed him, calling for retellings, asking comprehension questions, checking summary statements, and assessing background knowledge. Next, he was asked to rank the three passages from hardest to the easiest and to explain why each was ranked in that position.

Students at each grade level, two through eight, in almost each instance ranked the narrative passage as the easiest and the expository passages as harder. Depending on the reader's background knowledge and reading interests, the social studies and science passages changed positions between next easiest and hardest. It was interesting to note that most students quickly sensed the different writing styles, narrative or expository. Many referred to narrative text as *story* while the expository texts were often called *science* or *social studies facts*. In six instances, a social studies or science passage was ranked as the easiest, but only in cases where the readers had background knowledge from other reading or firsthand experiences.

The results of this study showed that students found expository text harder to read than narrative text. Without the structure of a story, readers reported that they had to expend more mental energy to recall and interpret the information in expository texts. The common complaints centered on the difficulty in recalling a series of details and pronouncing and understanding content area vocabulary. One sixth grader described his feelings about the Level 6 social studies passage:

> *After I read the first sentence, I had trouble getting the rest. Somehow I just kept forgetting the stuff. I had to stop and think at the end of each sentence, and then try to get it. It was like a mind twister!*

The students' comments about the passages proved to be revealing, not only about the issue of narrative versus expository text, but also about what readers do to acquire meaning. The table that follows reveals the thoughts that traveled through the minds of the students as they reflected about the passages.

Students' Comments Differentiating Narrative and Expository Passages (The information in parentheses following each comment identifies the title of each passage.)		
Passage Level	Form C: Narrative Passages	Forms S and SS: Expository Passages
2	• This is like a story. (The Busy Road)	• I didn't like to read this one. It was too hard. It was not like a story. (S: Hearing Sounds)
3	• This kind of thing happens a lot in neighborhoods. It's like a story. (Belonging to the Club)	• This one is not as easy as the clubhouse. We have heard about Thomas Jefferson before, though, and when you start to read about someone you know about your memory picks it up. (SS: Writing the *Declaration of Independence*)
4	• It's about a kid, his horse, and when his horse was sick. I have a pet. I can understand that. (A Sick Pony)	• The Jody story was the easiest. Really, it was hard for me to say which was the hardest. I love science! I read about it a lot. I saw all the stuff on TV about Halley's Comet. Wow! It was something! Well, I guess the Jody story was still easier to read. (S: A Comet) • This one was about an explorer like in history. Everything about history is hard for me. It's really hard for kids to know about things way back in the 1600s! (SS: French Explorers in North America)
5	• I like stories about racing, and this is a story! (A Woman Race Car Driver)	• When I read things that happened a long time ago, I get all messed up! (SS: The Civil War)
6	• The story caught my attention because the human body is very interesting. I think about being a doctor. (Open Heart Surgery)	• I didn't understand this one very well. But weaving, thread, machines, and inventions just aren't important to me. That's just my opinion. (SS: How the Industrial Revolution Changed the Textile Industry)

Passage Level	Form C: Narrative Passages	Forms S and SS: Expository Passages
7	• I think this story was sad. I have an older brother. I wanted the ending to be different. I think this one was the easiest because it was written in more of a story form, not so informational or with such big words. (Caring for His Brother)	• This one was too informational, and I found it to be the hardest. (S: Moving Forces and Inertia) • I thought this one was the next easiest to read because I'm interested in sports. Plus, when I read something new, the author explained what it was about and how it all tied together. (SS: The Birth of Public Education and Leisure Time)
8	• This one was the easiest because it flowed easily, and I could get a picture of what the author was saying. (The Science Project)	• This one was in the middle because it was informational, and the writer explained it in such a way that it made it more understandable for me. (SS: Vietnam War) • This one was the hardest to read because of all the big words. I don't know what all those words mean, and so I totally lost what was happening. (S: Cancer)

Expository and narrative elements differ from one another. As an examiner, you will need to know the difference. Narrative elements, referred to in the *ARI* as *story elements* (characters, time and place, problem, plot details, turning point resolution), are more commonly known; however, expository elements are less known. In their textbooks, reading experts (Brozo & Simpson, 2003; Heilman, Blair, & Rupley, 2002; Reutzel & Cooter, 2004) describe the elements identified by Meyer and Freedle (1984), recommending that teachers directly teach the elements to their students. Review Meyer's and Freedle's five expository elements and compare them to the narrative elements:

Expository Elements	All	Some	None
Description			
Collection			
Causation			
Problem/Solution			
Comparison			
Reader's Thumbnail Summary:			

- **Description** specifies something about a topic or presents an attribute or setting for a topic.
- **Collection** indicates a number of descriptions (specifics, attributes, or settings) presented together showing that the ideas are related to each other by a common factor or factors.
- **Causation** refers to text elements grouped in time sequence (before and after) with a specified causative relationship (earlier causes the later).
- **Problem/Solution** includes a caustive relationship (between a problem and its causes) and a solution set, one element of which can break the link between the problem and its cause.
- **Comparison** organizes text elements on the basis of their differences and similarities. Comparison does not contain elements of sequence or causality.

In a comprehensive assessment session, when assessing a reader using narrative passages, you will determine all four of a student's reading levels: independent, instructional, frustration, and listening. However, when assessing using expository passages, it is suggested that you administer only a grade level passage and determine at what reading level (independent, instructional, frustration) the reader functions with that passage. With expository text, it is important to know at what reading level each student functions. For example, in a classroom science textbook, it's not uncommon to have a few of your students functioning at the independent level, some at the instructional level, and some at the frustration level! Knowing this information, you can put together a collection of alternate texts that coordinate with the topics in the science and social studies textbooks, thus supporting the reading needs of all students in your classroom. You can determine multi-ability groupings as well.

PRACTICING 10 *ARI* ASSESSMENT COMPONENTS USING AUDIO TRAINING CD 2 AND STUDY PACKETS

An *ARI* assessment session is made up of 10 components. Each component is one essential element of a comprehensive assessment session. Column I of the *ARI* Overview Chart lists each component.

When the data from Component 1 through Component 8 are recorded and summarized, this information represents a comprehensive analysis of the standards and indicators that characterize reading competency. This analysis is called a *reader's multidimensional profile*. A comprehensive profile such as this provides the data essential for teaching standards-based reading lessons. To be a successful examiner, your task is to learn how to **record, analyze, synthesize,** and **summarize** the data. Components 9 and 10 describe examiner competencies, which are the essence of examiner expertise.

ARI Overview Chart	
Column I *ARI* **Components**	**Column II** **Reader and Examiner Standards and Indicators**
▣ **Component 1:**	**An examiner RECORDS the reader's . . .**
Component 1: Reading Interviews	**Reader Standard/Indicators: Reading Interests/Attitudes** • interests, attitudes, habits, beliefs • perceptions related to strategies applied to reading process
▣ **Components 2–8:**	**An examiner RECORDS a reader's ability to:**
Component 2: Word Lists/Initial Placement	**Reader Standard/Indicators: Phonics and Word Meaning** • decode and comprehend words in a list
Component 3: Prior Knowledge/ Prediction Analysis	**Reader Standard/Indicators: Prior Knowledge/Prediction** • access prior knowledge before reading • make a logical connection/prediction before reading • continue during reading to access prior knowledge and make logical predictions to recognize words, self-correct miscues, and comprehend text
Component 4: Oral Reading Miscue Analysis	**Reader Standard/Indicators: Phonics/Vocabulary and Language in Use** • decode and problem solve the pronunciation of words (assessment of omissions, insertions, substitutions, aided words, repetitions, and reversals) • make self-corrections to construct meaning of words and chunks of text • apply graphophonic, syntactic, and semantic cueing systems to decode or self-correct words and construct meaning of text

(continued)

Component 5: Fluency Analysis	**Reader Standard/Indicators: Fluency** • read smoothly, accurately, in meaningful phrases • use pitch, stress, and intonation to convey meaning of the text • repeat words or phrases using meaning to self-correct • use punctuation to divide text into units of meaning
Component 6: Retelling/Summary Statement Analysis	**Reader Standard/Indicators: Comprehension** • recall/retell a text to include all story structure elements—main character, time and place, problem, plot details in sequence, turning point, and resolution • recall/retell a text to include all expository text elements—description, collection, causation, problem/solution, comparison • summarize text including main idea and basic plot elements • retell in full sentences in language comparable to author's vocabulary and style
Component 7: Comprehension Question/Reader Text Relationship (RTR) Analysis	**Reader Standard/Indicators: Comprehension** • construct literal meaning of text • construct implied meaning of text • retain and put information together within and across paragraphs • access prior knowledge and connect it with meaning of text (context clues) • establish a personal opinion and substantiate it with information from text • reply in full sentences comparable to author's vocabulary and style
Component 8: Cueing Systems Miscue Analysis	**Reader Standard/Indicators: Phonics and Comprehension** • apply graphophonic, syntactic, and semantic cueing systems to decode words, self-correct miscues, and construct meaning of text

▦ **Components 9–10:**	An examiner **ANALYZES, SYNTHESIZES, AND SUMMARIZES the data developing a reader's multidimensional profile.**

Component 9:
Quantitative &
Qualitative
Analysis—
Developing a
Reader's
Multidimensional
Profile
	Examiner Standard/Indicators: Analysis/Synthesis
	• analyze and synthesize quantitative and qualitative data
	
	Quantitative **Qualitative**
	• # miscues • prior knowledge/prediction
	    • cueing systems
	• # comprehension • fluency
	  question errors • retelling/summary
	    • comprehension question responses
	      (RTR—literal and inferential)
	    • emotional status

Component 10: Summary of Results	**Examiner Standard/Indicators: Analysis/Synthesis/Summary** • articulate and synthesize quantitative and qualitative data for each narrative and expository passage • complete profile records in preparation for reporting data to student, parents, and educators • use findings to develop standards-based instructional plans and support

With another review of the *ARI* Overview Chart on the preceding pages you can begin to understand some important, yet more subtle, information—the relationship between an examiner's accountabilities to record, analyze, synthesize, and summarize data and the reader standards and indicators listed in Column II, Components 1–8. The relationship between the two actually defines a **dual ability** that qualifies examiner competency:

a. the ability to successfully record, analyze, synthesize, and summarize data

b. while listening to a reader, the ability to rapidly and accurately identify (in mind as well as on paper) standards and indicators the reader applies or defaults

This author refers to this dual ability as *thinking* and *responding*, both of which are essential during instruction and assessment. During instruction you must not only be able to listen and identify the instructional need, you must also be able to rapidly respond with standards-based recommendations. Although during assessment you do not respond with instructional recommendations, the repetitious experience of giving the *ARI* is the learning event that teaches you how to become competent at thinking and responding.

Take note that the administration of some *ARI* components is easier to master than others. As you work to learn how to give all of the assessment components, be comforted that a working knowledge of some components is generating competency with other components. For example, when beginning, even though you are administering all 10 components, focus specifically upon teaching yourself how to **record, analyze, synthesize,** and **summarize** data about a reader's fluency. Mastering fluency analysis is less demanding and simultaneously trains you to be efficient at recording, analyzing, synthesizing, and summarizing. Trust that as you master fluency analysis the know-how will prove useful as you turn your focus to a more demanding component such as quantitative and qualitative analysis. Additionally, trust that the process is preparing you with thinking and responding skills you need for instruction as well as assessment.

Understanding How to Use a Study Packet

Each of the 10 *ARI* components (pages 21 to 52) is organized into a study packet. The format of each study packet includes a listing of component standards and indicators, a component explanation, directions for practice, and a text box located in the left margin that itemizes study packet materials. A study packet materials list details the items you will refer to and/or copy. The list can include any combination of:

- *ARI* passages from the Examiner's Records
- charts included with the study packet
- CD tracks of students reading *ARI* passages
- passages in the *Reader's Passages* (thin spiral book)
- answer key pages located in the Appendix

The information that follows will introduce you to the study packet and Examiner's Record passage layout.

Use time, repeated assessment experience, and teaching experience to bring about a comfortable working knowledge of all standards-based *ARI* assessment components.

Trust that the process of giving the ARI *teaches you the dual ability, thinking and responding.* If well developed, this dual ability prepares you, for your entire career, to teach standards-based reading lessons.

Study Packet Materials

Any materials you need to copy or refer to are listed in a text box in the left margin next to study packet **directions.**

PASSAGE LAYOUT, COMPONENTS, STANDARDS, AND INDICATORS STUDY PACKET

Explanation

This practice session will introduce you to the layout of each reader's passage included in Section IV, Examiner's Records. The layout of each passage is conveniently organized so you can efficiently record standards-based data. During this practice opportunity you will become familiar with *ARI* Components 3–8 and the standards and indicators assessed by each component.

You will also be shown how to use a study packet that has been designed for each of the 10 *ARI* assessment components. The format of each study packet includes a list of component standards and indicators, a component explanation, directions for practice, and a list of study packet materials.

Directions
Examiner's Record Passage Layout, Components, Standards, and Indicators—Charts A, B, and C

1. Read carefully Charts A, B, and C, located on pages 18, 19, and 20.

2. If possible, lay Charts A, B, and C out in front of you, connecting one page to the next so you can see all three charts at once. Listen to CD 2, Track 2, Form C, Level 3, "Belonging to the Club" and follow along on the three charts.

3. With a partner, find each component located in a text box outside the passage. Name the component and describe the assessment purpose of each component, 3–8. For example, the name of Component 3 is Prior Knowledge/Prediction Analysis. The assessment purpose is to collect data about a reader's ability to access prior knowledge and make predictions to facilitate word recognition and comprehension. With a piece of scrap paper, cover the text boxes. As you point to each section of the reader's passage, can you name each component and describe its assessment function?

4. Return to Charts A, B, and C. Listen again to CD 2, Track 2. Stop the CD at each passage component and name the standard(s) and indicators written beneath the title of the component.

Cover each component text box on Charts A, B, and C. Listen to CD 2, Track 2 for the third time, stopping the CD (only for a few seconds) at each component. Name the component and recite the standards and indicators you heard the reader apply or default. After you finish, tell your partner what you thought and how you felt as you were required to **simultaneously listen for and determine** if you heard each standard and indicator.

5. With a partner, read the Case Study on pages 53 through 80. Notice how the data collection begins at a level of reader comfort (independent) and continues until the reader is at the frustration level.

Carefully review the Student Profile Summary on page 54. Talk with your partner and make a prediction about what data is represented in the grid on the top portion of the page. How do you think the examiner summarized the data from a series of passages onto the Student Profile Summary? Notice the grid on the lower portion of the profile summary. Can you locate each *ARI* assessment component on the grid?

Study Packet Materials

- Copy or refer to Charts A, B, and C (pages 18, 19, and 20).
- Copy or refer to *ARI* Overview Chart (pages 14 and 15).
- Refer to Case Study (pages 53–80).
- CD 2, Track 2

Refer to the subsection "Administering the *ARI*: Step-by-Step Instructions," and notice the assessment purpose is stated with each step. (pages 81–89).

CHART A ▣ Examiner's Record Passage Layout, Components, Standards, and Indicators

---

Component 3: Prior Knowledge/ Prediction Analysis

Prior Knowledge and Prediction

- access prior knowledge before reading
- make a logical prediction before reading
- continue during reading to access prior knowledge and make logical predictions to recognize words, self-correct miscues, and comprehend text

---

Component 4: Oral Reading Miscue Analysis (passage text lines 1–17)

Phonics/Vocabulary and Language in Use

- decode and problem solve the pronunciation of words (assessment of omissions, insertions, substitutions, aided words, repetitions, and reversals)
- make self-corrections to construct meaning of words and chunks of text
- apply graphophonic, syntactic, semantic cueing systems to decode or self-correct words, and construct meaning of text

---

FORM C, LEVEL 3   Reader's Passages page 36

Prior Knowledge/Prediction

☐ Read the title and predict what the story is about. *About somebody who belongs to a club.*

Q: What do you know about somebody who belongs to a club?
SR: My mom belongs to a club.

☐ Read the first two sentences and add more to your prediction.
There's a sign outside this club that says "For Neighborhood Triggers Only."

		O	I	S	A	Rp	Rv
	Be in Belonging (to) the Club						
1	This was the / sign that Jack read / as he stood outside the /						
2	*may SC* *club SC* neighborhood kids' clubhouse.		/				
	Triggers						
3	FOR NEIGHBORHOOD TIGERS ONLY!						
4	*SC* KNOCK ONE (HUNDRED) TIMES						
5	AND SAY THE SECRET WORD						
6	BEFORE ENTERING!						
7	*be in* Jack was a new boy, and he really wanted / to / belong (to) the club.	/	/	/			
8	*ask* "How can I get the kids to agree (to) let me belong?" (he) (thought.)	///		/			
9	*Soon* Suddenly, he / dashed home and (soon) returned with a bucket of	/		/			

The text is continued on the next page.

Prior Knowledge

☐ a lot
☑ some
☐ none

■ CHART B ■ Examiner's Record Passage Layout, Components, Standards, and Indicators

Cueing Systems

LINE #	Miscue	Graphophonically Similar I M F (word level)	Syntactically Acceptable Unacceptable (sentence level)	Semantic Change in Meaning (CM) No Change in Meaning (NCM) (sentence level)
3	*Triggers*	I F	A	*CM*
7	*be*	I	A	*NCM*
7	*in*	I	A	*NCM*
8	*ask*	I	A	*CM*
9	*seem*	I	A	*slight CM*
10	*some*	I	A	*slight CM*

Summary

☑ Most, ☐ few, ☐ no   miscues were graphophonically similar to the word in the passage.

☑ Most, ☐ few, ☐ no   miscues were syntactically matched.

☐ Most, ☑ few, ☐ no   miscues maintained the author's meaning.

☑ The self-corrections demonstrate that the reader monitors the meaning.

Component 8: Cueing Systems Miscue Analysis

Phonics and Comprehension

• apply graphophonic, syntactic, and semantic cueing systems to decode words, self-correct miscues, and construct meaning of text

---

Passage

Line		O	I	S	A	Rp	Rv	Text
1 0				/				yellow paint, one of black, and /*some* several brushes. He began pounding
1 1								on the clubhouse door.
1 2								"I'm / knocking one hundred times!" he shouted. "I don't know
1 3								*said SC* the secret word," he declared, "but I have something important to tell
1 4							/	everyone! I'm the new boy," he explained. "Since the name of your <u>club</u>
1 5						/		*Triggers* is / *Tigers*, I thought you might want to paint your clubhouse
1 6								*SC* yellow (with) <u>black stripes</u>!" All the kids thought this was a great idea
1 7								and / quickly invited Jack to belong!

TOTALS

Number of miscues ___13___   Number of self-corrections ___5___

Component 5: Fluency Analysis

Fluency

• read smoothly, accurately, in meaningful phrases

• use pitch, stress, and intonation to convey meaning of the text

• repeat words or phrases using meaning to self-correct

• use punctuation to divide text into units of meaning

Fluency: Does the Reader . . .

☐ read smoothly, accurately, (in meaningful phrases?)

☐ read (word-by-word) choppy, plodding?   *more than at Level 2*

☑ use pitch, stress, and intonation to convey meaning of the text?   *somewhat*

☑ repeat words and phrases because s/he is monitoring the meaning (self-correcting)?

☐ repeat words and phrases because s/he is trying to sound out words?   *most times*

☐ use punctuation to divide the text into units of meaning?   ☐ ignore the punctuation?   *belong? (line 8)*

Rating Scale: Circle One

4 = fluent reading / good pace   2 = choppy, plodding reading / slow pace

③ = fairly fluent / reasonable pace   1 = clearly labored, disfluent reading / very slow pace

CHART C ◼ Examiner's Record Passage Layout, Components, Standards, and Indicators

Retelling

It's about a boy who wants to belong to a club. And he got some paint and was banging on the door. He asked the kids if they wanted to paint the place yellow and black. And they thought it was a good idea, and they asked Jack to join.

Q: *Why do you think Jack chose yellow and black paint?*

SR: *He likes these colors.*

Note: Indicate any probing with a "P"

Story Elements	All	Some	None
Main Character(s)	✓		
Time and (Place)	✓		
Problem		✓	
Plot Details in Sequence		✓	
Turning Point		✓	
Resolution	✓		

Reader's Thumbnail Summary:

He wants to belong to the club.

Retelling Summary: ☐ many details, logical order ☑ some details, some order ☐ few details, disorder

Component 7: Comp. Question/ RTR Analysis

Comprehension
- construct literal meaning of text
- construct implied meaning of text
- retain and put information together within and across paragraphs
- access prior knowledge to construct meaning
- establish a personal opinion and substantiate it with information from the text
- reply in full sentences comparable to author's vocabulary and style

Comprehension Questions and Possible Answers

__+__ (RIF) 1. Who is the main character in this story? (Jack)

__=__ (PIT) 2. Why does Jack want to belong to the club? (he is the new boy and wants to make new friends) *He just does.*

__+__ (CAR) 3. What do you know about the word **belong?** (to be a member, to have a rightful place) *to be in something*
What does the word **belong** have to do with this story? (Jack wants to get the kids to agree to let him belong to the club) *be in the club*

__½__ (RIF) 4. What did Jack dash home to get? (bucket of yellow paint, one of black, and several brushes) *paint*

__½__ (PIT) 5. Why did Jack knock one hundred times on the clubhouse door? (the sign said to do that; he has something important to tell the club members) *He had something to tell the kids* *Nobody knows it but the kids in the club.*

__+__ (CAR) 6. What do you know about the phrase **secret word?** (clubs have a secret password, only members know the word)
What does the phrase **secret word** have to do with this story? (Jack says he doesn't know the secret word) *I don't*

__½__ (PIT) 7. What was Jack's clever idea? (because the club's name is Tigers, Jack thought they might want to paint the clubhouse yellow with black stripes) *He got the paint.*

__=__ (EAS) 8. In your opinion did it take courage to do what Jack did? (yes, it's hard to be the new kid and try to make friends)
You think this because . . . (he wanted to belong so bad that he thought of a clever idea to get the kids to like him) *Because it's hard to ask someone if you can join their club*

Reader Text Relationship (RTR)   From the Text ☑ adequate ☐ not adequate   From Head to Text ☐ adequate ☑ not adequate

Component 6: Retelling / Summary Statement Analysis

Comprehension
- recall/retell a text to include all story elements—main character, time and place, problem, plot details in sequence, turning point, resolution
- recall/retell a text to include all expository text elements— description, collection, causation, problem/ solution, comparison
- summarize text, including main ideas or basic plot elements
- retell in full sentences in language comparable to author's vocabulary and style

Scoring Guide Summary

WORD RECOGNITION

Independent ...... 1–2 *–13*
Instructional ...... 7–8 *Instr.*
Frustration ...... 15+

COMPREHENSION

Independent ...... 0–1 *–3 ½*
Instructional ...... 2 *Instr.*
Frustration ...... 4+

Emotional Status:

Less confident than at level 2.

COMPONENT 1 STUDY PACKET
READING INTERVIEW

Reader Standard/Indicators: Reading Interests/Attitudes

- interests, attitudes, habits, beliefs
- perceptions related to strategies applied to reading process

Explanation

Information derived from a reading interview helps you understand a student's reading interests, attitudes, habits, use of strategies, and perceptions about his or her reading ability. The interview can be given to a whole group; however, when given individually, it creates the relaxed, personalized environment that is central to informal assessment. The *ARI* offers two interviews developed by Laura Robb (Robb, 1995).

Directions

1. Read the interview called "Seven Questions About Reading" (page 92) and "The Reading Interview" (page 93). What do you think the purpose is for each interview?

<table>
<tr><td>Study Packet Materials</td></tr>
<tr><td>• Refer to Section III "Interviews and Profile Records" (pages 92–96).</td></tr>
</table>

COMPONENT 2 STUDY PACKET
WORD LISTS/INITIAL PLACEMENT

Reader Standard/Indicators: Phonics and Word Meaning

- decode and comprehend words in a list

Explanation

Narrative Forms A, B, and C each contain word lists, primer through level six. You will use the list to determine the reader's starting place in the passages. In addition to attending to the pronunciation of the words, you will check comprehension by asking the reader to use some of the words in sentences, ensuring that the reader is not word calling and serving as a validation for proper placement.

Directions

1. Listen to CD 1, Track 2, as Jenny reads the word lists from Form C. Code the word lists according to the step-by-step directions on page 82. Check your answers using the word lists from the Case Study on pages 55 and 56.

<table>
<tr><td>Study Packet Materials</td></tr>
<tr><td>• From Form C copy the word lists (pages 166–167).</td></tr>
<tr><td>• CD 1, Track 2</td></tr>
<tr><td>• Answer Key Case Study (pages 55, 56)</td></tr>
</table>

COMPONENT 3 STUDY PACKET
PRIOR KNOWLEDGE/PREDICTION ANALYSIS _____

Reader Standard/Indicators: Prior Knowledge/Prediction

▪ access prior knowledge before reading
▪ make a logical prediction before reading
▪ continue during reading to access prior knowledge and make logical predictions to recognize words, self-correct miscues, and comprehend text

Explanation

A good reader collects information about the content of a text and makes predictions based on prior knowledge. Titles, vocabulary, and phrases serve as clues for a reader who uses information to speculate about the potential meaning of the text (Blachowicz & Fisher, 2002; Nessell, 1987). Clues about story structure (who, where, when, and what) and expository elements (description, collection, causation, problem/solution, comparison) can be gathered when a reader skims the text. The reader then combines the skimmed data with prior knowledge to make a logical prediction. While reading, this prediction supports comprehension. Verification of an accurate prediction or revision of an inaccurate prediction are two strategies the reader uses to interpret meaning.

Directions

1. On page 106 (Form A, Level 2 "The Baseball Star"), look for the box called Prior Knowledge/Prediction. Notice the rating scale located inside the box. What purpose does it serve? What is the advantage of asking the reader to read the title and the first two sentences?

2. Read the passage "The Baseball Star" to yourself. Then, on CD 2, Track 3 listen to Patrick read the passage.

3. With a partner, discuss and answer this question: What happened to Patrick's reading when he read *basketball* for *baseball*? If you had been sitting next to him, you would have noticed his confused and stressed emotional status. Why do you think he was stressed?

4. How do you think the skills of prediction and prior knowledge work to help the reader? What does Patrick's reading of this passage teach us about the importance of this skill? In this instance, what is the advantage of informal assessment over a more formal assessment such as a standardized test?

Study Packet Materials

• Copy Form A, Level 2 "The Baseball Star" (pages 106, 107, and 108)—use this same material for Component 5.

• CD 2, Track 3

• Answer Key (page 264)

COMPONENT 4 STUDY PACKET
ORAL READING MISCUE ANALYSIS _____

Reader Standard/Indicators: Phonics/Vocabulary and Language in Use

▪ decode and problem solve the pronunciation of words (assessment of omissions, insertions, substitutions, aided words, repetitions, and reversals)
▪ make self-corrections to construct meaning of words and chunks of text
▪ use graphophonic, syntactic, and semantic cueing systems to decode or self-correct words and construct meaning of text

Explanation

A miscue is a deviation from the text. Miscue analysis serves as an opportunity to find out how the reader is decoding and comprehending text. Miscue analysis reveals the frequency of a miscue, the severity of a miscue, and the ability of a reader to self-correct.

Directions
Oral Reading Miscues Chart

Study Packet Materials Oral Reading Miscues Chart

• Copy or refer to Oral Reading Miscues Chart (page 24).

• Copy Form B, Level 1 "The Surprise Party" (page 138).

• Copy Form B, Level 6 "The First Gas Mask" (pages 152–153).

• CD 2, Track 4

• Answer Key (pages 264–265)

1. Work with a partner and study the descriptions and examples listed on the Oral Reading Miscues Chart (page 24). Note that some miscues are counted because they make up the word recognition quantitative score, which is tallied on the Scoring Guide Summary. Other miscues are not counted, but they are coded because they provide relevant information for the qualitative analysis. Both quantitative and qualitative data make up a reader's multidimensional profile. Make a copy of the Oral Reading Miscues Chart and use it as a study guide, placing it alongside a passage when you practice coding miscues.

2. Learning to code miscues can be discomforting because you must listen, write, and think—all at the same time. Repeated practice will bring ease and comfort.

Make copies of both of the following passages, "The Surprise Party" and "The First Gas Mask." In both passages each type of counted miscue is represented—omissions, insertions, substitutions, aided words, repetitions, and reversals. The coded but not counted miscues also occur—self-corrections, hesitations, and the ignoring of punctuation. Play each passage on CD 2, Track 4 and code each passage. Check your answers with the answer key found in the Appendix.

If you wish more coding practice, use other passages presented on CD 2, or use any of the passages from CD 1, Case Study. Locate the corresponding passages in the Examiner's Records and make copies.

3. Study the explanations as follows and those that continue on page 25 to clarify questions that will likely arise. Discuss the information with a partner. Use these explanations like a study guide as you practice coding miscues.

▪ Omissions
An omission occurs when a whole word is omitted from the text.

▪ Substitutions
If the student miscues the same word several times and the miscue does not change the meaning, it should be counted as one miscue. For example, if the student miscues *mom* for *mommy* and does it throughout the whole text, it should be counted as only one miscue. However, if the miscue

Oral Reading Miscues Chart

Abbr.	Miscue and Code	Example
O	**Omission:** Circle the word.	James Cornish lay (wounded) on the saloon floor.
I	**Insertion:** Write in the inserted word or words.	It was a hot and *very* humid day in Chicago in 1893.
S	**Substitution:** Write the substituted word. A substitution can be a real word or a non-word.	*house* The horse trotted along the road. *went* Pat went to the movies.
A	**Aided Word:** Draw a diagonal line through the word pronounced for the student.	She thought his condition seemed to be growing worse.
Rp	**Repetition:** Underline the repeated word or words. Sometimes a reader will repeat words or phrases because he or she is self-correcting. In this case, place SC over the miscue and do not count it.	All the kids thought this was a great idea and quickly invited Jack to belong.
Rv	**Reversal:** Use a curved line to indicate words or letters that have been reversed.	"Oh, no!" I shouted. It was a muggy, hot day.

The following miscues are coded but not added into the final miscue count.

Abbr.	Miscue and Code	Example
SC	**Self-Corrections:** Record as SC. Self-corrections show that the reader is first using semantic cues to monitor the meaning, then using graphophonic cues or background knowledge to correct the pronunciation.	*boy SC* An old beaver dam from upstream broke. *SC* No one could enter (the tunnel.)
/ (Fluency)	**Hesitations:** If a reader hesitates after words or at the ends of lines, it should be recorded as a /. Hesitations affect a reader's fluency.	I found a / lost / baby turtle. / I took him home so he / could / live in my house.
X (Fluency)	**Ignores Punctuation:** If a reader ignores end of sentence punctuation, use a ⌣ between the two sentences. If commas and/or other intra-sentence punctuation marks are ignored, place an X near them. Sometimes a reader ignores punctuation because he or she is not monitoring the meaning. Sometimes the reader repeats a phrase to self-correct, using the punctuation to convey the meaning and expression of the text.	"I'm knocking one hundred times!" he shouted. "I don't know the secret word," he declared X "but I have something important to tell everyone! I'm the new boy," he explained.

changes the meaning, such as *tricks* for *trash*, and is followed later in the text as *tricks* for *trash*, each attempt should be counted as a separate miscue. You would be wondering why the reader didn't self-correct. If the miscue is *tricks* for *trash*, then *tricks* for *trash*, then *tracks* for *trash*, the miscues total three.

In the case of proper nouns, if the reader miscues the name, such as *Trey* for *Terry*, and continues consistently throughout the text, it should be counted as one miscue, and you do not need to record it twice on the "Cueing Systems" grid. But, if the reader says *Trey* for *Terry* and then changes and says *Teresa* for *Terry*, it should be counted as two miscues.

If the reader omits part of a word, such as *fright* for *frightened*, count the miscue as a substitution and analyze it on the "Cueing Systems" grid.

A non-word substitution, such as *anter* for *anger*, is always counted. If the same non-word miscue is recurring, it should be counted each time because it obstructs the comprehension. A non-word substitution is always syntactically unacceptable and semantically changes the meaning.

Pronunciation related to articulation difficulties or regional dialects should not be counted as oral miscues, unless the reader has pronounced the word correctly previously in the passage.

■ Aided Words
Only when absolutely necessary should you provide pronunciation aid for a reader. It is best to allow the reader to problem solve the pronunciation of a word rather than to permit him or her to rely on your assistance. There are two common exceptions. One sometimes occurs at the beginning of an assessment session with a reluctant, nervous reader. You may need to assist him or her just to get the session started. Or, if a reader is clearly at the frustration level, you may provide aid because you plan to stop the reading at the end of the paragraph.

■ Repetitions
A repetition occurs when a reader repeats an entire word or phrase. If the reader repeats only part of a word, such as *neigh–neighborhood*, it should not be counted as a repetition. It is actually an attempt to sound the word out or to self-correct. If the reader repeats the same word or phrase several times without changing its pronunciation, underline it each time it occurs, but count it just as one miscue.

COMPONENT 5 STUDY PACKET
FLUENCY ANALYSIS

Reader Standard/Indicators: Fluency

■ read smoothly, accurately, in meaningful phrases
■ use pitch, stress, and intonation to convey meaning of the text
■ repeat words or phrases using meaning to self-correct
■ use punctuation to divide text into units of meaning

Explanation

Fluency refers to the reader's automatic control of text, taking into consideration phrasing, pitch, stress, and intonation, which indicate both word recognition and

Study Packet Materials

- Form A, Level 2 "The Baseball Star" (pages 106–108)—use copy from Component 3
- CD 2, Track 5
- Answer Key (page 265)

comprehension competency. After a passage is read, you will think about how the oral reading miscues and comprehension interact with the reader's fluency (Leu & Kinser, 2003; Walker, 2004). This information is recorded on the fluency grid attached to the bottom of a passage. Fluency analysis factors into the qualitative analysis and helps to establish the reader's multidimensional profile.

Directions

1. Study the fluency grid found on page 107, Form A, Level 2 "The Baseball Star." With a partner, discuss each of the qualities of fluency as described on the fluency grid.

2. On CD 2, Track 5, listen to the first reader, Caitlin. Can you hear in her voice each quality named on the grid? With only this little portion of information, what would be your prediction about Caitlin's reading level? Independent? Instructional? Frustration? Without other data, such as a retelling or responses to comprehension questions, an actual determination cannot be made, but in this instance, what telltale qualities of fluency cause you to predict the level you chose?

3. Listen to the second reader, Amanda. Listen again for the qualities that characterize fluency. Can you name each quality without looking at the grid? Jot them on the list below.

    a. _____   c. _____

    b. _____   d. _____

4. Look at the Fluency Rating Scale on page 107. Circle the number that best describes Amanda's fluency.

5. Make a tentative prediction about her reading level. Independent? Instructional? Frustration? Listen to her retelling and jot it down on page 108, and make a more data-driven guess about her reading level with this passage. Combine your fluency reasons with your retelling reasons and list them here.

_____

_____

6. Listen to Amanda again. Are you able to listen and simultaneously name the fluency indicators you hear her apply? Below write a phrase or sentence she read, and beside it write the fluency indicators. For example:

    a. "Strike one," called the man! I could feel my legs beginning to shake.

    Indicator: voice stress and intonation; use of punctuation to convey meaning

    b. _____

    Indicator: _____

    c. _____

    Indicator: _____

    How does it feel to listen and simultaneously name the indicators?

_____

_____

COMPONENT 6 STUDY PACKET
RETELLING/SUMMARY STATEMENT ANALYSIS ──────────

Reader Standard/Indicators: Comprehension

- recall/retell a text to include all story structure elements—main character, time and place, problem, plot details in sequence, turning point, resolution
- recall/retell a text to include all expository elements—description, collection, causation, problem/solution, comparison
- summarize text including main idea and basic plot elements
- retell in full sentences in language comparable to author's vocabulary and style

Story Elements	All	Some	None
Main Character(s)			
Time and Place			
Problem			
Plot Details in Sequence			
Turning Point			
Resolution			
Reader's Thumbnail Summary:			

Expository Elements	All	Some	None
Description			
Collection			
Causation			
Problem/Solution			
Comparison			
Reader's Thumbnail Summary:			

Study Packet Materials

- Copy Form C, Level 2, Case Study "The Busy Road" (pages 57, 58, 59)
- Copy Form C, Level 4, Case Study "The Beloved Horse" (pages 63–65)
- CD 2, Track 6
- Answer Key (pages 266, 267)

Explanation

After the student has read a passage, you will assess how thoroughly the reader comprehended the text. Before asking comprehension questions, ask the reader to retell as much as he can remember. It is recommended that you write the student's response in the box provided. To assist you in determining the thoroughness of the retelling, a checklist grid is included. The Story Elements grid used in Forms A, B, and C outlines the elements of narrative text, and the Expository Elements grid used in Forms S and SS outlines the elements of expository text. For a detailed explanation of the differences between the two types of passages and the grids, refer to pages 11–13, "Narrative and Expository Passages."

In addition to data about the reader's comprehension, a retelling provides important information about the reader's use of language. The reader's ability to construct a complete sentence, mimic the author's choice of words and style of language, and construct a logical, sequential retelling should be added to the narrative and expository elements information to render a thorough profile of the reader's comprehension.

Asking readers to retell a text is an essential instructional practice as well as an assessment tool (Morrow, 1988). Children who practice retelling become better at both comprehension and recall. They also gain the ability to organize and retain text information (Gambrell, Pfeiffer, & Wilson, 1985; May, 2006).

Directions

1. Listen to CD 2, Track 6, as Jenny reads Form C, Level 2 "The Busy Road" and follow along in the Case Study, pages 57–58. Pause the CD immediately after she finishes reading the text (after she reads, "Please hurry so we can save him!"). Based upon what you have heard, although you don't know for certain, can you predict the quality of her retelling?

Now, turn to page 59 and read her retelling. Does she identify each story element? Draw a line from the name of the element listed in the Story Elements grid to the corresponding element in her retelling. Are the elements sequenced in a logical order?

Notice the Retelling Summary at the bottom of the grid. Do you agree that her retelling includes: ☐ many details, logical order? _____

Did Jenny retell using any of the author's words and style of language? _____

What is the quality of the Reader's Thumbnail Summary statement?

_____

2. Release the pause button on your CD player and listen to Jenny read Form C, Level 4 "The Beloved Horse" (pages 63–65). Based upon what you heard and read, although you don't know for certain, predict the quality of her retelling.

Now turn to page 65 and read the retelling. Does she identify each story element? Draw a line from the name of the element listed in the Story Elements grid to the corresponding element in her retelling. Notice how the examiner had to *probe* to get Jenny to give more information. Notice how an examiner's probe is an open-ended question designed to cause the reader to think and probe his or her own mind.

Notice the Retelling Summary at the bottom of the grid. Do you agree that her retelling includes: ☐ few details, disorder? _____

Are the elements sequenced in a logical order? _____

Did Jenny retell using any of the author's words and style of language? _____

What is the quality of the Reader's Thumbnail Summary statement?

_____

3. List four specific contrasting features you notice between the retellings for "The Busy Road" and "The Beloved Horse."

<u>Busy</u>   <u>Beloved</u>

a. _____   a. _____

b. _____   b. _____

c. _____   c. _____

d. _____   d. _____

COMPONENT 7 STUDY PACKET
COMPREHENSION QUESTION/READER TEXT
RELATIONSHIP (RTR) ANALYSIS ─────────────

Reader Standard/Indicators: Comprehension

- construct literal meaning of text
- construct implied meaning of text
- retain and put information together within and across paragraphs
- access prior knowledge and connect to in-text information (context cues)
- establish a personal opinion and substantiate it with information from text
- reply in full sentences comparable to author's vocabulary and style

Explanation

The comprehension questions used in the *ARI* are divided into two overarching categories: questions that cause responses primarily *from the text* at the literal level and questions that cause the reader to respond *from head to text,* or at a higher level

QAR/RTR Equivalencies

QAR	RTR
In the Book	**From the Text**
• Right There	• RIF
• Think and Search	• PIT (literal)
In My Head	**From Head to Text**
• Author & You	• PIT (inferential) CAR
• On My Own	• EAS (must substantiate from text)

such as inferential or evaluative (Heilman, Blair, & Rupley, 1998). Based upon how a question is worded, the reader will use different thinking skills to generate a response. The difference in thinking can be observed when the reader responds to comprehension questions. The *ARI* refers to this demonstration as the *reader text relationship (RTR)*.

For example, when dealing with a question that activates literal thinking, the reader's mind searches for one or more facts to produce a response, focusing mostly on information from the text. However, when dealing with a question that is inferential or evaluative, the reader's mind journeys back and forth between the content of the text and his or her prior knowledge (*from head to text*) in order to deduce, infer, connect, and evaluate (Heilman, Blair, & Rupley, 2002; Leu & Kinzer, 2003; Raphael, 1982, 1986). Examiner listening skills should be fine-tuned to know what type of comprehension question elicits what level of thinking.

Types of *ARI* Comprehension Questions and Reader Text Relationship Chart

Type	Description	Indicator(s)	RTR
RIF	The reader **retells in fact** one or two explicitly stated listing of facts.	• retells literal facts	• from the text
PIT	The reader **puts information together,** combining two or more explicitly stated facts from the text, either in the same location or in different parts of the text. In contrast to list-like **RIF** responses, **PIT** responses have a relationship to each other.	• combines & connects literal facts directly from same part of the text	• from text
	In some instances, PIT questions require the reader to combine information that is not explicitly stated, yet is strongly implied (deducted). Thus, a PIT question can be a transition question, guiding the reader from explicit restating, accessing of prior knowledge, and/or combining of facts toward higher level thinking.	• combines & connects information from various parts of the text	• from text
		• connects implied information to prior in-head knowledge	• from head to text
CAR	The reader **connects author and reader,** combining in-head prior knowledge with the author's choice of words and phrases (vocabulary) to interpret the author's intended meaning. The mental journey can be back and forth between in-head knowledge and use of in-text context clues.	• connects information from text, accesses prior knowledge, and uses context to acquire the meaning	• back and forth from head to text
EAS	The reader **evaluates and substantiates** assessing and judging to generate an opinion, an emotional response, or prediction based upon a personal interpretation inferred from the text. Finally, the reader substantiates the interpretation with explicit information from the text.	• evaluates and substantiates	• back and forth from head to text

Directions

1. With a partner study the Types of *ARI* Comprehension Questions and Reader Text Relationship Chart on the previous page.

2. Open the *Reader's Passages* book to page 5 and read the text. Read the questions, respond to them, identify the question type and indicators in application, and circle the correct RTR.

Question & Response	Type	Indicator(s)	RTR
1. Who are the two main characters in this story?			from head? head to text?
2. Where is Pat sitting?			from head? head to text?
3. What is Pat's problem?			from head? head to text?
4. What do you know about the word *work*? What does the word *work* have to do with the story?			from head? head to text?
5. What did Pat decide to do about this problem?			from head? head to text?
6. Where did Pat hide and why?			from head? head to text?
7. Do you think Pat's mom will find him? You think this because . . .			from head? head to text?

COMPONENT 8 STUDY PACKET
CUEING SYSTEMS: MISCUE ANALYSIS

Reader Standard/Indicators: Phonics and Comprehension

■ apply graphophonic, syntactic, and semantic cueing systems to decode words, self-correct miscues, and construct meaning of text

Explanation

When you conduct miscue analysis, you learn how the reader uses three of the cueing systems: graphophonic, syntactic, and semantic (Reutzel & Cooter, 2004). It's important to know if a reader is balancing the use of cueing systems or overrelying on one. For example, you can find out if a reader is: (1) focusing too much on graphophonic cues and calling words that are not associated with the meaning of the text; (2) overusing background knowledge and not carefully attending to the graphophonic cues; or (3) searching for meaning and self-correcting by using a triangulation of graphophonic, syntactic, and semantic cues to pronounce the word. Additionally, miscue analysis helps you determine the seriousness of a miscue. "Does the miscue support or detract from the meaning of the text?" you ask yourself. Miscue analysis provides the specific qualitative analysis you need to appropriately focus instructional advice.

Graphophonic

The graphophonic (*grapho*–written letters; *phonic*–spoken language sounds) cueing system concerns the relationship between letters and the sounds of the letters (Goodman & Burke, 1976; Reutzel & Cooter, 2004). On the Cueing Systems grid, you will look for graphophonic similarity in the Initial (I), Medial (M), and/or Final (F) positions of the word. For example, if a reader said *wert* for *went* (Pat went to the movies), the miscue is similar in the initial (I) and final (F) positions of the word. This non-word substitution shows that the reader is focusing on the graphophonic features. If the reader said *want* for *wait* (I will wait for you.), again the miscue is similar in the initial (I) and final (F) positions, and the reader is still focusing on graphophonic cues. If the student read *they* for *these* (I think these children are too noisy!), the miscue is similar only in the initial (I) part. Think about this miscue, *breath* for *breathing* (The pony's condition was growing worse as his breathing grew louder and harder.). In this instance the reader attended to the initial (I) and the medial (M) portions of the word even though the vowel sound is different. With the miscue *much* for *wait* (I will wait for you.), there is no graphophonic similarity. In this case, leave the cell in the grid blank.

Syntactic

The syntactic cueing system relates to the reader's knowledge about how language is ordered in the structure of a sentence. Syntactic knowledge demonstrates a reader's intuitive sense of the grammatical structure of his or her first language. A syntactically unacceptable miscue occurs when the reader substituted a word that is a different part of speech or a non-word. For example, the reader reads *straight* for *stood* (The boy stood for hours.). In this case, the reader substitutes an adjective for a verb, causing the miscue to be syntactically unacceptable because the sentence does not make sense.

Semantic

Constructing meaning is the central reason for engaging in the act of reading (Reutzel & Cooter, 2004). An analysis of a miscue from the semantic viewpoint reveals the reader's ability to focus on the meaning of the text. Background knowledge, interests, attitudes, and perspectives constitute a reader's mental schemata. Such a schemata is the foundation of a reader's ability to think and comprehend. An example of a semantic miscue might be substituting the word *large* for *big* (I will hide by this big tree.). A reader can make a substitution such as this, and semantically there is little or no significant change in meaning. Caution should be taken, however, because a recurring inattention to graphophonic cues could prevent a reader from comprehending an author's intended meaning. For example, substituting the word *laughed* for *snickered* (The girl snickered, so no one heard.) distorts the specific meaning intended by the author. Some might code this miscue "NCM" (No Change in Meaning); however, a competent reader accurately reads the author's word choices, which reflect the subtleties and innuendos of meaning. If near-miss miscues like this persist, the problem should be noted. A non-word substitution such as *anter* for *anger* is always coded as "CM" (Change in Meaning).

Directions

1. Study the description of each cueing system—graphophonic, syntactic, and semantic. As you read the description of each system, use the examples to fill out this Cueing Systems grid. Notice that the miscue is in italics and the actual text in parentheses. Discuss each miscue with a partner.

Cueing Systems				
L I N E #	Miscue	Grapho-phonically Similar I M F (word level)	Syntactically Acceptable Unacceptable (sentence level)	Semantic Change in Meaning (CM) No Change in Meaning (NCM) (sentence level)

2. Refer to the Case Study Form C, Level 2 "The Busy Road." Read the passage and note the various types of miscues. Next, study the miscues recorded in the Cueing Systems grid on page 57. With a partner discuss the significance of each miscue. Read the "Cueing Systems Summary" on page 58. What is the significance of the reader's self-corrections?

COMPONENT 9 STUDY PACKET
QUANTITATIVE AND QUALITATIVE ANALYSIS
DEVELOPING A READER'S MULTIDIMENSIONAL
PROFILE

Examiner Standard/Indicators: Analysis/Synthesis

▣   analyze and synthesize quantitative and qualitative data

Quantitative	Qualitative
• # miscues • # comprehension question errors	• prior knowledge/prediction • cueing systems • fluency • retelling/summary • comprehension question responses (RTR–literal and inferential) • emotional status

> The term *reading level* refers to the reader's level of ability with a given passage: independent, instructional, frustration, or listening.
>
> The term *passage level* refers to the calculated level of difficulty of an *ARI* passage–for example, Form C, Level 2 "The Busy Road."

Explanation

When administering the *ARI*, you will determine a reader's four reading levels: independent, instructional, frustration, and listening. Each reading level reflects data about the reader's mastery or nonmastery of standards and indicators. In the past, informal reading inventory examiners determined a reading level only by counting miscues and comprehension question errors. In other words, only the quantitative data was used to determine the reader's reading level. However, without the qualitative data, the significance and severity of the miscues and comprehension errors were unknown. Now we know that the combination of the quantitative and qualitative (Q & Q) data reveals a more accurate determination of reading level and in the final analysis represents all factors that make up the reader's multidimensional profile.

The best way to learn to instantly recognize the qualitative factors is to listen for and identify them as a student reads a passage at a given reading level. At each reading level the reader demonstrates recognizable behaviors. For example, at the independent level the reader's emotional status is calm and the oral reading is fluent. The reader therefore demonstrates at that level a high amount of control over both Q & Q factors. As the reader progresses from independent to frustration level, an examiner can hear and see changes in the amount of control a reader exhibits. Your ability to listen for and identify both Q & Q factors at each reading level is essential during assessment and is of equal importance during reading instruction.

When giving the *ARI*, you will start a reader at the independent reading level, continue through the two instructional levels, and stop at the frustration level. To obtain a listening level, you will read a passage to the reader, assessing his or her prior knowledge/prediction, retelling, and responses to comprehension questions. To accurately determine a reading level, you must know both the Q & Q factors at each level and be able to recognize them as you hear the reader apply or default the standards and indicators.

**Directions
Quantitative and Qualitative Data Chart for Four
Reading Levels**

1. With a partner study the Quantitative and Qualitative Data Chart for Four Reading Levels on page 35. Name each level and jot notes in the grid below that characterize the quantitative and qualitative factors at each level.

Reading Level	Quantitative Factors	Qualitative Factors

2. You found out that qualitative factors refer to _____ _____.

3. You found out that quantitative factors refer to _____ _____.

4. Why do you think it is important to assess both types of data? _____ _____

5. Read the background information in the bottom row of the chart and discuss it with a partner.

6. Test yourself. With a piece of scrap paper, cover the Quantitative and Qualitative columns on the chart. Begin with the independent reading level and describe both Q & Q factors. Then, repeat this process with the instructional, frustration, and listening levels.

Quantitative and Qualitative Data Chart for Four Reading Levels

Reading Level*	Quantitative Factors	Qualitative Factors
Independent	The reader reads with no more than one uncorrected miscue in 100 running words of text (99%) and with 90% accuracy for comprehension. In some cases, the reader may exceed the criterion for miscues if comprehension is maintained at 90% or higher. • Word Recognition = 99–100% • Comprehension = 90–100%	The reader gathers information from the text and accesses prior knowledge and context clues to make a meaningful prediction. The reader almost always self-corrects miscues. Uncorrected miscues don't change the meaning. The reading is fluent and expressive with accurate attention to punctuation. A retelling contains all text elements and is well organized in language that is comparable to the author's. The summary statement is concise and focused. When answering comprehension questions the reader thinks both literally and inferentially (RTR). The reader is at ease and confident.
Instructional	The reader reads with no more than five uncorrected miscues in 100 words of text (95%) and with at least 75% comprehension. In some cases, the number of miscues may exceed this criterion if comprehension is higher than 75%. • Word Recognition = 95–99% • Comprehension = 75–89%	The reader gathers information from the text and accesses prior knowledge and context clues to make a meaningful prediction. The reader miscues, yet often self-corrects. Sometimes miscues change the meaning. Sometimes assistance is required. The reader is mostly fluent. A retelling and summary statement are for the most part adequate. Most of the time the reader uses language comparable to the author's. When asked comprehension questions, some of the time the reader thinks both literally and inferentially (RTR). The reader is sometimes confident, challenged but not frustrated. At this level a reader can achieve maximum growth when supported by appropriate instruction and materials.
Frustration	The reader is struggling so much that little or no meaning is achieved. Miscues exceed 10% (less than 90% correct) with comprehension at or below 50%. • Word Recognition = 90% or below • Comprehension = 50% or below	The reader fails to gather information from the text and also fails to access prior knowledge or context clues to make a meaningful prediction. The reader miscues frequently and rarely self-corrects. Most miscues change the meaning. The reading is disfluent. The retelling is disorganized and incomplete, and the language used is disorganized and seldom comparable to the author's. The summary statement is inadequate. Responses to comprehension questions are mostly inadequate, and the reader seldom thinks inferentially (RTR). The reader is nervous and frustrated.
Listening	The reader comprehends 75% of the material that has been read aloud by the examiner. This comprehension score is equal to the oral instructional level score. Sometimes this level is called the *level of reading potential*. A large gap between the oral reading frustration level and listening level indicates that the reader could achieve growth in reading with appropriate instructional strategies and books. • Reading Potential Comprehension = 75%	The reader gathers information from the text and accesses prior knowledge and context clues to make a meaningful prediction. The quality of the retelling is equal to or better than at the oral instructional level. When responding to comprehension questions, most of the time the reader thinks both literally and inferentially (RTR). When responding to retelling and comprehension questions, the reader is at ease with few or no signs of stress.

*Each level reflects the percentages established by Betts (Beldin, 1970; Pikulski, 1974). However, a study by Powell (1970) and Powell and Dunkeld (1971) challenged Betts's numerical standard; their findings suggested that the word recognition criteria of 95% at the instructional level was too high for primary readers. Then, Pikulski (1974) disputed Powell's and Dunkeld's challenge. Additionally, Ekwall (1976a, 1976b) presented strong evidence that the Betts's standard should be maintained. Finally, Johnson and Kress (1965) in *Informal Reading Inventories* also recommended the Betts's standard. Therefore the standard of Betts et al. was used in the *ARI*.

The qualitative factors outlined on each reader's chart are:

- Prior Knowledge/ Prediction
- Cueing Systems Summary
- Fluency
- Retelling, Story Element Summary, Summary Statement
- Comprehension Questions and Possible Answers, RTR
- Emotional Status

7. In this portion of the study packet, you will hear five readers each reading a different passage at a different reading level: independent, instructional, frustration, and listening. The purpose of this portion of the study packet is to train you to:

  a. name and know the qualitative factors that characterize each reading level

  b. listen for and identify the qualitative factors while a student is reading at a given level

  c. compare and contrast differences in the amount of control a reader has at the independent, instructional, and frustration levels

  If you need a review of the qualitative factors, refer to the Quantitative and Qualitative Data Chart on page 35.

8. Find Form A, Level 3 "Exploring a Cave" in the *Reader's Passages* book, p. 8. Place the text next to Reader #1 Chart, Freddie, Independent Level (p. 37), so that you can easily see the passage as you follow the information on the chart. Listen to CD 2, Track 8, and follow Freddie's responses for each factor outlined on his chart, Reader #1.

  When listening for the Cueing Systems factors, follow your copy of the passage from the *Reader's Passages* book, noticing miscues but not coding them (unless you choose to do so). Focus on the qualitative factors rather than the quantitative factors. Listen for evidence that verifies the check or comment made in the box, Cueing Systems Summary.

  As you listen to the comprehension questions asked by the examiner, notice that questions are not asked if the information was included in the retelling. As you listen, note the qualitative factors in the reader's responses, such as how the reader structures sentences and uses the author's style and words. Note also if the RTR is both *from text* and *from head to text*.

9. With a partner, listen again to CD 2, Track 8. As you hear each qualitative factor, point to it on the reader's chart and pause the CD. Name the qualitative factor and discuss the quality of Freddie's response.

10. Repeat directions 7, 8, and 9 with each reader's chart:

  Reader #2
  Reader #3
  Reader #4
  Reader #5

  Note that the Study Packet Materials box, which lists all items you need, is located in the top left corner of each reader's chart.

Purpose: Listen for and identify the qualitative factors at a given reading level.

Study Packet Materials

- Reader #1 Chart Directions 7–9 (p. 36)
- copy Reader's Passages Form A, Level 3 "Exploring a Cave" (p. 8)
- CD 2, Track 8

PRIOR KNOWLEDGE/PREDICTION

☐ Read the title and predict what the story is about.
It's gonna be a boy in a cave and looking for lots of stuff. Probe: *What do you know about going in caves and looking for lots of stuff?*
Response: *There's going to be cave monsters and all that stuff.*

☐ Read the first two sentences and add more to your prediction.
That he is gonna find his dog Boxer exploring lots of stuff—finding stuff.

Prior Knowledge
☐ a lot
☑ some
☐ none

CUEING SYSTEMS SUMMARY

☐ Most	☐ few	☐ no	miscues were graphophonically similar to the word in the passage.
☐ Most	☐ few	☐ no	miscues were syntactically matched. *only 1 miscue*
☐ Most	☐ few	☐ no	miscues maintained the author's meaning.

☑ The self-corrections demonstrate that the reader monitors the meaning. *SC from far off*

Fluency: Does the Reader . . .

☐ read smoothly, (accurately, in meaningful phrases?)

☐ read word-by-word, choppy, plodding?

☑ use pitch, stress, and intonation to convey meaning of the text? *(near end)*

☑ repeat words and phrases because s/he is monitoring the meaning (self-correcting)?

☐ repeat words and phrases because s/he is trying to sound out words?

☐ use punctuation to divide the text into units of meaning? ☑ ignore the punctuation?

(Freddie read rapidly in a monotone voice—glided through most punctuation, but none of this affected the quality of comprehension, retelling, or RTR-self-corrected the for that)

Rating Scale: Circle One

4 = fluent reading / good pace   2 = choppy, plodding reading / slow pace
③ = fairly fluent / reasonable pace   1 = clearly labored, disfluent reading / very slow pace

RETELLING

He went into this cave and the farther he walked the darker it grew. Then he, then his dog, Boxer, went to explore on his own, and then he went into this cave holding his candle really high. Then it blew out. The very first match he lit, it blew out. Then suddenly he holded it up real high and then he found this thing that was moving, and then he saw dark glowing eyes. Then he shouted it was his dog, Boxer. And then he said, "Let's get out of here!"
(Freddie used well structured sentences, some in exact author's style and words.)

Story Elements Sum
- retold with all story elements

Summary Statement
- exploring a cave (adequate)

EMOTIONAL STATUS
- confident
- calm
- focused
- attentive
- successful

Retelling Summary ☑ many details, logical order   ☐ some details, some order   ☐ few details, disorder

COMPREHENSION QUESTIONS AND POSSIBLE ANSWERS:

+ (RIF) 1. Who are the two main characters in this story? (a boy named Mark and his dog, Boxer) *(questions 1-5 in retelling)*
+ (PIT) 2. What is the problem in this story? (Mark and Boxer walked into a cave that is getting darker and darker)
+ (RIF) 3. When they first went into the cave, what did Boxer do? (ran off to explore on his own) *because he couldn't see*
+ (PIT) 4. Why did Mark light the candle the first time? (it was dark; he couldn't see; he grew fearful)
+ (RIF) 5. What did Mark do when the candle went out? (tried to light it; but the first match went out)
+ (EAS) 6. How do you think Mark felt when the candle went out? (scared) You think this because the text said ... (his hand was shaking)
+ (CAR) 7. What do you know about the word **recognize?** (you **know** something, maybe you've seen it before) What does the word **recognize** have to do with this story? (it said Mark *recognized* Boxer)
+ (EAS) 8. Do you think Mark was smart to go into the cave alone? (no, you'd get scared and fall, get hurt, and no one could find you) You think this because the story said ... (Mark got scared; his candle went out)

#6–8

Reader Text Relationship (RTR) From the Text ☑ adequate ☐ inadequate   From Head to Text ☑ adequate ☐ not adequate

READER #2 CHART: KALA   INDEPENDENT LEVEL

Purpose: Listen for and identify the qualitative factors at a given reading level.

Study Packet Materials

- Reader #2 Chart
  Directions 7–9 (p. 36)
- *Reader's Passages*
  Form A, Level 5
  "The Bicycle Race"
  (p. 10)
- CD 2, Track 9

PRIOR KNOWLEDGE/PREDICTION

☐ Read the title and predict what the story is about.
It's probably about a couple of kids who want to have a bicycle race and it works out. They get to have the race.
P: *What do you know about bicycle races?* Res: *They can be fun and dangerous if you fall off your bike and hurt your knee or something.*
☐ Read the first two sentences and add more to your prediction.
Sheila probably hits a fence or a tree and probably hurts her hand or leg.

Prior Knowledge
☑ a lot
☐ some
☐ none

CUEING SYSTEMS SUMMARY

☐ Most	☐ few	☐ no	miscues were graphophonically similar to the word in the passage.
☐ Most	☐ few	☐ no	miscues were syntactically matched.
☐ Most	☐ few	☐ no	miscues maintained the author's meaning.

☑ The self-corrections demonstrate that the reader monitors the meaning. *all miscues SC*

Fluency: Does the Reader . . .

☐ read smoothly, (accurately, in meaningful phrases?)

☐ read word-by-word, choppy, plodding?

☑ use pitch, stress, and intonation to convey meaning of the text?

☑ repeat words and phrases because s/he is monitoring the meaning (self-correcting)?

☐ repeat words and phrases because s/he is trying to sound out words?

☐ use punctuation to divide the text into units of meaning?   ☐ ignore the punctuation?

(Kala read rapidly and confidently. She repeated some phrases to self-correct. She said "Oh!" when she read about the injury. She glided over some punct., but still had perfect comp.)

Rating Scale: Circle One
④ = fluent reading / good pace   2 = choppy, plodding reading / slow pace
3 = fairly fluent / reasonable pace   1 = clearly labored, disfluent reading / very slow pace

---

RETELLING

It's about Sheila Young and she hits into this bicycle, bicycler, actually the bicycle hits into her. The other bicycler is going 40 miles per hour and she has a big 9 inch gash on her head. And she didn't have time to get it stitched up because she wants to win the race. And so she just tells the doctor that is probably there at the track to staple it up and put a bandage over it. And then at the end of the race she wins it.
(Kala used well structured sentences—some in the exact author's style and words.)

Story Elements Sum
- *retold with all story elements*

Summary Statement
- *adequate*

EMOTIONAL STATUS
- *confident*
- *focused*
- *attentive*
- *tense but in control*
- *successful*

Retelling Summary   ☑ many details, logical order   ☐ some details, some order   ☐ few details, disorder

---

COMPREHENSION QUESTIONS AND POSSIBLE ANSWERS:

+ (RIF)   1. Who is the main character in this story? (Sheila Young) *(# 1 and 2 in retelling)*
+ (PIT)   2. What is the problem in this story? (She was bumped by another racer.)
+ (CAR)   3. What do you know about the word **challenger?** (someone who is racing against you; another competitor)
            What does **challenger** have to do with this story? (Shelia saw her challenger's bike come too close.)
+ (PIT)   4. How do you know the crash was dangerous? (it was horrifying; the crash occurred at 40 mph)
+ (RIF)   5. What injury did Sheila receive in the crash? (a 9 inch gash on her head)
+ (RIF)   6. Why didn't Sheila want to quit the race? (she could only think of winning)
+ (CAR)   7. What do you know about the phrase **intense pain?** (strong pain, agony) What does the word **intense pain** have to do with this story? (tears rolled down Sheila's face from the intense pain)
+ (EAS)   8. In your opinion, how important was this race to Sheila? (extremely important)
            You think this because the story said ... (despite being injured, she still wanted the gold medal)

Reader Text Relationship (RTR)   From the Text   ☑ adequate ☐ inadequate   From Head to Text   ☑ adequate ☐ not adequate

READER #3 CHART: PATRICK   INSTRUCTIONAL LEVEL

Purpose: Listen for and identify the qualitative factors at a given reading level.

Study Packet Materials

- Reader #3 Chart
  Directions 7–9 (p. 36)
- copy *Reader's Passages*
  Form A, Level 1
  "The Crowded Car" (p. 6)
- CD 2, Track 10

PRIOR KNOWLEDGE/PREDICTION

☐ Read the title and predict what the story is about.

It's going to be about a car and the people getting in it, and there is not going to be much room in it.

☐ Read the first two sentences and add more to your prediction.

Some more of it is going to be about somebody and people bringing stuff in to share with their class and stuff. P: There's not much room in them. You can't fit much stuff in it. P: They bring stuff in to share and tell at least 3 things about what they brought in.

Prior Knowledge
☐ a lot
☑ some
☐ none

CUEING SYSTEMS SUMMARY

☑ Most ☐ few ☐ no   miscues were graphophonically similar to the word in the passage.
☐ Most ☐ few ☐ no   miscues were syntactically matched.
☐ Most ☐ few ☑ no   miscues maintained the author's meaning.
☐ The self-corrections demonstrate that the reader monitors the meaning.

Fluency: Does the Reader . . .

☐ read smoothly, accurately, in meaningful phrases?

☐ read (word-by-word,) choppy, plodding?

☐ use pitch, stress, and intonation to convey meaning of the text?

☐ repeat words and phrases because s/he is monitoring the meaning (self-correcting)?

☐ repeat words and phrases because s/he is trying to sound out words?

☐ use punctuation to divide the text into units of meaning?   ☑   ignore the punctuation?

*(Patrick read rapidly in a monotone voice—glided through some punctuation, and it did affect the comp. He made several omissions, only correcting one—**little**. He never corrected **Terry**.)*

Rating Scale: Circle One

4 = fluent reading / good pace   ②= choppy, plodding reading / slow pace
3 = fairly fluent / reasonable pace   1 = clearly labored, disfluent reading / very slow pace

RETELLING

People got into the car and they went to school. And there are 4 and 5 people got into the car. And 4 or 5 of them, almost all of them brought stuff to share and a few of them brought their stuff in paper bags.

(Patrick used simple, run-on sentences with information from his background, but sometimes not the text. He kept using the word stuff instead of the author's words. This reading is at the low instructional level.

Retelling Summary   ☐ many details, logical order   ☑ some details, some order   ☐ few details, disorder

Story Elements Sum
- *includes most story elements*
Summary Statement
- *adequate but not in complete sentence*

EMOTIONAL STATUS
- *persevering*
- *attentive*
- *nervous*
- *some stress*

COMPREHENSION QUESTIONS AND POSSIBLE ANSWERS:

+ (RIF)   1. Who is the main character in this story? (Terry) *Trey - miscue*
+ (RIF)   2. What does each child have? (a big paper bag with something for Show and Tell) *(in retelling)*
+ (CAR)   3. What do you know about the phrase **Show and Tell?** (kids take something to school to show and talk about)
          What does the phrase **Show and Tell** have to do with this story? (they had things for Show and Tell in paper bags)
+ (PIT)   4. What is the problem in this story? (the little car is crowded; the kids have big paper bags)
− (PIT)   5. Why did the children laugh? (Terry made a joke; he said, "The little car is getting fat!") *I don't remember.*
− (EAS)   6. Do you think Terry's joke was funny? You think this because ...
          (yes, a car can't really get fat, that's funny!) (no, it's silly talking about a car getting fat)

Reader Text Relationship (RTR)   From the Text   ☑ adequate ☐ inadequate   From Head to Text   ☐ adequate ☑ not adequate

Purpose: Listen for and identify the qualitative factors at a given reading level.

<table>
<tr><td>

Study Packet Materials

- Reader #4 Chart
  Directions 7–10 (p. 36)
- copy *Reader's Passages*
  Form A, Level 2
  "The Baseball Star" (p. 7)
- CD 2, Track 11

</td><td>

PRIOR KNOWLEDGE/PREDICTION

☐ Read the title and predict what the story is about.
Baseball. Probe: *What do you know about baseball?*
Response: *The boy hits a ball. Somebody hits a home run.*
☐ Read the first two sentences and add more to your prediction.
No response

</td><td>

Prior Knowledge
☐ a lot
☑ some
☐ none

</td></tr>
</table>

CUEING SYSTEMS SUMMARY

☑ Most   ☐ few   ☐ no   miscues were graphophonically similar to the word in the passage.
☐ Most   ☐ few   ☐ no   miscues were syntactically matched.
☐ Most   ☐ few   ☐ no   miscues maintained the author's meaning.
☐ The self-corrections demonstrate that the reader monitors the meaning.

Fluency: Does the Reader . . .

☐ read smoothly, accurately, in meaningful phrases?

☑ read word-by-word, choppy, plodding?

☐ use pitch, stress, and intonation to convey meaning of the text?

☐ repeat words and phrases because s/he is monitoring the meaning (self-correcting)?

☑ repeat words and phrases because s/he is trying to sound out words?

☐ use punctuation to divide the text into units of meaning?   ☑ ignore the punctuation?

(Andrew read slowly and labored. He pronounced words hesitantly, without confidence. Comprehension was affected.)

Rating Scale: Circle One

4 = fluent reading / good pace
3 = fairly fluent / reasonable pace

2 = choppy, plodding reading / slow pace
①= clearly labored, disfluent reading / very slow pace

RETELLING

The boy hits a ball. He was nervous.
Probe: *Anything else you want to say?*
Response: *No.*
(Andrew's sentences are simply structured—not retold in author's words or style of language—retelling could have been from background knowledge)

Retelling Summary   ☐ many details, logical order   ☐ some details, some order   ☑ few details, disorder

Story Elements Sum
• *void of most story elements*
Summary Statement
• *inadequate*

EMOTIONAL STATUS
• *confused*
• *nervous*
• *giving up*
• *lethargic*
• *frustrated*

COMPREHENSION QUESTIONS AND POSSIBLE ANSWERS:

I don't know.

+ (RIF)   1. Who is the main character in this story? (the batter) *the boy*
– (PIT)   2. After strike one, how do you think the batter felt? (nervous) You think this because ... (his legs began to shake)
– (RIF)   3. After strike two what did the batter plan to do? (planned to smack the ball) *another strike*
– (CAR)   4. What did it mean when the batter said, "I'll kill the ball"? (hit the ball real hard; get a home run)
– (PIT)   5. Why was the last pitch good? (because it went right over the plate)
– (EAS)   6. Do you think it was good or bad to hit the ball right out of the park? Because ... (good ... it's a homer; it will go far, and the batter can run all bases) (bad because if you only have one ball, then it's gone)
– (EAS)   7. How do you think the batter felt after hitting the ball? (felt good, confident) You think this because ... (the story said everyone yelled because s/he was a baseball star)   *surprised*

Reader Text Relationship (RTR)   From the Text   ☐ adequate ☑ inadequate   From Head to Text   ☐ adequate ☑ not adequate

Purpose: Listen for and identify the qualitative factors at a given reading level.

Study Packet Materials

- Reader #5 Chart Directions 7–9 (p. 36)
- copy *Reader's Passages* Form A, Level 4 "Crossing the River" (p. 9)
- CD 2, Track 12

PRIOR KNOWLEDGE/PREDICTION

☐ Read the title and predict what the story is about.
Crossing a river
☐ Read the first two sentences and add more to your prediction.
There is going to be some dogs and a cat who cross the river.
Probe: *What do you know about crossing a river?*
Res: *It would be hard. Cats don't like water.*

Prior Knowledge
☐ a lot
☑ some
☐ none

CUEING SYSTEMS SUMMARY

☐ Most   ☐ few   ☐ no   miscues were graphophonically similar to the word in the passage.
☐ Most   ☐ few   ☐ no   miscues were syntactically matched.
☐ Most   ☐ few   ☐ no   miscues maintained the author's meaning.   *n/a*
☐ The self-corrections demonstrate that the reader monitors the meaning.

Fluency: Does the Reader . . .

☐ read smoothly, accurately, in meaningful phrases?

☐ read word-by-word, choppy, plodding?

☐ use pitch, stress, and intonation to convey meaning of the text?

☐ repeat words and phrases because s/he is monitoring the meaning (self-correcting)?

☐ repeat words and phrases because s/he is trying to sound out words?

☐ use punctuation to divide the text into units of meaning?   ☐ ignore the punctuation?

No fluency data is available. This passage was read to Abi for a listening level.

Rating Scale: Circle One

4 = fluent reading / good pace
3 = fairly fluent / reasonable pace

2 = choppy, plodding reading / slow pace
1 = clearly labored, disfluent reading / very slow pace

RETELLING

One of the dogs got caught in the water, and so the cat jumped in trying to get to him, and a log came and hit him, and it threw him away to where he couldn't get to the dog.
Probe: *Anything else?* Response: *No.*
Abi used run-on type sentences, without using the author's exact words or style. Her retelling was void of most details. This reading may be at the low instructional level.

Retelling Summary   ☐ many details, logical order   ☑ some details, some order   ☐ few details, disorder

Story Elements Sum
• *void of most story elements*
Summary Statement
• *adequate*

EMOTIONAL STATUS
• *confused*
• *tense*
• *shy*

COMPREHENSION QUESTIONS AND POSSIBLE ANSWERS:

+ (RIF)   1. Who are the main characters in this story? (<u>older dog, younger dog, and a cat</u>)
+ (PIT)   2. What is the problem in this story? (the animals are tired; they have to swim across a wide, deep river)
− (CAR)   3. What do you know about the word **suffering?** (to experience pain or injury) *he can't have medicine—wait*
        What does **suffering** have to do with this story? (the older dog was weak and suffering with pain)
+ (RIF)   4. Why did the younger dog bark at the older dog and the cat? (<u>he wanted them to follow him into the water</u>)
− (CAR)   5. Explain what you know about the phrase **wailing with fear.** (<u>to cry out in fear</u>)
        What does **wailing with fear** have to do with this story? (the cat ran up and down the bank wailing with fear)
+ (EAS)   6. How do you think the cat felt? (<u>afraid, scared, panicked</u>) You think this because ... (the cat was alone; afraid to get across)
− (PIT)   7. After the cat jumped in, what happened? (an old beaver dam broke; a log came hurling downstream and hit the cat)
− (RIF)   8. Why did a large log come hurling downstream? (the force of the water from the beaver dam hurled the log, made it go fast)
                                it fell

Reader Text Relationship (RTR)   From the Text   ☑ adequate ☐ inadequate   From Head to Text   ☐ adequate   ☑ not adequate

11. When you have finished Readers' Charts #1–5, read the Five Readers' Qualitative Summary Chart on page 43. Use the information provided on each reader's chart to fill out the five readers' summary chart. After you have completed the summary chart, compare the variance in the amount of control a reader has at the independent level, instructional level, and finally the frustration level. Jot your observations on the grid below, talk with a partner, and make a summary statement about the differences in control.

Amount of Reader Control Grid						
Q Factor ⟶ R. Level ⬇	Prior Knowledge/ Prediction	Cueing Systems	Fluency	Retelling/ Summary Statement	Comp. Ques. RTR	Emotional Status
Independent						
Instructional						
Frustration						

Make a summary statement about the differences in control.

_____

_____

_____

Five Readers' Qualitative Summary Chart

QUALITATIVE FACTORS ↓	Reader #1: Freddie Independent Level	Reader #2: Kala Independent Level	Reader #3: Patrick Instructional Level	Reader #4: Andrew Frustration Level	Reader #5: Abi Listening Level
PRIOR KNOWLEDGE	☐ a lot ☐ some ☐ none	☐ a lot ☐ some ☐ none	☐ a lot ☐ some ☐ none	☐ a lot ☐ some ☐ none	☐ a lot ☐ some ☐ none
PREDICTION	☐ logical ☐ uses context and adds more info. ☐ complete sentence	☐ logical ☐ uses context and adds more info. ☐ complete sentence	☐ logical ☐ uses context and adds more info. ☐ complete sentence	☐ logical ☐ uses context and adds more info. ☐ complete sentence	☐ logical ☐ uses context and adds more info. ☐ complete sentence
CUEING SYSTEMS (Miscue Analysis) *Most miscues are . . .*	☐ graphophonically similar ☐ a syntactic match ☐ maintain author's meaning (sem.) ☐ self-corrections for meaning	☐ graphophonically similar ☐ a syntactic match ☐ maintain author's meaning (sem.) ☐ self-corrections for meaning	☐ graphophonically similar ☐ a syntactic match ☐ maintain author's meaning (sem.) ☐ self-corrections for meaning	☐ graphophonically similar ☐ a syntactic match ☐ maintain author's meaning (sem.) ☐ self-corrections for meaning	☐ graphophonically similar ☐ a syntactic match ☐ maintain author's meaning (sem.) ☐ self-corrections for meaning
FLUENCY	☐ fluent ☐ fairly fluent ☐ choppy ☐ disfluent Rating =	☐ fluent ☐ fairly fluent ☐ choppy ☐ disfluent Rating =	☐ fluent ☐ fairly fluent ☐ choppy ☐ disfluent Rating =	☐ fluent ☐ fairly fluent ☐ choppy ☐ disfluent Rating =	☐ fluent ☐ fairly fluent ☐ choppy ☐ disfluent Rating =
RETELLING	☐ all story elements ☐ some story ele. ☐ few story ele. ☐ organized ☐ disorganized ☐ well-constructed sentences; author's style and words	☐ all story elements ☐ some story ele. ☐ few story ele. ☐ organized ☐ disorganized ☐ well-constructed sentences; author's style and words	☐ all story elements ☐ some story ele. ☐ few story ele. ☐ organized ☐ disorganized ☐ well-constructed sentences; author's style and words	☐ all story elements ☐ some story ele. ☐ few story ele. ☐ organized ☐ disorganized ☐ well-constructed sentences; author's style and words	☐ all story elements ☐ some story ele. ☐ few story ele. ☐ organized ☐ disorganized ☐ well-constructed sentences; author's style and words
SUMMARY STATEMENT	☐ adequate ☐ scanty	☐ adequate ☐ scanty	☐ adequate ☐ scanty	☐ adequate ☐ scanty	☐ adequate ☐ scanty
COMPREHENSION QUESTIONS RTR	☐ RTR from text adequate ☐ RTR from head to text adequate ☐ well-constructed sentences; matches author's vocab.	☐ RTR from text adequate ☐ RTR from head to text adequate ☐ well-constructed sentences; matches author's vocab.	☐ RTR from text adequate ☐ RTR from head to text adequate ☐ well-constructed sentences; matches author's vocab.	☐ RTR from text adequate ☐ RTR from head to text adequate ☐ well-constructed sentences; matches author's vocab.	☐ RTR from text adequate ☐ RTR from head to text adequate ☐ well-constructed sentences; matches author's vocab.
EMOTIONAL STATUS	☐ relaxed/confident ☐ some stress ☐ high stress	☐ relaxed/confident ☐ some stress ☐ high stress	☐ relaxed/confident ☐ some stress ☐ high stress	☐ relaxed/confident ☐ some stress ☐ high stress	☐ relaxed/confident ☐ some stress ☐ high stress

Scoring Guide Summary
<u>Word Recognition</u>
Independent 1–2
Instructional 7–8
Frustration 15+
<u>Comprehension</u>
Independent 0–1
Instructional 2   (−3½)
Frustration 4+
Emotional Status:
Less confident than at level 2
Form C, Level 3, "Belonging to the Club"

12. Take a close look at the numbers that indicate each level in the Scoring Guide Summary to the left. Notice that Word Recognition (WR) is 7 – 8 allowable miscues at the instructional level, and then 15+ allowable miscues at frustration. Did you notice the gap between the number of miscues allowed at instructional and frustration levels? Knowing how the numbers or range of numbers at each level were determined and what they represent will help you to understand why there are gaps.

Review Betts's percentages for word recognition and comprehension at each level in the following table. Reread the research information in the last row of the Quantitative and Qualitative Data Chart for Four Reading Levels (page 35).

Reading Levels Percentages and Qualitative Factors			
Independent	*Instructional*	*Frustration*	*Listening*
• WR = 99%	• WR = 95%	• WR = 90%	• WR = N/A
• Comp = 90%	• Comp = 75%	• Comp = 50%	• Comp = 75%
• Qualitative Factors	• Qualitative Factors	• Qualitative Factors	• Qualitative Factors

<u>*Formula used to determine Scoring Guide numbers or range of numbers:*</u>
• Passage word count × (100–99%) = number of errors at independent level. (In "Belonging to the Club" there are 149 words.)
• Number of comprehension questions × (100–75%) = number of errors allowable at Instr. level. ("Belonging to the Club" has 8 comp. questions.)

Review the Scoring Guide Summary again. The numbers at each level in the Scoring Guide Summary equate to the percentages that Betts established for each reading level. Note this:

   a. In the passage, Form C, Level 3 "Belonging to the Club," 7–8 word recognition errors equate to the percentage at the Instructional Level—95% of the words are read accurately.

   b. the 15+ errors equate to the percentage at the Frustration Level—90% of the words are accurate.

There are actually two instructional levels, definite and transitional.

13. Questions emerge about the accurate determination of a reading level because sometimes a reader's miscue count is out of sync with numbers indicated on the Scoring Guide Summary. For example, the Scoring Guide Summary above notes the WR at −13 and the Comprehension at −3½. The WR error count doesn't align with the range of numbers, and the comprehension count doesn't match the number. As you know, a final determination will be made by considering both quantitative and qualitative factors.

Ambiguities occur most often at the instructional level. Once again, review the Scoring Guide Summary above. According to the miscue count, 13, word recognition errors appear to be at the instructional level; however, with so many errors, you should be wary. The number of comprehension errors, 3½, is more than 2 but less than 4. The instructional level is in question.

Eldon E. Ekwall clarifies this confusion about the instructional level in an article entitled, "Informal Reading Inventories: The Instructional Level*." Ekwall explains that when Betts et al. established the quantitative percentages for the reading levels, they actually created two instructional levels:

*The information and the source for the graph are from an article entitled, "Informal Reading Inventories: The Instructional Level" by Eldon Ekwall.

The Reading Teacher, Volume 29, No. 7, April 1976.

- a definite instructional level
- a questionable instructional level

Study the graph below. Instead of referring to the second instructional level as the **questionable instructional level**, the *ARI* has renamed it the **transitional instructional level**.

To make an accurate determination at any reading level, both quantitative and qualitative factors must be considered.

Reading Levels Graphic

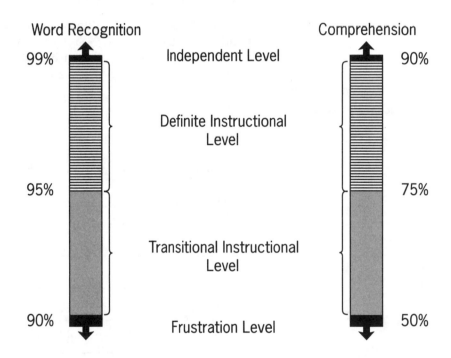

If both quantitative scores fall within the *definite* instructional level (WR = 95% through 98%; Comprehension = 75% through 89%), and the qualitative data supports the quantitative data, the reader is clearly performing at the *definite instructional level.*

However, sometimes one or both of the quantitative scores may fall in the *transitional* range: WR = 91% through 94%; Comprehension = 51% through 74%. This would be the *transitional instructional level.*

In the passage "Belonging to the Club," by quantitative counts alone (WR = −13 and comp. = −3½), the reader is in the low transitional range. Without the qualitative information, however, you cannot, as yet, understand the severity of the miscues and the reader's strategic strength.

14. The purpose of this practice is to teach you how to accurately determine a student's *definite* and *transitional* instructional levels.

The Two Instructional Levels Chart (page 47) contains four scoring guide summaries that represent information about a student's reading across four passages of increasing difficulty. On each scoring guide summary, the reader's miscues and comprehension errors are recorded. The qualitative data from each passage is listed beneath the scoring guide.

Your task is to analyze the quantitative and qualitative data from each passage. The experience of thinking about a student's reading across a series of passages of increasing difficulty should help you to notice a behavioral progression that would be less evident within a single passage. For example, when the passages reflect a progression from the independent to the frustration reading levels, you will notice the difference in the reader's emotional status. The differences in the quality of the fluency, retellings, and other qualitative factors will also be noticeable. Behavioral changes and the behavioral consistencies found across passages are key indicators to supporting a final determination of a reading level.

Some examiners process the information by "talking themselves through" the data, while others jot notes as they review the data taken from each passage.

15. Based upon the quantitative and qualitative data included in the Scoring Guide Summary and the Qualitative Factors chart, determine this reader's independent level, definite and transitional instructional levels, and frustration level. Record your answers below:

Form C: Level 1 _____   Form C: Level 2 _____

Form C: Level 3 _____   Form C: Level 4 _____

16. Talk with a partner and describe the progression of behaviors across passages.

17. Did you come up with a rule of thumb when considering both quantitative and qualitative factors? _____

_____

_____

_____

_____

Two Instructional Levels Chart

Quantitative Factors	Scoring Guide Sum. Form C, Level 1	Scoring Guide Sum. Form C, Level 2	Scoring Guide Sum. Form C, Level 3	Scoring Guide Sum. Form C, Level 4
	Word Recognition Ind. 0–1 Instr. 3–4 (–2) Frust. 7–8+	**Word Recognition** Ind. 1 Instr. 6 (–8) Frust. 12+	**Word Recognition** Ind. 1–2 Instr. 7–8 (–8) Frust. 15+	**Word Recognition** Ind. 2 Instr. 7–8 (–14) Frust. 15+
	Comprehension Ind. 0 Instr. 1–2 (–0) Frust. 3+	**Comprehension** Ind. 0 Instr. 1–2 (–2) Frust. 3+	**Comprehension** Ind. 0–1 Instr. 2 (–3) Frust. 4+	**Comprehension** Ind. 0–1 Instr. 2 (–4) Frust. 4+

Qualitative Factors	Form C, Level 1	Form C, Level 2	Form C, Level 3	Form C, Level 4
• quality of prediction	• good	• good	• okay, but less information	• not good; too much prior knowledge
• application of prior knowledge	• some	• some	• some	• a lot
• self-correction of substitutions	• all	• some	• some	• only 2
• quality of miscues	• substitutions = no changes in meaning	• substitutions = few changes in meaning	• substitutions = more changes in meaning	• most substitutions = changes in meaning
• all factors included in fluency	• read smoothly most of the time, repeated phrases to self-correct • voice pitch and stress conveyed meaning • used punctuation for meaning	• hesitations, yet still in meaningful phrases • voice pitch and stress for meaning mostly • used punctuation for meaning	• many hesitations and word-by-word reading • voice pitch and stress used less for meaning • some punctuation ignored	• a lot of hesitations • choppy word-by-word phrasing • little voice pitch and stress used • punctuation ignored
• all factors related to the quality of the retelling	• all story elements • all details • logical order	• all story elements • many details • logical order	• few story elements (missing "where") • some details • less logical order	• few story elements • few details • disorganized
• summary statement	• good	• good	• okay	• missed most information
• language structure used in retelling and responses to comprehension questions	• well-constructed sentences • used author's language	• well-constructed sentences • less use of author's language	• well-constructed sentences • less use of author's language	• disorganized, poorly constructed sentences • little of author's language • mostly background information
• emotional status	• confident	• confident	• less confident	• nervous

COMPONENT 10 STUDY PACKET
SUMMARY OF RESULTS

Examiner Standard/Indicators: Analysis, Synthesis, Summary

- articulate and synthesize quantitative and qualitative data for each narrative and expository passage
- complete profile records in preparation for reporting data to student, parents, and educators
- use findings to develop standards-based instructional plans and support

Explanation

The *ARI* includes three comprehensive and organized forms to make it easy for you to summarize the results. The Student Profile Summary form is designed to summarize all components of an *ARI* assessment session serving as a synopsis of the results. Many teachers include the Student Profile Summary in the student's literacy portfolio because it is so comprehensive. The Class Profile Summary provides a means of reviewing whole class data for decisions about grouping and selection of materials. The *ARI* Profile Card is a convenient and quick short form that can be placed in a student's records for the benefit of a forthcoming teacher. The information reported on this card identifies the student's instructional level.

School psychologists and reading specialists who are preparing an individual education plan (IEP) must write an assessment narrative. The final pages of the case study (pages 78–80) contain an assessment narrative.

Directions
Profile Records

1. With a partner, carefully study the Student Profile Summary located in Section III (page 94). Then, answer the following questions:

- What data is recorded in the top portion of the grid?
- What information is recorded in the bottom portion of the grid? What components of an *ARI* assessment session are represented on the grid?

Turn to the case study Student Profile Summary found in Section II (page 54). Review it to verify your responses to the previous questions.

2. Study the Class Profile Summary in Section III (page 95). This sheet contains spaces for summarizing assessment data for 12 students, so you will need two or more sheets for a whole class. Filling out this form you will ask yourself questions like: "What flexible grouping decisions can I make from this data?" "What different kinds of books should I select?"

3. Review the *ARI* Profile Card in Section III (page 96). The data is reported at the student's instructional level. If the student were new in your classroom, what information would you know about his reading ability?

Study Packet Materials

- Refer to the Case Study Profile Narration (pages 78–80).
- Refer to the case study Form C, Level 2 "The Busy Road" (pages 57–59).
- Refer to the case study Form C, Level 3 "Belonging to the Club" (pages 60–62).
- Answer Key (pages 270–271)

4. **An examiner's ability to synthesize quantitative and qualitative data is the mark of examiner expertise.** Read the Case Study Profile Narration (pages 78–80). This narration serves as an example of the articulation *(a talk-through)* done when reviewing the data from each assessment component. *Talking through the data,* one component at a time, one passage at a time, serves as a process for synthesizing quantitative and qualitative data.

Prior to filling out the Student Profile Summary, you will review the data from each passage the student read—component by component. As you review each passage, you will think about the data represented in each component. Talking through the data serves as a means of organizing your thoughts.

The following Sample Talk-Through Chart contains a talk-through (an articulation) that reveals the examiner's thoughts about the first case study passage. Copy this chart and place it alongside the case study Form C, Level 2 "The Busy Road" (pages 57–59). Read the passage aloud and then read the sample talk-through.

Sample Talk-Through Chart

Component	Example of Examiner's Thoughts Form C, Level 2 "The Busy Road"
Prior Knowledge/Prediction	Jenny had specific background knowledge, and she made a logical prediction. I wonder if she accessed and applied that background knowledge during the reading of the passage? If so, it should show up in her ability to recognize words, make self-corrections, retell, and respond to comprehension questions.
Word Recognition Oral Miscues Cueing Systems	The four self-corrections show that she is really trying to monitor the meaning. It feels like she is self-correcting because she is looking at the word (***Thad*** to ***Thud,*** str to ***straight***). However, I wonder if she is using her prediction and her knowledge of syntax to monitor the meaning as well (***nose*** to ***noise, scar*** to ***scared***)? Will this prove to be a pattern in the next passage?
# Miscues = 6 # Self-Corrections = 4	Most of the six miscues are substitutions. When I jot them down in the Cueing Systems grid, I find that she seems to be looking mostly at the initial portion of the word. I wonder why ***ready*** for ***right*** wasn't self-corrected? She certainly didn't rely on the meaning of the context or her background in this case. Yet, ***hold*** for ***fight***—she was attending to the meaning, but not looking carefully. Why didn't she self-correct the miscue ***street*** when she got farther into the sentence? Given her background knowledge and what I know about her sentence structure, I would have thought she'd have corrected those miscues. So far it seems like what is going on in her head is a mix of looking at the word and sometimes accessing and applying background (both personally and from the reading). I wonder if that pattern will hold in the next passages. So, is she relying mostly on graphophonic cues? Syntactic? Semantic? Right now it looks like graphophonic. Will that become a pattern in the next passage?
Fluency Final Rating	Number 4 on the rating scale, fluent reading and good pace describe the fluency of this passage. She used pitch, stress, and intonation to show that she understood the meaning. I'm still curious why she didn't self-correct the miscues.
Retelling Summary Statement	The retelling and summary statement are right on! All story elements are there, and the retelling has many details logically ordered. She even uses the author's exact words. Curious, then why weren't those miscues self-corrected.

(continued)

Component	Example of Examiner's Thoughts Form C, Level 2 "The Busy Road"
Comprehension Questions # wrong = 0 RTR: From the Text = adequate From Head to Text = adequate	The questions were all answered correctly. RTR was flexible showing that she can interpret literal and implied meaning—at least in this context.
Emotional Status	With this passage she is confident and comfortable. Her energy sustains throughout. Will this become a pattern?

Overall I wonder . . .
I wonder why the miscues weren't corrected? Is she relying mostly on graphophonic cues? If she knows background information and knows some of the context, why didn't she correct more of the miscues? I wonder if these patterns will continue.

5. Read case study Form C, Level 3 "Belonging to the Club" (pages 60–62). Based upon what you learned from "The Busy Road" talk-through, with a partner talk through the data from this passage. Jot your comments on the Blank Copy Talk-Through Chart that follows. Compare your responses to those in the Answer Key, pages 270 and 271.

Blank Copy Talk-Through Chart

Component	Examiner's Talk-Through Comments Form:_____ Level:_____ Passage Title:_____
Prior Knowledge/Prediction	

Word Recognition
  Oral Miscues
  Cueing Systems
 	
# Miscues = 	
# Self-Corrections = 		

Fluency Final Rating	
Retelling Summary Statement	
Comprehension Questions # wrong = RTR: From the Text = From Head to Text =	
Emotional Status	
Overall I wonder . . .	

6. Briefly jot notes from your talk-through comments about the two passages on the following chart. Make a summary statement about what happens to Jenny's reading ability between Levels 2 and 3. Check your responses with the Answer Key, page 271.

Component	NOTES Level 2 "The Busy Road"	NOTES Level 3 "Belonging to the Club"
Prior Knowledge/ Prediction		
Word Recognition Oral Miscues Cueing Systems		
Fluency		
Retelling Summary Statement		
Comprehension Questions		
Emotional Status		

Summary Statement:

_____

_____

_____

PRACTICING A CASE STUDY
USING AUDIO TRAINING CD 1
AND STUDY PACKET

Explanation

In this case study, a fourth grader, Jenny, reads word lists for initial placement, narrative passages from the independent to frustration levels, and grade level expository passages.

This case study includes practice opportunities for components 2–10 of an *ARI* assessment:

- word lists/initial placement
- prior knowledge/prediction analysis
- oral reading miscue analysis
- fluency analysis
- retelling/summary analysis
- comprehension question/RTR analysis
- cueing systems miscue analysis
- quantitative and qualitative analysis
- summary of results

During this practice opportunity your task is to listen to CD 1 and use this study packet to learn how to give the *Analytical Reading Inventory*. After you have reviewed the CD and study packet, you will independently record the data. In preparation for independent practice, run blank copies of those passages from Section IV Examiner's Records listed in the textbox on this page.

> **Study Packet Materials**
>
> Run blank copies of the following passages:
>
> From the Examiner's Records copy:
> - Form C Word Lists (pages 166–167)
> - Form C Level 2 "The Busy Road" (pages 174–176)
> - Form C Level 3 "Belonging to the Club" (pages 177–179)
> - Form C Level 4 "The Beloved Horse" (pages 180–182)
> - Form B Level 4 "The Small Pony" (pages 146–148)
> - Form C Level 5 "A Woman Race Car Driver" (pages 183–185)
> - Form S Level 4 "A Comet" (pages 208–210)
> - Form SS Level 4 French Explorers . . ." (pages 236–238)
> - Student Profile Summary (page 94)
> - CD 1 Practicing a Case Study

Directions

1. As you listen to CD 1, to familiarize yourself with the case study content quickly read through the case study, found on pages 54–80. List four things you discovered about an *ARI* assessment session, and discuss your findings with a partner.

_____

_____

_____

_____

2. Using the copies of the passages you have prepared and CD 1, begin your independent documentation. As you listen to each passage, note that the time it takes for the examiner to write Jenny's responses has been deleted. Information about how to fast forward and back up a CD player within a track is located adjacent to the CDs, which are attached inside the back cover.

3. Use the study packet documentation (pages 54–77) as an answer key.

STUDENT PROFILE SUMMARY

Student __Jenny Stapp__   Grade __4__   Sex __F__   Age _9 yrs./10 mos._ (yrs./mos.)

School __Merrill Elementary__   Examiner __M.L. Woods__   Date _25 Sept. 05_

◊ *Indicates Column for Final Score or Level*

Passage Level	◊ Word Lists			◊ Narrative Reading Level		◊ Expository at Grade Level
FORM —	% correct	Word Recognition	Comprehension	Listening and/or Silent		**Science, Form S** Level _4_
Preprimer	- - - - - -					W.R. _frustration_
Primer	95					Comp. _frustration_
Level 1	100					Listening, Passage Level _____
Level 2	100	-6 def. instr.	-0 independent		independent	Comp. _____
Level 3	85	-13 trans. instr.	-3½ trans. instr.		trans. instructional	**Social Studies, Form SS**
Level 4	40 (10)	-18 frustration	-4½ frustration	silent -7 frust.	frustration	Level _4_
Level 5				lis. -2½ def. ins.	definite listening	W.R. _frustration_
Level 6						Comp. _frustration_
Level 7	- - - - - -					Listening, Passage Level _____
Level 8	- - - - - -					Comp. _____
Level 9	- - - - - -					

OVERVIEW OF READING BEHAVIORS

1. Predictions
   ☑ Reader most often made a logical prediction from the title.

   ☑ Reader most often made a logical prediction from the first two sentences.

2. Reader had prior knowledge of
   ☐ many passages

   ☑ some passages

   ☐ few passages

3. Types of Oral Reading Miscues
   ☑ Omissions   ☐ Insertions
   ☑ Substitutions   ☐ Aided words
   ☑ Repetitions   ☐ Reversals

   Reader Self-Corrects
   ☐ a lot   ☑ sometimes   ☐ seldom

4. Fluency Analysis
   1 = labored, disfluent reading/very slow pace
   2 = slow and choppy reading/slow pace
   3 = fairly fluent/reasonable pace
   4 = fluent/good pace

   _4_ independent
   _3_ instructional
   _1_ frustration

5. Cueing Systems: Miscue Analysis
   Graphophonic Similarities
   ☑ Initial   ☐ Medial   ☐ Final

   Syntactic: Most miscues were
   ☑ acceptable   ☐ unacceptable

   Semantic: Most miscues caused
   ☑ change in meaning   ☑ no change in meaning
   at upper passages   *at lower passages*

6. Retelling Analysis: The reader most often retold
   ☐ many details, logical order
   ☑ some details, some order
   ☐ few details, disorder

   Reader most often summarizes
   ☑ adequately   ☐ not adequately

7. Comprehension Questions Analysis
   The examiner
   ☐ asked few   ☑ asked many

   Reader's Strength(s)
   ☑ Retells In Fact (RIF)
   ☑ Puts Information Together (PIT)
   ☐ Combines Author and Reader (CAR)
   ☐ Evaluates and Substantiates (EAS)

   Reader Text Relationship (RTR)
   Reader responds adequately
   ☑ From the Text   ☐ From Head to Text

8. Emotional Status at Various Reading Levels
   Reader was
   ☐ relaxed/confident
   ☐ slightly nervous
   ☐ stressed/little confidence

   Independent Level _confident_

   Instructional Level _less confident_

   Frustration Level _stressed_

   Listening Level _relaxed, attentive_

Form C, Primer

1. about ___ +
2. can ___ +
3. who ___ +
4. with ___ +
5. some ___ +
6. goat ___ +
7. out ___ +
8. trees ___ +
9. father ___ +
10. red ___ +
11. green ___ +
12. make ___ +
13. is ___ +
14. yes ___ +
15. saw ___ +
16. get ___ +
17. ball ___ +
18. and ___ +
19. down _do_ +
20. are ___ +

Sentences:

My father is very tall.

Comprehends: ☑ a lot ☐ some ☐ none

Form C, Level 1

1. ice ___ +
2. before ___ +
3. another ___ +
4. children ___ +
5. stopped ___ +
6. hurry ___ +
7. drop ___ +
8. friend ___ +
9. balloon ___ +
10. when ___ +
11. where ___ +
12. those ___ +
13. picnic ___ +
14. laugh ___ +
15. farm ___ +
16. airplane ___ +
17. tomorrow ___ +
18. wagon ___ +
19. made ___ +
20. surprise ___ +

Sentences:

I had to hurry to get ready for school on time.

Tomorrow is Wednesday.

Comprehends: ☑ a lot ☐ some ☐ none

Form C, Level 2

1. goose ___ +
2. mouse ___ +
3. library ___ +
4. teacher ___ +
5. kite ___ +
6. cart ___ +
7. different ___ +
8. anyone ___ +
9. feather ___ +
10. pie ___ +
11. sidewalk ___ +
12. straight ___ +
13. telephone ___ +
14. clean ___ +
15. remember ___ +
16. wood ___ +
17. summer ___ +
18. bell ___ +
19. gun ___ +
20. matter ___ +

Sentences:

I found a feather on the ground.

We walk in a straight line.

Comprehends: ☑ a lot ☐ some ☐ none

Form C, Level 3

1. clap ___ +
2. fright ___ + _SC_
3. diamond _die-a-mond_
4. silence _slice_
5. nurse ___ +
6. wiggle ___ +
7. precious _precoe_
8. salt ___ +
9. bread ___ +
10. breath _beth_
11. fellow ___ +
12. several ___ +
13. unusual ___ +
14. overhead ___ +
15. driven ___ +
16. fool ___ +
17. darkness ___ +
18. honor ___ +
19. screen ___ +
20. they'll ___ +

Sentences:

It was unusual that the rabbit wiggled his tail.

miscues?

Comprehends: ☐ a lot ☑ some ☐ none

Form C, Level 4

1. canoe _can't_
2. hasn't _+_
3. dozen _+_
4. motion _magic_
5. pride _+_
6. vicious _vi_
7. concern _+_
8. harvest _harvest_
9. sample _simple_
10. official _office_
11. windshield ___
12. human ___
13. humor ___
14. decorate ___
15. slender ___
16. seventh ___
17. parachute ___
18. good-bye ___
19. dignity ___
20. trudge ___

Sentences:
Stopped after 10.

Comprehends: ☐ a lot ☐ some ☐ none

Form C, Level 5

1. prevent ___
2. kindle ___
3. grease ___
4. typical ___
5. foam ___
6. blur ___
7. mumps ___
8. telegram ___
9. vision ___
10. sandal ___
11. argument ___
12. hail ___
13. halt ___
14. region ___
15. manager ___
16. sleet ___
17. yarn ___
18. parallel ___
19. coconut ___
20. dissolve ___

Sentences:

Comprehends: ☐ a lot ☐ some ☐ none

Form C, Level 6

1. midstream ___
2. lens ___
3. bail ___
4. college ___
5. failure ___
6. falter ___
7. width ___
8. graceful ___
9. somewhat ___
10. privacy ___
11. microphone ___
12. particle ___
13. clutter ___
14. applaud ___
15. vapor ___
16. reluctant ___
17. contract ___
18. nephew ___
19. insurance ___
20. fund ___

Sentences:

Comprehends: ☐ a lot ☐ some ☐ none

FORM C, LEVEL 2 — Reader's Passages page 35

Prior Knowledge/Prediction

- ☐ Read the title and predict what the story is about. *About a road, it's got a ~~lot~~ lot of cars.*
  - Q: *What do you know about a busy road?*
  - SR: *We live near a road that has a lot of cars.*
- ☐ Read the first two sentences and add more to your prediction.
  - *The boy yells at his dog because he's going to get hit.*
  - Q: *What do you know about a dog getting hit on a road?*
  - SR: *I had a dog that got hit when she ran across the road.*

Prior Knowledge
- ☑ a lot
- ☐ some
- ☐ none

	The Busy Road (*Buzzy SC*)	O	I	S	A	Rp	Rv
1	"Look out, you'll get hit!" I/yelled as my dog ran across/the						
2	busy road./*Thud* (*Thad SC*) was the noise (*nose*, *no SC*) I heard, and then I saw my pup/						
3	lying in the street. "Oh, no!" I shouted. I felt scared (*scar SC*) inside. "Rex is						
4	my best friend!" I wanted to cry out. I knew that he was hurt, but						
5	he'd be all right/if (*ready*) I could get help fast. I knew I had to be brave.			/			
6	"Mom! Dad!" I/yelled as I ran/straight (*str SC*) home. I tried to fight (*hold*)			/			
7	back the tears. They (*The*)/started (*st*, *street*) rolling down my face/(anyway) as I	/		//			
8	blasted (*to*) through the door. "Rex has been hit, and he needs help/			/			

The text is continued on the next page.

Cueing Systems

LINE #	Miscue	Grapho-phonically Similar I M F (word level)	Syntactically Acceptable Unacceptable (sentence level)	Semantic Change in Meaning (CM) No Change in Meaning (NCM) (sentence level)
5	*ready*	*I*	*A*	*CM*
6	*hold*		*A*	*NCM*
7	*The*	*IM*	*U*	*CM*
7	*street*	*I*	*U*	*CM*
8	*to*	*I*	*A*	*CM*

The cueing system grid is continued on the next page.

Cueing Systems

L I N E #	Miscue	Grapho-phonically Similar I M F (word level)	Syntactically Acceptable Unacceptable (sentence level)	Semantic Change in Meaning (CM) No Change in Meaning (NCM) (sentence level)

Summary

☑ Most, ☐ few, ☐ no   miscues were graphophonically similar to the word in the passage.

☑ Most, ☐ few, ☐ no   miscues were syntactically matched.

☐ Most, ☑ few, ☐ no   miscues maintained the author's meaning.

☑ The self-corrections demonstrate that the reader monitors the meaning.

Form C, Level 2

	O	I	S	A	Rp	Rv
9						
now!" I cried out. "Please hurry so we can save him!"						
TOTALS					1	5

Number of miscues ___6___   Number of self-corrections ___4___

Fluency: Does the Reader . . .

☐ read smoothly, accurately (in meaningful phrases?)

☐ read word-by-word, choppy, plodding?

☑ use pitch, stress, and intonation to convey meaning of the text?

☐ repeat words and phrases because s/he is monitoring the meaning (self-correcting)?

☑ repeat words and phrases because s/he is trying to sound out words?   *wrile, straight*

☐ use punctuation to divide the text into units of meaning? ← *most times*   ☐ ignore the punctuation?

Rating Scale: Circle One

4 = fluent reading / good pace

③ = fairly fluent / reasonable pace

2 = choppy, plodding reading / slow pace

1 = clearly labored, disfluent reading / very slow pace

Retelling *Well, this is a story about a dog and the boy yells at his dog, "Look out, you're gonna get hit." The dog runs across the busy road, and he gets hit anyway. The boy feels real scared. He starts to cry. If he can get help fast, it will be okay. Then he runs home to tell his mom and dad. If they hurry up, they can save the dog.*

Retelling Summary: ☑ many details, logical order ☐ some details, some order ☐ few details, disorder

Note: Indicate any probing with a "P"

Story Elements	All	Some	None
Main Character(s)	✓		
Time and Place	✓		
Problem	✓		
Plot Details in Sequence	✓		
Turning Point	✓		
Resolution	✓		

Reader's Thumbnail Summary:
A dog gets hit on a busy road.

Scoring Guide Summary

WORD RECOGNITION
Independent 1   −6
Instructional 6
Frustration ...... 12+

COMPREHENSION
Independent 0   −0
Instructional 1-2
Frustration ...... 3+

Emotional Status:
confident

Form C, Level 2

Comprehension Questions and Possible Answers

+ _(RIF)_ 1. Who is the main character in this story?   (a child, boy or girl)

+ _(PIT)_ 2. What is the problem in the story?   (the dog ran across a busy street and got hit)

+ _(PIT)_ 3. Do you think the dog is an old dog or a young one?   (a young dog, the child calls the dog a pup) *He said that it's a pup.*

+ _(CAR)_ 4. What do you know about the phrase **fight back the tears?**   (you try not to cry, you try to be brave, you try to keep the tears from rolling down your cheeks)   What does the phrase **fight back the tears** have to do with this story? *It's when you don't want to cry.*
(when the child ran home to get mom and dad, he/she tried to fight back the tears) *The boy held back his tears.*

+ _(PIT)_ 5. Why did the child run home?   (to get help fast so he/she could save the dog)

+ _(EAS)_ 6. Do you think the dog will be all right? You think this because . . .   *because the story said that if he can get help*
(yes, the child is getting help fast; no, maybe they can't hurry fast enough) *fast, it will be okay.*

Reader Text Relationship (RTR)   From the Text ☑adequate ☐ not adequate   From Head to Text ☑adequate ☐ not adequate

---

FORM C, LEVEL 3 — Reader's Passages page 36

Prior Knowledge/Prediction

- ☐ Read the title and predict what the story is about. *About somebody who belongs to a club.*
  Q: What do you know about somebody who belongs to a club?
  SR: My mom belongs to a club.
- ☐ Read the first two sentences and add more to your prediction.
  There's a sign outside this club that says "For Neighborhood Triggers Only".

Prior Knowledge

- ☐ a lot
- ☑ some
- ☐ none

	~~Belonging~~ (*Be in*) (to) the Club	O	I	S	A	Rp	Rv
1	This was the/sign that Jack read/as he stood outside the/						
2	neighborhood (*nay SC*) kids' clubhouse (*club SC*).						
3	FOR NEIGHBORHOOD TIGERS (*Triggers*) ONLY!			/			
4	KNOCK ONE/(HUNDRED) (*SC*) TIMES						
5	AND SAY THE SECRET WORD						
6	BEFORE ENTERING!						
7	Jack was a new boy, and he really wanted/to/belong (*be in*) (to) the club.	/	/	/			
8	"How can I get the kids to agree (*ask*) (to) let me belong?" (he) (thought.)	///		/			
9	Suddenly, he/dashed home and (soon) (*Soon*) returned with a bucket of	/		/			
	The text is continued on the next page.						

Cueing Systems

LINE #	Miscue	Grapho-phonically Similar I M F (word level)	Syntactically Acceptable Unacceptable (sentence level)	Semantic Change in Meaning (CM) No Change in Meaning (NCM) (sentence level)
3	*Triggers*	*IF*	*A*	*CM*
7	*be*	*I*	*A*	*NCM*
7	*in*		*A*	*NCM*
8	*ask*	*I*	*A*	*CM*
9	*soon*	*I*	*A*	*slight CM*
10	*some*	*I*	*A*	*slight CM*

The cueing system grid is continued on the next page.

Cueing Systems

	Miscue	Grapho-phonically Similar I M F (word level)	Syntactically Acceptable Unacceptable (sentence level)	Semantic Change in Meaning (CM) No Change in Meaning (NCM) (sentence level)
L I N E #				

Summary

☑ Most, □ few, □ no — miscues were graphophonically similar to the word in the passage.

☑ Most, □ few, □ no — miscues were syntactically matched.

□ Most, ☑ few, □ no — miscues maintained the author's meaning.

☑ The self-corrections demonstrate that the reader monitors the meaning.

Form C, Level 3

Reading passage with coding (columns: O I S A Rp Rv)

Line	Text	O	I	S	A	Rp	Rv
1 0	yellow paint, one of black, and /several brushes. He began pounding (*some* above /several)	/					
1 1	on the clubhouse door.						
1 2	"I'm /knocking one hundred times!" he shouted. "I don't know						
1 3	the secret word," he declared, "but I have something important to tell (*said SC* above)						
1 4	everyone! I'm the new boy," he explained. "Since the name of your <u>club</u>						
1 5	is /Tigers, I thought you might want to paint your clubhouse (*Triggers* above)			/			
1 6	yellow (with) black stripes!" All the kids thought this was a great idea (*SC* above)						
1 7	and /quickly invited Jack to belong!						/
	TOTALS	5	1	6			1

Number of miscues ___13___   Number of self-corrections ___5___

Fluency: Does the Reader . . .

- □ read smoothly, accurately (in meaningful phrases?)
- □ read (word-by-word), choppy, plodding?   *more than at Level 2*
- ☑ use pitch, stress, and intonation to convey meaning of the text?   *somewhat*
- ☑ repeat words and phrases because s/he is monitoring the meaning (self-correcting)?
- □ repeat words and phrases because s/he is trying to sound out words?   *most times*
- □ use punctuation to divide the text into units of meaning?   □ ignore the punctuation?   *belong? (line 8)*

Rating Scale: Circle One

4 = fluent reading / good pace   2 = choppy, plodding reading / slow pace

(3)= fairly fluent / reasonable pace   1 = clearly labored, disfluent reading / very slow pace

Note: Indicate any probing with a "P"

Story Elements	All	Some	None
Main Character(s)	✓		
Time and (Place)	✓		
Problem		✓	
Plot Details in Sequence		✓	
Turning Point		✓	
Resolution	✓		

Reader's Thumbnail Summary:
He wants to belong to the club.

Scoring Guide Summary

WORD RECOGNITION
Independent ...... 1-2 _-13_
Instructional 7-8
Frustration .... 15+

COMPREHENSION
Independent ...... 0-1 _-3 1/2_
Instructional 2
Frustration .... 4+

Emotional Status:
Less confident than at level 2.

Form C, Level 3

Retelling *It's about a boy who wants to belong to a club. And he got some paint and was hanging on the door. He asked the kids if they wanted to paint the place yellow and black. And they thought it was a good idea, and they asked Jack to join.*

Q: Why do you think Jack chose yellow and black paint?
SR: He likes these colors.

Retelling Summary: ☐ many details, logical order ☑ some details, some order ☐ few details, disorder

Comprehension Questions and Possible Answers

+ (RIF)   1. Who is the main character in this story?   (Jack)

− (PIT)   2. Why does Jack want to belong to the club?   (he is the new boy and wants to make new friends) *He just does.*

+ (CAR)   3. What do you know about the word **belong?**   (to be a member, to have a rightful place)
  What does the word **belong** have to do with this story?   (Jack wants to get the kids to agree to let him belong to the club)
    to be in something → *be in the club.*

1/2 (RIF)   4. What did Jack dash home to get?   (bucket of yellow paint, one of black, and several brushes) → *paint*

1/2 (PIT)   5. Why did Jack knock one hundred times on the clubhouse door?   (the sign said to do that; he has something important to tell the club members)   *He had something to tell the kids.*

+ (CAR)   6. What do you know about the phrase **secret word?**   *Nobody knows it but the kids in the club.* (clubs have a secret password, only members know the word)
  What does the phrase **secret word** have to do with this story?   (Jack says he doesn't know the secret word) *I don't*

1/2 (PIT)   7. What was Jack's clever idea?   (because the club's name is Tigers, Jack thought they might want to paint the clubhouse yellow with black stripes)   *He got the paint.*

− (EAS)   8. In your opinion did it take courage to do what Jack did?   (yes, it's hard to be the new kid and try to make friends)
  You think this because ... (he wanted to belong so bad that he thought of a clever idea to get the kids to like him)
    Because it's hard to ask someone if you can join their club.

Reader Text Relationship (RTR)   From the Text   ☑ adequate ☐ not adequate   From Head to Text   ☐ adequate ☑ not adequate

Prior Knowledge/Prediction

☐ Read the title and predict what the story is about. *A horse that somebody loves.*

Q: What do you know about horses?

SR: I've never been on a horse.

☐ Read the first two sentences to yourself and add more to your prediction.

Jody was really worried because her horse was sick.

Prior Knowledge

☐ a lot
☐ some
☑ little to none

The Beloved Horse

	Text	O	I	S	A	Rp	Rv
1	Jody was so/worried that she had/stayed in the barn all day						
2	to take care of her sick/horse, Gabe. She thought his/condition *(cold)*		/		/		
3	*(breath)* (seemed to be)growing worse. His/breathing grew louder and harder.		/	/		/	
4	*(night / horse SC)* At nightfall, Jody/brought a blanket from the house so she could sleep		/		/	/	
5	*(loved / wind SC)* near her/beloved animal. In the/middle of the night/the wind whipped around		/		/	/	
6	the barn/(rattling)windows, and the barn door shook as if it would break into	/					
7	*(excited / slep)* splinters. She had been so/exhausted that she/slept through all the noise.		/	/			
8	*(came)* When the(dawn)light poured/through the windows, Jody stirred. Bits of		/				
9	*(stray SC)* straw stuck in her hair and onto her/wrinkled clothes. Where was the sound of	/					

The text is continued on the next page.

Cueing Systems

LINE #	Miscue	Grapho-phonically Similar I M F (word level)	Syntactically Acceptable Unacceptable (sentence level)	Semantic Change in Meaning (CM) No Change in Meaning (NCM) (sentence level)
2	*cold*	I	A	CM
3	*breath*	IM	A	slight CM
4	*night*	IM	A	slight CM
5	*loved*	MF	U	CM
6	*excited*	IF	A	CM
8	*came*		A	CM
10	*breath*	IM	A	slight CM
10	*jet*	IF	U	CM
10	*heal*	IM	U	CM

The cueing system grid is continued on the next page.

Cueing Systems

Miscue	Grapho-phonically Similar I M F (word level)	Syntactically Acceptable Unacceptable (sentence level)	Semantic Change in Meaning (CM) No Change in Meaning (NCM) (sentence level)
L I N E #			

		O	I	S	A	Rp	Rv
1 0	*breath* *jolt* *heal* the/sickly breathing? She sat up with a jolt! Then she saw Gabe/healthy and			III			
1 1	strong, standing by the open door. To her/surprise it looked like he was saying,					/	
1 2	"Let's go for a run!"						
	TOTALS	3	1	9	1	4	0

Number of miscues __18__   Number of self-corrections __3__

Fluency: Does the Reader . . .

☐ read smoothly, accurately, in meaningful phrases?

☑ read word-by-word, choppy, plodding?

☐ use pitch, stress, and intonation to convey meaning of the text?

☑ repeat words and phrases because s/he is monitoring the meaning (self-correcting)?   *some* ↗

☑ repeat words and phrases because s/he is trying to sound out words?   *some WR difficulties are beginning to interfere.*

☑ use punctuation to divide the text into units of meaning?   ☐ ignore the punctuation?

Rating Scale: Circle One

4 = fluent reading / good pace

3 = fairly fluent / reasonable pace

②= choppy, plodding reading / slow pace

1 = clearly labored, disfluent reading / very slow pace

Summary

☑ Most, ☐ few, ☐ no   miscues were graphophonically similar to the word in the passage.

☑ Most, ☐ few, ☐ no   miscues were syntactically matched.

☐ Most, ☑ few, ☐ no   miscues maintained the author's meaning.

☐ The self-corrections demonstrate that the reader monitors the meaning.

Form C, Level 4

Retelling *It's about a pony. Jody is really worried about her pony. It's sick. The barn door shook.*
She was really tired.

Q: *Can you tell more?*
SR: *That night Jody stayed with her horse. She took a blanket to the barn.*

Q: *Can you tell more?*
SR: *No*

Retelling Summary: ☐ many details, logical order ☐ some details, some order ☑ few details, disorder

Note: Indicate any probing with a "P"

Story Elements	All	Some	None
Main Character(s)	✓		
Time and Place		✓	
Problem		✓	
Plot Details in Sequence			✓
Turning Point			✓
Resolution			✓

Reader's Thumbnail Summary:

A sick pony.

Scoring Guide Summary

WORD RECOGNITION

Independent 2   *-18*
Instructional 7-8
Frustration ...... 15+

COMPREHENSION

Independent 0-1
Instructional 2   *-4*
Frustration ...... 4+

Emotional Status:
Less confident than at level 3.
...confused at times

Form C, Level 4

Comprehension Questions and Possible Answers

+ (RIF)   1. Who is the main character in this story?   (Jody)

+ (RIF)   2. Where does this story take place?   (in a barn, in the country)

+ (PIT)   3. What is the problem in this story?   (Jody's horse is sick)

– (CAR)   4. What do you know about the phrase **his condition seemed to be growing worse?** (state of health; his health was poor)
What does the phrase **his condition seemed to be growing worse** have to do with this story? (his condition seemed to be growing worse;
his breathing grew louder and harder) *He's sick.*   *with her horse*
       He has a cold.

+ (RIF)   5. Why did Jody take a blanket to the barn? (so she could sleep near her sick horse)

– (RIF)   6. Why did the windows rattle and the barn door shake? (in the middle of the night the
wind whipped around the barn) *It's loose.*

– (CAR)   7. What do you know about the word **dawn?**   (sunrise, the start of the day)
What does the word **dawn** have to do with this story? (the dawn light poured through the windows of the barn) *I don't know.*
       I don't know.

– (EAS)   8. Do you think Jody's horse will be all right? You think this because the text said…(yes, Gabe stood by the barn door looking
healthy and strong; no, he just looks healthy and strong, he's still sick)

Reader Text Relationship (RTR)   From the Text   ☑ adequate ☐ not adequate   From Head to Text   ☐ adequate ☑ not adequate

Cueing Systems

L I N E #	Miscue	Grapho-phonically Similar I M F (word level)	Syntactically Acceptable Unacceptable (sentence level)	Semantic Change in Meaning (CM) No Change in Meaning (NCM) (sentence level)

The cueing system grid is continued on the next page.

Prior Knowledge/Prediction

☐ Read the title and predict what the story is about.   *A small pony.*

☐ Read the first two sentences and add more to your prediction.
This boy's father was going to surprise him by buying him a pony. He's going to get the money.

Prior Knowledge
☐ a lot
☐ some
☑ none

	O	I	S	A	Rp	Rv

The Small Pony

Silent Reading Sample.

1. A long time ago a strong horse was important to a farmer,

2. so it was no surprise that Joel's father was storming mad. Mr. Goss

3. had sent Joel to a nearby town to collect some money a man owed him.

4. Joel had returned with a pony instead of the money! The news had

5. spread that the pony was small. People were already laughing.

6. What good was a small pony when there was heavy farm work to do?

7. Joel hoped to calm his father's anger by telling him about the

8. pony's unusual strength. Mr. Goss would not listen. He pounded

9. his fist on the table shouting several commands! The pony could not stay

The text is continued on the next page.

*This passage is retelling from the novel, *Justin Morgan Had a Horse*, by M. Henry.

Cueing Systems

	Miscue	Grapho-phonically Similar I M F (word level)	Syntactically Acceptable Unacceptable (sentence level)	Semantic Change in Meaning (CM) No Change in Meaning (NCM) (sentence level)
L I N E #				

Summary

☐ Most, ☐ few, ☐ no   miscues were graphophonically similar to the word in the passage.

☐ Most, ☐ few, ☐ no   miscues were syntactically matched.

☐ Most, ☐ few, ☐ no   miscues maintained the author's meaning.

☐ The self-corrections demonstrate that the reader monitors the meaning.

Form B, Level 4

	O	I	S	A	Rp	Rv
1 0	on his land! In the morning he would take his son to the saw mill					
1 1	and ask if Joel could live and work there. Joel felt shocked and hurt.					
1 2	How could he leave his home and also lose the pony he loved?					

TOTALS

Number of miscues _____   Number of self-corrections _____

Silent Reading Sample

Fluency: Does the Reader . . .

☐ read smoothly, accurately, in meaningful phrases?

☐ read word-by-word, choppy, plodding?

☐ use pitch, stress, and intonation to convey meaning of the text?

☐ repeat words and phrases because s/he is monitoring the meaning (self-correcting)?

☐ repeat words and phrases because s/he is trying to sound out words?

☐ use punctuation to divide the text into units of meaning?   ☐ ignore the punctuation?

Rating Scale: Circle One

4 = fluent reading / good pace   2 = choppy, plodding reading / slow pace

3 = fairly fluent / reasonable pace   1 = clearly labored, disfluent reading / very slow pace

Note: Indicate any probing with a "P"

Story Elements	All	Some	None
Main Character(s)		✓	
Time and Place			✓
Problem			✓
Plot Details in Sequence			✓
Turning Point			✓
Resolution			✓

Reader's Thumbnail Summary:
About a boy who lost his money.

Scoring Guide Summary

WORD RECOGNITION
Independent.......1-2
Instructional.....7-8   *N/A*
Frustration.......15+

COMPREHENSION   *-5 of*
Independent.......0-1   *6 asked*
Instructional.....2
Frustration.......4+

Emotional Status:
confused and stressed

Form B, Level 4

Retelling   *It's about this boy. His dad is mad because he lost his money.*
Q: Can you tell any more?
SR: No

Retelling Summary: □ many details, logical order □ some details, some order ☑ few details, disorder

Comprehension Questions and Possible Answers

+ (RIF)   1. Who are the two main characters in this story?   (Joel and his father, Mr. Goss)   *a boy and his dad*

– (RIF)   2. Where does this story take place?   (on a farm, in the country)   *I don't know.*

– (PIT)   3. Why was Joel's father storming mad?   (he had sent Joel to collect a debt and Joel returned with a small pony)   *He lost his money.*

– (PIT)   4. Why were people laughing about the pony?   (a farmer needed a strong horse, and a small pony could not do the heavy farm work)   *They thought it was funny.*

– (RIF)   5. How had Joel hoped to calm his father's anger?   (by convincing Mr. Goss of the pony's unusual strength)   *I don't know—finding his money.*

– (CAR)   6. What do you know about the phrase **shouting several commands**? What does the phrase **shouting several commands** have to do with this story?   (To yell out many orders one after the other)   (Mr. Goss pounded his fist on the table shouting several commands)   *I don't know. Maybe to yell.*

(PIT)   7. What did Mr. Goss command?   (the pony could not stay on the property; Joel had to leave his house and get a job working and living at the saw mill)
not asked

(EAS)   8. Do you think Joel's father's behavior was right? You think this because the text said...   (no, he should have let his son show how strong the pony was; yes, Joel should not have disobeyed his father by not bringing back the money)

SECTION II   ▪   Learning How to Use the *ARI*

Cueing Systems

L I N E #	Miscue	Grapho-phonically Similar I M F (word level)	Syntactically Acceptable Unacceptable (sentence level)	Semantic Change in Meaning (CM) No Change in Meaning (NCM) (sentence level)

The cueing system grid is continued on the next page.

FORM C, LEVEL 5	Reader's Passages page 38

Prior Knowledge/Prediction

□ Read the title and predict what the story is about. *A lady who drives race cars.*

Q: What do you know about a lady who drives a race car? SR: Well, there was a lady who drove in the Indy 500.   Q: Have you ever seen the Indy 500?   SR: I saw it on tv.

□ Read the first two sentences and add more to your prediction.

That she wants to go 500 miles per hour.   Q: Do they go 500 miles per hour at the Indy 500?   SR: I don't know.

Prior Knowledge
□ a lot
☑ some
□ none

		O	I	S	A	Rp	Rv
	A Woman Race Car Driver			*Listening Level*			
1	"I want to be the fastest woman top fuel car driver in the world,"						
2	stated Shirley Muldowney. "I want to go 500 miles per hour!" In those						
3	days, top fuel cars were the fastest, the most powerful, and the most carefully						
4	built machines in the car racing sport.						
5	At last the day of Shirley's big race arrived. The engines roared and						
6	Shirley blasted forward just like she was the top challenger in the						
7	country! It wasn't long before the speedometer read 220 miles per hour,						
8	and as Shirley's determination kicked in, the car seemed to propel forward.						
9	Her mind raced as she whizzed around the track. "I can accomplish						

The text is continued on the next page.

Cueing Systems

L I N E #	Miscue	Grapho-phonically Similar I M F (word level)	Syntactically Acceptable Unacceptable (sentence level)	Semantic Change in Meaning (CM) No Change in Meaning (NCM) (sentence level)

Summary

- ☐ Most, ☐ few, ☐ no miscues were graphophonically similar to the word in the passage.
- ☐ Most, ☐ few, ☐ no miscues were syntactically matched.
- ☐ Most, ☐ few, ☐ no miscues maintained the author's meaning.
- ☐ The self-corrections demonstrate that the reader monitors the meaning.

	O	I	S	A	Rp	Rv
1 0	anything I set out to do!" At 230 miles per hour her confidence and					
1 1	her nerves of steel began to push the car faster.					
1 2	Then, at 242 miles per hour, she established a record speed that no					
1 3	other top fuel driver had reached. Seconds later, her car rushed over the					
1 4	victory line! "Finally," she thought as she pulled into Victory Lane, "now people					
1 5	will think of me as a top race car driver and not just as a woman who					
1 6	drives a race car!"					

TOTALS

Number of miscues _____   Number of self-corrections _____

Listening Level   Fluency: Does the Reader . . .

- ☐ read smoothly, accurately, in meaningful phrases?
- ☐ read word-by-word, choppy, plodding?
- ☐ use pitch, stress, and intonation to convey meaning of the text?
- ☐ repeat words and phrases because s/he is monitoring the meaning (self-correcting)?
- ☐ repeat words and phrases because s/he is trying to sound out words?
- ☐ use punctuation to divide the text into units of meaning?   ☐ ignore the punctuation?

Rating Scale: Circle One
4 = fluent reading / good pace   2 = choppy, plodding reading / slow pace
3 = fairly fluent / reasonable pace   1 = clearly labored, disfluent reading / very slow pace

Note: Indicate any probing with a "P"

Story Elements	All	Some	None
Main Character(s)	✓		
Time and Place			✓
Problem			✓
Plot Details in Sequence			✓
Turning Point			✓
Resolution		✓	

Reader's Thumbnail Summary:
This lady drives a fast race car.

Scoring Guide Summary

WORD RECOGNITION   *Listening*
                              Level
Independent 2
Instructional 9-10
Frustration .... 19+

COMPREHENSION
Independent 0-1
Instructional 2   *-2 1/2*
Frustration ...... 4+

Emotional Status:
more relaxed than
at Level 4

Retelling   *This lady drives a race car, and she wants to go 500 miles per hour.*

Q: *Can you remember anything else?*
SR: *Yes, she wins a race.*
Q: *Any more?*
SR: *No*

Retelling Summary: ☐ many details, logical order ☐ some details, some order ☑ few details, disorder

Comprehension Questions and Possible Answers

+ _(RIF)_ 1. Who is the main character in this story?   (Shirley Muldowney)

+ _(RIF)_ 2. What is Shirley's goal?   (she wants to be the fastest woman driver in the world; to go 500 miles per hour)
                                              fast and powerful

+ _(PIT)_ 3. What were top fuel cars like?   (fastest, most powerful, and among the most carefully built machines)

— _(CAR)_ 4. What do you know about the phrase **top challenger?** (someone who competes against someone else and is the best, the top one) What does the phrase **top challenger** have to do with the story? (Shirley started the race like she was the top challenger in the whole country) *I don't know what that means.*

                                              It's in your car. It tells you how fast you're going.
1/2 _(CAR)_ 5. What do you know about the word **speedometer?**   (it is the instrument that measures the speed of a car, how fast it is going) What does **speedometer** have to do with the story? (the speedometer read 220 miles per hour)   *No response*
                                              She has a speedometer in her car.

— _(PIT)_ 6. What happened when Shirley's determination kicked in?   (the car seemed to propel forward)

+ _(EAS)_ 7. In your opinion, what was so unusual about Shirley's being a top fuel driver?   (in the story, she said, "Finally, now people will think of me as a top race car driver and not just as a woman who drives a race car!")   *She's a woman who wins races.*

+ _(PIT)_ 8. Why won't people think of her "just as a woman who drives a race car?"   *She won a race!*
             (she wins races; she has confidence and nerves of steel, she is a top fuel driver)

Reader Text Relationship (RTR)   From the Text   ☑ adequate ☐ not adequate   From the Head to Text   ☐ adequate ☑ not adequate

Cueing Systems

L I N E #	Miscue	Graphophonically Similar I M F (word level)	Syntactically Acceptable Unacceptable (sentence level)	Semantic Change in Meaning (CM) No Change in Meaning (NCM) (sentence level)
1	*got*		A	NCM
1	*bright*	IM	U	CM
2	*even*	IM	U	CM
3	*signs*	IM	A	CM
3	*they*	I	U	CM
4	*comets*	I	U	CM
5	*in*	I	U	CM
5	*parts*	IM	A	NCM
6	*came*	IF	A	NCM
6	*outs*	IM	U	CM
6	*stars*	I	U	CM
7	*even*	I	U	CM
8	*passed*	I	A	CM
9	*some*		A	CM
10	*passes*	IF	A	CM

The cueing system grid is continued on the next page.

Prior Knowledge/Prediction

☐ Read the title and predict what the text is about. *Comets*

Q: *What do you know about comets?*

SR: *They're bright in the sky at night. They have a tail.*

☐ Read the first two sentences and add more to your prediction.

People were scared of a comet. They thought it made an earthquake.

Prior Knowledge
☐ a lot
☑ some
☐ none

	A Comet	O	I	S	A	Rp	Rv
1	A long time ago/people/ *got became*/frightened when they saw a comet.			//			
2	They/thought a comet was a/sign that(unpleasant)events/ *such as* an /		/	/			
3	*signs they* earthquake/would/take place. Scientists (now)know that these ideas(are)(not)		//	//			
4	*comets* correct.			/			
5	*in parts* A comet/is(a)space(object)made up of ice particles/mixed/with dust.		//	/			
6	*came outs stars* Comets(probably)come from the far, outer/edge/of(our)(solar)(system). Comets		///	///			
7	*even* can be seen(only)when they are close enough to the sun/to/reflect its light.		//	/			
8	*passed* A comet has two parts: the head and the/tail. The tail is present(only)		/	/			
9	*some* when the/comet is heated by the sun. The tail is made of fine dust and gas.		/	/			

The text is continued on the next page.

Cueing Systems

LINE #	Miscue	Graphophonically Similar (I M F) (word level)	Syntactically Acceptable / Unacceptable (sentence level)	Semantic Change in Meaning (CM) / No Change in Meaning (NCM) (sentence level)
10	*miles*	IF	A	CM
11	*parts*	IF	A	NCM

Summary

☑ Most, ☐ few, ☐ no — miscues were graphophonically similar to the word in the passage.

☐ Most, ☑ few, ☐ no — miscues were syntactically matched.

☐ Most, ☑ few, ☐ no — miscues maintained the author's meaning.

☐ The self-corrections demonstrate that the reader monitors the meaning.

Form S, Level 4

	O	I	S	A	Rp	Rv
10	//	//	//			//
11	/ /	/ /				
12	/		/			/
13			//			
14			/			

praises / *miles*
10 A comet's/tail/always points away from the sun. It can be/millions (of kilometers)/

up / *parts* / *meat SC*
11 long. The head is made of ice (frozen) gases, and particles of rock/and/metal.

12 It could be (described) as a dirty snowball. The heads of most comets are/only a /

re
13 few/kilometers wide. As they/near the sun/reflected sunlight makes them

14 appear/large.

TOTALS — O 16 | I 1 | S 17 | A 3 | Rv 6

Number of miscues ___43___   Number of self-corrections ___1___

Fluency: Does the Reader . . .

☐ read smoothly, accurately, in meaningful phrases?

☑ read word-by-word, choppy, plodding?

☐ use pitch, stress, and intonation to convey meaning of the text?

☐ repeat words and phrases because s/he is monitoring the meaning (self-correcting)?

☑ repeat words and phrases because s/he is trying to sound out words?

☐ use punctuation to divide the text into units of meaning?   ☑ ignore the punctuation?

Rating Scale: Circle One

4 = fluent reading / good pace   2 = choppy, plodding reading / slow pace

3 = fairly fluent / reasonable pace   ①= clearly labored, disfluent reading / very slow pace

Note: Indicate any probing with a "P"

Expository Elements	All	Some	None
Description			✓
Collection			✓
Causation			✓
Problem/Solution			✓
Comparison			✓

Reader's Thumbnail Summary:

About a comet.

Scoring Guide Summary

WORD RECOGNITION

Independent 1-2
Instructional 8-9   *-43*
Frustration ..... 17+

COMPREHENSION

Independent 0-1
Instructional 2   *-6*
Frustration ..... 4+

Emotional Status:
very stressed, whole body tense

Form S, Level 4

Retelling   *It's about comets. They have a tail.*

Q: Anything else?
S.R.: *No, that's all.*

Retelling Summary: ☐ many details, logical order ☐ some details, some order ☑ few details, disorder

---

Comprehension Questions and Possible Answers

+ (RIF)   1. In relation to the sun, where does a comet's tail always point?   (away from the sun)

+ (PIT)   2. What happened a long time ago when people saw comets?   *They got scared.*
(they became frightened because they thought comets were signs of unpleasant events)

− (EAS)   3. In your opinion, a long time ago why did people become frightened of a comet?   (a long time ago,   *I don't know.*
before telescopes were invented, people didn't know what a comet was; they were superstitious)
You think this because . . . (the text said scientists now know these fears were not correct)

− (RIF)   4. What is a comet?   (a space object made of ice particles with dust)   *It's in space.*

− (RIF)   5. Where do comets come from?   (probably come from the outer edge of our solar system)   *space*

− (PIT)   6. When can you see the comet?   (when it is close enough to the sun to reflect the sun's light)   *at night*

− (CAR)   7. What do you know about the phrase **reflect the sun's light?**   (when the sun shines on something like a glass car
window, the light bounces off of it) What does the phrase **reflect the sun's light** have to do with this text?   *No response*
(the text said the sun shines on the comet and the light bounces off of it and then we can see it)

− (PIT)   8. Why is a comet described as a dirty snowball?   (the tail is made from dust and gas; the head is ice,
frozen gases, and particles of rock and metal)   *I don't know.*

Reader Text Relationship (RTR)   From the Text ☐ adequate ☑ not adequate   From Head to Text ☐ adequate ☑ not adequate

---

FORM SS, LEVEL 4 — Reader's Passages page 57

Prior Knowledge/Prediction

☐ Read the title and predict what the text is about. *French explorers in North America.*

Q: *What do you know about French explorers in North America?*
SR: *Not much.*

☐ Read the first two sentences and add more to your prediction.
A long time ago, some guys went to New France.

Prior Knowledge
☐ a lot
☐ some
☑ none

French Explorers in North America

#	Text	O	I	S	A	Rp	Rv
1	During the 1600s, the French settled much of eastern Canada. They	//		/	/		
2	called this land New France. They had heard stories about a large body of	/					
3	water to the west. The French thought it might be the Pacific Ocean. They			/			
4	wanted more land to add to the French Empire. Soon they began to look for	///		//			
5	the great body of water. This journey took them to regions that are now part	//			/		
6	of the United States. Some went south instead of west.			/			
	Examiner stopped the session.						
7	In 1679, a Frenchman, La Salle, began a second journey to explore						
8	the Great Lakes region. He started at the south end of Lake Michigan. He						
9	followed the Illinois River to the place where it met the Mississippi River.						

The text is continued on the next page.

Cueing Systems

LINE #	Miscue	Graphophonically Similar I M F (word level)	Syntactically Acceptable/Unacceptable (sentence level)	Semantic Change in Meaning (CM) No Change in Meaning (NCM) (sentence level)

The cueing system grid is continued on the next page.

Cueing Systems

L I N E #	Miscue	Grapho-phonically Similar I M F (word level)	Syntactically Acceptable Unacceptable (sentence level)	Semantic Change in Meaning (CM) No Change in Meaning (NCM) (sentence level)

Summary

☐ Most, ☑ few, ☐ no   miscues were graphophonically similar to the word in the passage.

☐ Most, ☐ few, ☐ no   miscues were syntactically matched.

☐ Most, ☐ few, ☐ no   miscues maintained the author's meaning.

☐ The self-corrections demonstrate that the reader monitors the meaning.

Form SS, Level 4

	O	I	S	A	Rp	Rv
1 0	By 1682, he had gone all the way down the Mississippi to where it flowed into					
1 1	the Gulf of Mexico. He claimed the lands on both sides of the river. He also					
1 2	claimed the rivers that flowed into the land. He named the region Louisiana in					
1 3	honor of Louis XIV, the French king.					
TOTALS		9	5	2		

Number of miscues __16__   Number of self-corrections __1__

Fluency: Does the Reader . . .

☐ read smoothly, accurately, in meaningful phrases?

☑ read word-by-word, choppy, plodding?

☐ use pitch, stress, and intonation to convey meaning of the text?

☐ repeat words and phrases because s/he is monitoring the meaning (self-correcting)?

☑ repeat words and phrases because s/he is trying to sound out words?

☐ use punctuation to divide the text into units of meaning?   ☑ ignore the punctuation?

Rating Scale: Circle One

4 = fluent reading / good pace   2 = choppy, plodding reading / slow pace

3 = fairly fluent / reasonable pace   ①= clearly labored, disfluent reading / very slow pace

Note: Indicate any probing with a "P"

Expository Elements	All	Some	None
Description			
Collection			
Causation			
Problem/Solution			
Comparison			

Reader's Thumbnail Summary:

Scoring Guide Summary

WORD RECOGNITION *-16 in first*
Independent .... 2 *first paragraph*
Instructional .... 8–9 *paragraph*
Frustration .... 17+ *Frust*

COMPREHENSION *N/A*
Independent 0–1
Instructional 2
Frustration .... 4+

Emotional Status:
very stressed, clearly frustrated

Form SS, Level 4

Retelling *Not asked.*

Retelling Summary: □ many details, logical order □ some details, some order □ few details, disorder

Comprehension Questions and Possible Answers *Not asked.*

___(PIT) 1. What did the French do during the 1600s? (they explored and settled most of eastern Canada)

___(CAR) 2. What do you know about the word **settled?** (to take permanent residence, to stay and live in one spot)
What does the word **settled** have to do with the text? (they settled eastern Canada)

___(RIF) 3. What did the French call eastern Canada? (New France)

___(RIF) 4. What did the French think the large body of water to the west was? (the Pacific Ocean)

___(PIT) 5. Why were the French so eager to explore farther west? (they wanted more land to add to the French Empire)

___(RIF) 6. Where did La Salle's second journey take him? (Great Lakes region; Lake Michigan all the way down the Mississippi River to the Gulf of Mexico)

___(CAR) 7. What do you know about the phrase **claimed the lands?** (he said the land belonged to France, took ownership of the land) What does the phrase **claimed the lands** have to do with the text? (La Salle claimed the land on both sides of the Mississippi River)

___(EAS) 8. In your opinion was La Salle loyal to his country and his king? You think this because . . . (yes, his journeys were dangerous and he probably risked his life; he always claimed the land in the name of the French Empire; he named the land near the Gulf of Mexico Louisiana in honor of the French king)

Reader Text Relationship (RTR) From the Text □ adequate □ not adequate From Head to Text □ adequate □ not adequate

Refer to Sample
Talk-Through Chart
on pages 49 and 50.

Case Study Profile Narration
Narrative Passages, Form C
Expository Passages, Forms S and SS

• Level 2, The Busy Road

•Prediction/Prior Knowledge

Jenny's predictions were focused and based upon a lot of prior knowledge.

• Word Recognition (−6 miscues; 4 SC)

Jenny was searching for meaning as she read. For example, she self-corrected (SC) some miscues (*nose* for *noise; scar* for *scared*), showing that she was attending to the meaning, applying her prediction, and/or using context clues to select the correct word. Even though the miscue count was 6, and even though most miscues changed the meaning within the sentence, her overall grasp of the meaning was accurate, causing the word recognition score to be definite instructional.

• Fluency (Rating 4)

Even though Jenny's reading appeared somewhat choppy, she did read in meaningful phrases. In some instances intonation was used to convey the meaning of the text. Some repetitions were made because she was sounding out the words. Punctuation was effectively used to divide the text into units of meaning. At this level her reading was fairly fluent and maintained a good pace.

• Comprehension (Retelling, Summary, + Quest.)

The retelling was very thorough and reflected all the story elements. Jenny used complete, well-structured sentences and in some instances used the author's exact words. The summary statement was complete. Responses to the comprehension questions (–0) were accurate and in the language of the author as well as the retelling.

• Scoring Guide Sum. Grid (Emotional Status)

Jenny was confident and relaxed.

• Summary

Word Recognition = definite instructional

Comprehension = independent

Overall = independent

• Level 3, Belonging to the Club

• Prediction/Prior Knowledge

Jenny had some background knowledge about club membership; however, the miscue in the first two sentences (*triggers* for *tigers*) caused her to lose the chance for a meaningful prediction.

• Word Recognition (−13 miscues; 5 SC)

She made some word substitutions that were close choices (*be in* for *belong, ask* for *agree, soon* for *suddenly*), which shows that she was continuing to search for meaning, but she did not self-correct (SC) these miscues. The Cueing Systems Miscue Analysis showed that her strength is in using the initial portion of the word, but that medial and final portions are not often attended to. The number of self-corrections did not markedly increase based upon the increase of total words.

• Fluency (Rating 3)

The reading was choppier than at Level 2, but still many of the words were grouped into meaningful phrases. In some cases intonation was used to convey the meaning. Some words or phrases were repeated because Jenny was attempting to self-correct. Most of the time punctuation was used effectively.

• Comprehension (Retelling, Summary, + Quest.)

Despite the fact that the number of miscues increased, Jenny retold some of the story; however, some important information was omitted (Jack was new to the neighborhood.). Her failure to correct the word *Triggers* for *Tigers* caused her to miss an important concept in the story (the connection between the yellow and black paint and the name of the club). The summary statement was incomplete. The responses to some of the comprehension questions didn't contain enough information (−3½).

• Scoring Guide Sum. Grid (Emotional Status)

She did not have the same confidence as she did reading Level 2. Her posture became more slumped, and her breathing less relaxed, yet she persisted with determination.

• Summary

Word Recognition = transitional instructional

Comprehension = transitional instructional

Overall = transitional instructional

- *Level 4, A Beloved Horse*

- Prediction/Prior Knowledge

Jenny added to her prediction after reading the first two sentences, but it was limited because she had little prior knowledge about ponies.

- Word Recognition (−16 miscues; 3 SC)

Substitutions and repetitions comprised the majority of miscues. Only 3 self-corrections were made, indicating that Jenny was less able to use context clues and was more confounded by word recognition difficulties. At this level she used both initial and medial portions of the words, but for the most part the miscues changed the meaning. Two miscues, *breath* for *breathing* and *night* for *nightfall,* caused a slight change in meaning. Other miscues (6) were totally inaccurate, such as *cold* for *condition.* A pattern emerged with substitutions: omitting the final portions of words (*breath* for *breathing, night* for *nightfall, heal* for *healthy*). For the first time, a word had to be aided.

- Fluency (Rating 2.5)

The reading was word-by-word. Jenny repeated some phrases in an attempt to clarify the meaning, but in many instances attempts to pronounce words slowed the fluency. The use of intonation to convey meaning was less evident at this level. For the most part, punctuation was used to divide the text into units of meaning.

- Comprehension (Retelling, Summary, + Quest.)

Jenny's retelling was scanty and poorly organized. The summary statement was weak. Responses to most comprehension questions were incorrect (−4).

- Scoring Guide Sum. Grid (Emotional Status)

Jenny did not look like or sound like a confident reader. She showed physical signs of stress—hands were tightly fisted, and her breathing became short and choppy. Sometimes she appeared confused. She was reluctant to take any risks such as making meaningful word substitutions.

- Summary

Word Recognition = frustration

Comprehension = frustration

Overall = frustration

- *Level 4, Form B, The Small Pony* (silent reading)

- Prediction/Prior Knowledge

Jenny predicted that the passage would be about a pony, but she seemed to have no background information. After reading the first two sentences she picked up incorrect information.

- Silent Reading Behavior

Jenny read through the text rapidly. It looked like she was running from line to line in a fast manner without careful attention to the text.

- Comprehension (Retelling, Summary, + Quest.)

The retelling was scanty with incorrect information. (Joel had lost his father's money.). Incorrect responses were given to five of the six comprehension questions.

- Scoring Guide Sum. Grid (Emotional Status)

She seemed more relaxed than with the oral reading at Level 4, but with more inaccurate information.

- Summary

Word Recognition = N/A

Comprehension = frustration

Overall = frustration

- *Level 5, A Woman Race Car Driver* (listening)

- Prediction/Prior Knowledge

Jenny's prediction was adequate and she had prior knowledge about women race car drivers.

- Comprehension (Retelling, Summary, + Quest.)

The retelling was scanty and her summary statement contained only partial information. Her responses to the comprehension questions showed that she remembered a lot of the story (−2½) and responded often in the language of the author.

- Scoring Guide Sum. Grid (Emotional Status)

Jenny retold in a confident manner. Her responses to the comprehension questions were given in a more relaxed, direct manner. Her voice conveyed more certainty. Her body straightened, and her hands relaxed.

- Summary (listening level)

Word Recognition = N/A

Comprehension = definite instructional

Overall = definite instructional

- *Form S, Level 4, A Comet*
- Prediction/Prior Knowledge

The prediction was weak, and Jenny had little prior knowledge about comets.

- Word Recognition (−43 miscues; 1 SC)

The miscues were mostly omissions, substitutions, and repetitions. There was only one self-correction. The analysis of the substitutions showed that Jenny relies mostly upon the use of initial consonants and blends as a key strategy to pronounce the words. Toward the end of the passage she was so frustrated that it was necessary to aid three words.

- Fluency (Rating 1)

Jenny's reading was clearly labored, disfluent reading, with a very slow pace.

- Comprehension (Retelling, Summary, + Quest.)

The retelling was scanty. The retelling contained the same information as the prediction with no new information from the text. The summary statement was incomplete. Most comprehension question responses were incorrect (−6).

- Scoring Guide Sum. Grid (Emotional Status)

Jenny showed all the obvious signs of frustration.

- Summary

Word Recognition = frustration

Comprehension = frustration

Overall = frustration

- *Form SS, Level 4, French Explorers in North America*
- Prediction/Prior Knowledge

The prediction was inadequate, and she had no prior knowledge about French explorers.

- Word Recognition (incomplete)

The miscues were so numerous that Jenny was unable to complete the passage. She made 16 miscues in the first paragraph and asked for help with so many words that it was necessary to stop the session.

- Fluency (Rating 1)

Jenny's reading was not fluent.

- Comprehension (Retelling, Summary, + Quest.)

Did not complete the passage.

- Scoring Guide Sum. Grid (Emotional Status)

Jenny showed all the obvious signs of frustration.

- Summary

Word Recognition = incomplete

Comprehension = incomplete

Overall = frustration

ADMINISTERING THE *ARI:* STEP-BY-STEP INSTRUCTIONS

This subsection provides detailed instructions for administering a comprehensive *ARI* assessment session. When first learning, it is recommended that you listen to the CD 1 tracks and follow along with the corresponding case study documentation (pages 53–80), using these instructions as a study guide or checklist. When administering the *ARI* to a student, you can also use these instructions like a checklist. As you become more experienced and confident, use the Short Form Checklist of Step-by-Step Instructions (page 89) like a short form guide.

As you journey through the process of administering the *ARI,* note that you will: **establish** rapport, **record** data, **determine** assessment status, and **analyze, synthesize,** and **summarize** data.

Step 1: Establish Rapport

<table>
<tr><td>

From the subsection "Acquiring Background Knowledge," read Examiner or Teacher Behaviors (page 9).

</td></tr>
</table>

The assessment purpose is to **establish** the tone for an informal, personalized, and interactive assessment session.

☐ During informal assessment establish rapport by setting the reader at ease while both you and the reader work through the procedures. Informal assessment is suited to a relaxed, conversational style of interaction. Tell the reader that the results of the assessment will be shared with him or her as well as with others. Tell the reader that he or she is the most important person in this process because unlike other tests/assessments, the results will identify strengths and needs and help the two of you to set goals for change. Explain that you will be writing data while he or she reads, retells, and answers questions.

☐ Many examiners tape-record the entire session, enabling them to verify coding and comprehension responses. If you use a tape recorder, set the reader at ease by explaining why and how it is being used.

Step 2: Conduct a Reading Interview

<table>
<tr><td>

To review Component 1, Reading Interview, read "Seven Questions About Reading" and "Reading Interview" in Section III (pages 92–93).

</td></tr>
</table>

The assessment purpose is to **record** data about the reader's:

- reading interests, attitudes, and habits
- strategies for book selection and reading
- perceptions regarding his or her reading ability

☐ Section III includes two reading interviews, "Seven Questions About Reading" and "Reading Interview" (Robb, 1995). These two surveys provide important information about the student's reading behaviors. You may choose to give these interviews individually, using the time to establish an informal, personalized tone for an assessment session—or you may choose to give the interviews as a whole class event. Regardless of the manner in which you administer the surveys, it is important that you **report** the results to each reader. Reporting the results will help you set the expectation that each reader is to establish goals for reading growth. It is important that your students recognize the significance of the process of reflection and goal setting.

- If you wish to review how to administer Component 2, Word Lists/Initial Placement, refer to the case study word lists (pages 55, 56).
- Listen to CD 1, Track 2, as you review the case study word lists.

Step 3: Ask Student to Read Word Lists

The assessment purpose is to **determine**

- if the reader pronounces and comprehends the words
- the first narrative level passage the student is to read

☐ Select the narrative form you plan to use: Form A, B, or C.

☐ Open the *Reader's Passages* book to the word lists and place that page in front of the reader. Use a small sheet of scrap paper to cover all lists but the one the student will read.

☐ Ask the student to begin reading the words in the Primer word list. Mark a "+" if the word is pronounced correctly. If the word is pronounced incorrectly, write the word the reader said on the line adjacent to the word. If the reader does not attempt a pronunciation or says he doesn't know the word, mark "DK." If the reader miscues and then self-corrects, write the miscue and mark "SC" next to it.

☐ When words are pronounced in isolation, you don't really know if the reader is just *calling* words or is actually comprehending them. After the student has completed a list, select some words from the list and ask the reader to put them into a sentence. For example, say, "Make up a sentence that uses numbers fifteen and seventeen from list three. You can put them into one sentence or two sentences." Jot the sentence(s) down in the space at the bottom of the word list. This quick assessment will help you to know if the student comprehends the words; therefore, you will make an accurate decision about which narrative passage to select as the starter.

☐ Have the reader continue pronouncing words until he or she miscues 5 or does not attempt 5 of the 20 words in a list. Ask the reader to stop reading the words in any list when the fifth word is miscued. Sometimes a student will plunge on despite the difficulties. Honor the student's perseverance, but do not begin another list.

☐ To select the starting place in the narrative reading passages, **find the highest level at which the student pronounced all 20 words correctly.** For example, if all 20 words were pronounced correctly at Level 3, and if the reader's sentences demonstrated adequate comprehension, ask the student to begin reading the narrative Level 3 passage. However, if the sentences reflected little comprehension, you should select Level 2 as the initial passage. If any words were miscued on the primer level list, begin the reader in the preprimer passage.

Read the Explanation for Component 3, Prior Knowledge/Prediction Analysis (page 22).

Step 4: Ask Student to Read the Passage and Access Prior Knowledge/Prediction

The assessment purpose is to **determine** if the reader

- has prior knowledge about the text
- accesses prior knowledge and applies it to make a meaningful prediction before reading the text
- uses prior knowledge/prediction skills throughout the reading of the text to impact word recognition and comprehension

☐ Open the *Reader's Passages* book to the first narrative passage to be read by the reader. Open your Examiner's Record to the corresponding passage. Show the student your copy and his copy. Point to the corresponding items on both copies, giving the reader an overview of what is expected. You should say:

☐ "First, you will read the title and make a prediction.

☐ Next, you'll read the first two sentences and I'll ask you to add more to your prediction.

☐ Then, I'll ask you to tell what you already know about things in the passage.

☐ Then, you'll read the whole passage while I write notes on my copy.

☐ After reading, I will close your book, and you will retell as much as you can remember about the passage. I'll record your retelling.

☐ Finally, I'll ask you some comprehension questions."

☐ Point to the title and ask the student to read it aloud. If the reader hesitates or miscues, allow a short amount of time for self-correction. If the reader does not quickly self-correct, aid the word or words. An aided word in the title does not factor into the total miscue count.

☐ After the title has been read, ask the student to predict. Say, "You think this story will be about . . ." Jot the prediction in the box above the passage. After the prediction, find out if the reader has any prior knowledge by asking, "So what do you know about . . . ?"

☐ Next, ask the student to read the first two sentences in the passage. Point to the end of the second sentence so the reader knows where to stop. Provide aided words only in extreme cases of anxiety or if you know the reader is at the frustration level. After the two sentences have been read say, "After you read the title you said this story is going to be about . . . , now can you add more to your prediction?" If the reader adds more to the prediction, you can inquire again for more prior knowledge. Ask again, "So, what do you know about . . . ?"

☐ Finally, rate the amount of prior knowledge you think the reader has by checking the scale located to the right of the predictions.

Step 5: Code Oral Reading Miscues

The assessment purpose is to **record** data about the reader's

- miscues (types and frequency)
- use of all cueing systems (graphophonic, syntactic, and semantic)
- word recognition level—independent, instructional, or frustration
- self-correcting behavior

☐ Before the student begins to read remind him or her, "After you read the passage, I will ask you to retell as much as you can remember about the passage, and then I'll ask you some comprehension questions." This statement lets the reader know your expectations and reminds him or her to concentrate on more than just the pronunciation of words.

☐ As the student reads, record all miscues in the space provided above the text. It is important to notice the student's emotional status. Is he or she relaxed or nervous? Confident or uncertain? Persevering or giving up? Observations about a reader's emotional status provide important qualitative data. Knowing how to combine qualitative and quantitative data enables you to make an accurate decision about the student's reading level.

- If you wish to review coding, refer to Component 4, Oral Reading Miscue Analysis, the Oral Reading Miscues Chart (page 24).

- If questions arise, refer to the Miscue Coding Questions information (pages 23 and 25).

- Read the Explanation for Component 5, Fluency Analysis (pages 25 and 26).
- Review the coded but not counted miscues explained in the Oral Reading Miscues Chart (page 24).

Step 6: Check for Fluency

The assessment purpose is to **record** data about the reader's ability to

- read smoothly, accurately, in meaningful phrases
- use pitch, stress, and intonation to convey meaning
- repeat words and phrases using meaning to self-correct
- use punctuation to divide text into units of meaning

☐ As the student reads, record fluency data by coding hesitations, the ignoring of punctuation marks, and self-corrections.

☐ After the reader completes the passage, make a quick fluency assessment using the descriptions in the box located beneath the reader's passage. Later you can make a more thorough analysis.

☐ After you have completed the fluency assessment, circle the appropriate rating in the scale at the bottom of the fluency grid.

- Read the Explanation for Component 6, Retelling Analysis (page 27).
- You may wish to review CD 2, Track 6, which distinguishes the quality of retellings.

Step 7: Ask for a Retelling and Summary Statement

The assessment purpose is to **record** the reader's

- comprehension of the text elements
- summary statement
- language structure

☐ After the reader has read the passage, close the *Reader's Passages* book or remove it from view. Say, "Retell everything you can remember from the passage, and I will write down what you say." Record the retelling in the box marked, "Retelling." Some examiners use the time-saving convenience of the computer and word processing software, typing as the reader retells. Later the text is cut and pasted into the passage retelling grid.

☐ Sometimes a student doesn't retell much information from the text. When this happens you should *probe* (P) to find out if the reader actually knows more but just hasn't said it. Rather than asking a focused question that may give away information, you should ask an open-ended probe because the purpose is to see if the reader can tell more, not to prompt him. "Can you tell more?" "And?" "More?" are appropriate open-ended probes.

☐ Quickly assess the retelling and check the appropriate "Retelling Summary" box located at the bottom of the retelling grid.

☐ Next check the appropriate columns: "All," "Some," or "None," located on the Story Elements or Expository Elements grid.

☐ Finally, ask the reader to make a summary statement. Say, "In one or two short sentences, tell what this passage is about." This summary is called the Reader's Thumbnail Summary. It is recorded in the bottom cell of the elements grid.

Read the Explanation for
Component 7, Compre-
hension Question/RTR
Analysis (pages 28 and
29). Note the QAR
equivalencies (page 29).

Step 8: Ask Comprehension Questions

The assessment purpose is to **record** data about the reader's

- comprehension
- level of thinking, literal and implied (Reader Text Relationship)
- language structure

☐ Eliminate the comprehension questions that reiterate information already included in the retelling. Put a plus (+) on the line next to those questions indicating that credit has been given for that question. Mark correct responses with a plus (+) and incorrect responses with a minus (−). If the response contains half of the correct answer, give half credit for that question.

☐ When a reader responds to a question, he may not give the exact answer listed in the Examiner's Record. Probe first, and then use educated judgment to decide what is acceptable. Think about these responses from Form C, Level 4 "The Beloved Pony" (Case Study, page 65).

> QUESTION 5: Why did Jody take a blanket to the barn? (so she could sleep near her sick horse)
> RESPONSE: *So she could sleep with her horse.*

Even though the response to question 5 is not stated in the exact words of the suggested response, you should determine that the student knows why Jody took the blanket to the barn and give full credit for the response.

> QUESTION 6: Why did the windows rattle and the barn door shake? (in the middle of the night the wind whipped around the barn)
> RESPONSE: *It's loose.*

The response to question 6 demonstrates that the reader doesn't know why the door shook. No credit can be given for a reader's response that comes from background knowledge without substantiating it with information from the text. The reader's response was not text related.

> QUESTION 8: Do you think Jody's horse will be all right? You think this because the text said . . . (yes, Gabe stood by the barn door looking healthy and strong; no, he just looked healthy and strong, he's still sick)
> RESPONSE: *I don't know.*

In question 8, the reader makes no effort to express an opinion or to substantiate it with information from the text; thus, no credit can be given.

☐ Finally, below the comprehension questions, check the boxes to indicate the nature of the Reader Text Relationship (RTR).

Refer to Component 9, Quantitative and Qualitative Analysis, "Taking a Closer Look at the Scoring Guide Summary, Two Instructional Levels" (pages 44–46).

Step 9: Use the Scoring Guide Summary

The assessment purpose is to **estimate** the reading level as independent, instructional, or frustration to **determine** whether to stop or continue the oral reading.

☐ At this point you must determine if the reader should continue to the next passage. Quickly total the number of miscues and comprehension errors. Do this discreetly so you don't make the student feel uncomfortable. In pencil, circle the appropriate levels for word recognition and for comprehension in the Scoring Guide Summary, which is located to the right of the comprehension questions.

In some cases, the word recognition totals and comprehension totals match and the overall level is clear. However, sometimes, they don't match, or the miscue or comprehension error count exceeds or falls short of the range indicated on the Scoring Guide Summary. Refer to "Taking a Closer Look at the Scoring Guide Summary, Two Instructional Levels" (pages 44–46) earlier in this section for clarification.

☐ If you determine that the reader has not reached the frustration level, continue with the next oral reading passage.

From the subsection Acquiring Background Knowledge, read Oral and Silent Reading (page 9).

Step 10: Assess the Student's Silent Reading

The assessment purpose is to **determine** if the reader is more successful as a silent reader than as an oral reader.

☐ If you determine that the reader should read silently, change to another narrative form and select a silent reading passage. For example, if a reader is experiencing difficulty at Level 4, Form A, then use Level 4, Form B as the silent reading passage. Refer to the subsection on "Oral and Silent Reading" (page 9) for more information on this topic.

☐ After you have chosen the form and passage, say:
"Please read the title silently and make an oral prediction."
"Now, read the first two sentences silently and add to the prediction."
"What do you know about . . . ?"
Record all information in the Prediction/Prior Knowledge grid.

☐ Ask the reader to read the whole text silently. Remind him or her that you will ask for a retelling and comprehension questions.

As the student reads, does he or she skim through the text rapidly, seemingly paying little attention to words or punctuation with little reflection about the meaning? Or, does the reader attentively read and reflect? What is the nature of his or her emotional status? Jot this information on the passage.

☐ After the student has read the passage, ask for a retelling, a summary statement, and finally ask comprehension questions. Record the student's responses in the appropriate places. Was the retelling complete or inadequate? Was the language of the retelling disorganized or well sequenced? Was it in language that matched the author's vocabulary and style? Were responses to the comprehension questions adequate? What was the RTR? Was the reader stressed or relaxed?

- Read about the listening level on the Quantitative and Qualitative Data Chart (page 35).

- If you wish a review, listen to CD 2, Track 12, and follow along on Reader #5 Chart: Abi Listening Level (page 41).

Step 11: Determine Listening Level

The assessment purpose is to **determine** the reader's level of comprehension when he is not reading, rather when listening to the examiner read the text.

☐ The listening level identifies the reader's ability to comprehend a passage without the stress of word recognition. Select a passage at the same or one level above the student's frustration level. You may choose the passage within the same form or change to a different form.

☐ Say, "Now, you may relax and listen carefully while I read to you."
  • "First, I'll read the title and then ask you to make a prediction."
Was the prediction adequate?

  • "Now, I'll read the first two sentences and ask you to add to the prediction."
Did the reader add more information to his prediction?

  • "What do you know about . . . ?"
Did the reader have any prior knowledge?

  • "Now, I'll read the whole passage. When I've finished reading you will retell as much information as you can remember."
Was the retelling complete or inadequate? Was the language of the retelling disorganized or well sequenced? Was the retelling in language that matches the author's vocabulary and style? Was the summary statement sufficient?

  • "Now, I will ask you comprehension questions."
Were responses to the comprehension questions adequate? Was the reader's RTR adequate? Was the student stressed or relaxed?

☐ It is suggested that you stop reading to the student when he reaches the instructional level (75% comprehension); however, the data is so revealing that you may choose to continue reading until the reader reaches the frustration level.

Knowing the size of the gap between the student's oral reading frustration level and his listening level is significant information. For example, if a reader's oral reading frustration level is at passage level 4, and her listening level is at passage level 5, you know the student is weak in both word recognition and comprehension. However, if a reader's oral reading frustration level is at passage level 4 and his listening level is at passage level 7, you know that he comprehends far beyond his oral reading frustration level. This implies that word recognition is a weakness, but that comprehension is a strength. This important information should influence the selection of materials such as books to read aloud; it should also cause you to make informed decisions about multi-ability groupings.

Step 12: Assess Reading Level for Expository Passages

From the subsection "Acquiring Background Knowledge," read "Narrative and Expository Passages" (pages 11–13).

The assessment purpose is to **determine** the reader's at-grade-level expository reading level—independent, instructional (definite/transitional), or frustration.

☐ After you have determined the student's listening level using the narrative passages, Forms A, B, or C, switch to the expository passages. Before the student begins to read, say, "You will be reading two passages. The first is a science passage, and the second a social studies passage. One passage is like our science book and the other like our social studies book."

Follow Steps 4–9 of the instructions on pages 82–86, which are used for the narrative passages. When analyzing the student's ability to process the expository passages, you should be thinking:

- At what reading level—independent, instructional, or frustration—does the student read the grade level expository passage?
- What strengths and difficulties is the student experiencing when reading the grade level expository passage?

☐ If the student is frustrated or reading at a transitional instructional level with the grade level passage, what is his listening level with expository text? When you read aloud, can most of your students comprehend the information? To find the science or social studies listening level, read aloud the grade level passage and follow the instructions for Step 11. If you want to find out if the listening level is above grade level, choose the passage above grade level and follow the same instructions.

It is important to know at what reading level—independent, instructional, or frustration—each student functions with the science and social studies text used in your classroom. Some students will be able to read the text at the independent level, while others are at the frustration level. If you know this important information, you will be able to effectively determine multi-ability, flexible reading groups.

You can also put together a collection of alternate texts that coordinate with the topics in the science and social studies textbooks, thus supporting the reading needs of all students in your classroom. The data should raise the following questions. What is the most effective way to use the science or social studies textbook in my class? Should alternate texts be used in conjunction with the text? Can I find narrative texts that support the content of the science or social studies textbooks? Should some of the alternate texts be used as read-aloud texts? Can some be used as books for sustained silent reading?

Step 13: Summarize Results

The assessment purpose is to **analyze, synthesize,** and **summarize** data in preparation for reporting data to the reader, the reader's parents, and other educators.

☐ Review all passages the student read. To do this some teachers *talk through* the data. The process of talking through the data causes you to articulate the information; therefore, you can discover across several passages, consistent applications or repetitious defaults of standards and indicators.

In the process of talking through the data, you will fill in the Cueing Systems grid located to the right of each passage. After filling out the grid, summarize the data by checking the information in the Summary box at the bottom of the grid. Ask yourself these questions:

- Did the reader make many self-corrections?
- Did those self-corrections affect the quality and accuracy of the retelling?
- Did self-corrections continue throughout all passages?

The answer to these questions can play an important role in the final summarization of the data.

☐ Fill out the Student Profile Summary. This summary is so comprehensive that it is but a staple away from portfolio ready. To gain a whole class perspective, fill out the Class Profile Summary. Finally, complete the *ARI* Profile Card, which is placed in a student's file for the student's forthcoming teachers.

- Refer to Component 10, Summarizing Results, Directions 4–6 "Talking Through the Data" (pages 49–50).

- Read the explanation for Component 8, Cueing Systems Analysis (pages 30–32).

- Review the Case Study passages, reading the Cueing Systems grid to the right of each passage (pages 57–77).

- Review the Case Study Student Profile (page 54) and Case Study Profile Narration (pages 78–80), to know how a final summary is documented.

- From the subsection "Acquiring Background Knowledge," read "Portfolio and the *ARI*" (page 10).

Short Form Checklist of Step-by-Step Instructions	✓
Step 1: Establish Rapport—establish: • the tone for an informal, personalized, and interactive assessment session	
Step 2: Conduct a Reading Interview—record data about the reader's: • reading interests, attitudes, and habits • strategies for book selection and reading • perceptions related to his or her reading ability	
Step 3: Ask Student to Read Word Lists—determine: • if the reader pronounces and comprehends the words (reads words in list and puts words in sentences) • the first narrative passage level the student is to read	
Step 4: Ask Student to Read Passage and Access Prior Knowledge/Prediction—determine if the reader: • has prior knowledge about the text (reads title and predicts; reads first two sentences and adds to prediction) • accesses the prior knowledge and applies it to make a meaningful prediction • uses prior knowledge/prediction skills throughout the text to impact word recognition and comprehension	
Step 5: Code Oral Reading Miscues—record data about the reader's: • miscues (types and frequency) • word recognition level–independent, instructional, frustration • self-correcting behavior	
Step 6: Check for Fluency—record data about the reader's ability to: • read smoothly, accurately, in meaningful phrases • use of pitch, stress, and intonation to convey meaning • repeat words and phrases using meaning to self-correct • use of punctuation to divide text into units of meaning	
Step 7: Ask for a Retelling and Summary Statement—record the reader's: • comprehension of the text • summary statement • language structure	
Step 8: Ask Comprehension Questions—record data about the reader's: • comprehension • level of thinking, literal and implied–RTR • language structure	
Step 9: Use the Scoring Guide Summary—estimate: • the reading level as independent, instructional, or frustration to determine whether to stop or continue the oral reading	
Step 10: Assess the Student's Silent Reading—determine: • if the reader is more successful as a silent reader than as an oral reader	
Step 11: Determine Listening Level—determine the reader's: • level of comprehension when he or she is listening to the examiner read the text	
Step 12: Assess Reading Level for Expository Text—determine the reader's: • at-grade-level expository reading level–independent, instructional (definite/transitional), or frustration	
Step 13: Summarize Results—analyze, synthesize, and summarize data: • in preparation for reporting data to the reader, the reader's parents, and other educators	

SECTION III

Interviews and Profile Records

Seven Questions About Reading*

Name: _____   Date: _____   Grade: _____

• Why do you read?

• What benefits do you see in reading? How do you think reading helps you?

• What do you do well as a reader?

• Do you read at home? How often? What do you read?

• How does reading make you feel?

• What are some of your favorite books?

• Do you have a favorite author? Why do you enjoy this author's books?

*From *Reading Strategies That Work* by Laura Robb, pages 20, 21, and 22. Scholastic
Professional Books, 1995. Copyright © by Laura Robb. Used by permission.

Reading Interview*

Name: _____   Date: _____   Grade: _____

- **Book Selection Strategies**

Why do you check out a book to read?

How do you know if you can read the book?

- **Before Reading Strategies**

Now that you have a book to read, do you do anything before you start reading?

- **During Reading Strategies**

If you are alone and can't pronounce a word, what do you do?

If you are alone and don't know what a word means, what do you do?

What do you do if you don't understand a paragraph or an entire page?

- **After Reading Strategies**

Now that you've completed the book, what do you do?

- **Examiner's Notes:**

*From *Reading Strategies That Work* by Laura Robb, pages 20, 21, and 22. Scholastic Professional Books, 1995. Copyright © by Laura Robb. Used by permission.

STUDENT PROFILE SUMMARY

Student_____ Grade _____ Sex _____ Age _____ (yrs. + mos.)

School _____ Examiner _____ Date _____

◊ *Indicates Column for Final Score or Level*

Passage Level	◊ **Word Lists**			◊ **Narratiave Reading Level**		◊ **Expository at Grade Level**
FORM ___	% correct	Word Recognition	Comprehension	Listening and/or Silent		**Science, Form S**
Preprimer	- - - - - -					Level ___
Primer						W.R. _____
Level 1						Comp. _____
Level 2						Listening, Passage Level _____
Level 3						Comp. _____
Level 4						**Social Studies, Form SS**
Level 5						Level ___
Level 6						W.R _____
Level 7	- - - - - -					Comp. _____
Level 8	- - - - - -					Listening, Passage Level _____
Level 9	- - - - - -					Comp. _____

OVERVIEW OF READING BEHAVIORS

1. Predictions
☐ Reader most often made a logical prediction from the title.

☐ Reader most often made a logical prediction from the first two sentences.

2. Reader had prior knowledge of
☐ many passages

☐ some passages

☐ few passages

3. Types of Oral Reading Miscues
☐ Omissions ☐ Insertions
☐ Substitutions ☐ Aided words
☐ Repetitions ☐ Reversals

Reader Self-Corrects
☐ a lot ☐ sometimes ☐ seldom

4. Fluency Analysis
1 = labored, disfluent reading/very slow pace
2 = slow and choppy reading/slow pace
3 = fairly fluent/reasonable pace
4 = fluent/good pace

_____ independent
_____ instructional
_____ frustration

5. Cueing Systems: Miscue Analysis
Graphophonic Similarities
☐ Initial ☐ Medial ☐ Final

Syntactic: Most miscues were
☐ acceptable ☐ unacceptable

Semantic: Most miscues caused
☐ change in meaning ☐ no change in meaning

6. Retelling Analysis: The reader most often retold
☐ many details, logical order
☐ some details, some order
☐ few details, disorder

Reader most often summarizes
☐ adequately ☐ not adequately

7. Comprehension Questions Analysis
The examiner
☐ asked few ☐ asked many

Reader's Strength(s)
☐ Retells In Fact (RIF)
☐ Puts Information Together (PIT)
☐ Combines Author and Reader (CAR)
☐ Evaluates and Substantiates (EAS)

Reader Text Relationship (RTR)
Reader responds adequately
☐ From the Text ☐ From Head to Text

8. Emotional Status at Various Reading Levels
Reader was
☐ relaxed/confident
☐ slightly nervous
☐ stressed/little confidence

Independent Level _____

Instructional Level _____

Frustration Level _____

Listening Level _____

ARI CLASS PROFILE SUMMARY

Teacher: _____   Grade: _____

Students' Names	Date 1st assessment / 2nd assessment	Narrative Reading Level			Listening Level		Expository Reading Level (Ind. Inst. Frust.)		List of Alternate Expository Texts
		Ind.	Inst.	Frust.			Science	Social Studies	

ARI PROFILE CARD

Student: _____   Grade: _____   School: _____

Date of administration of *ARI*: _____/_____/_____   Teacher: _____

Instructional Level Passage, Form _____, Level _____   ☐ above grade level   ☐ at grade level   ☐ below grade level

Reader's Profile at Instructional Level	Instructional Interventions Grouping Description

Word Recognition
 Self-Corrections
    Reader self-corrects ☐ a lot ☐ sometimes ☐ seldom
 Miscues / Cueing Systems
    Graphophonic: Reader attends to ☐ initial ☐ medial ☐ final sounds
    Semantic: ☐ many miscues cause a change in meaning
            ☐ few miscues cause a change in meaning	

Comprehension
 Retelling
   ☐ many details / logical order ☐ some details / some order ☐ few details / disorder
   ☐ uses complete sentences   ☐ does not use complete sentences
   ☐ parallels author's language   ☐ does not parallel author's language
 Questions
   From the Text (mostly literal) ☐ adequate ☐ not adequate
   From Head to Text (higher level) ☐ adequate ☐ not adequate	

Fluency
   ☐ 4 = fluent reading / good pace
   ☐ 3 = fairly fluent / reasonable pace
   ☐ 2 = choppy, plodding reading / slow pace
   ☐ 1 = clearly labored, disfluent reading / very slow pace	

Emotional Status ☐ confident ☐ less confident ☐ stressed	

SECTION IV

Examiner's Records

▣ FORM A ▣

Word Lists and Narrative Passages, Preprimer—Nine

FORM A

Form A, Primer

1. not _____
2. funny _____
3. book _____
4. thank _____
5. good _____
6. into _____
7. know _____
8. your _____
9. come _____
10. help _____
11. man _____
12. now _____
13. show _____
14. want _____
15. did _____
16. have _____
17. little _____
18. cake _____
19. home _____
20. soon _____

Sentences:

Comprehends: ☐ a lot ☐ some ☐ none

Form A, Level 1

1. kind _____
2. rocket _____
3. behind _____
4. our _____
5. men _____
6. met _____
7. wish _____
8. told _____
9. after _____
10. ready _____
11. barn _____
12. next _____
13. cat _____
14. hold _____
15. story _____
16. turtle _____
17. give _____
18. cry _____
19. fight _____
20. please _____

Sentences:

Comprehends: ☐ a lot ☐ some ☐ none

Form A, Level 2

1. mile _____
2. fair _____
3. ago _____
4. need _____
5. fourth _____
6. lazy _____
7. field _____
8. taken _____
9. everything _____
10. part _____
11. save _____
12. hide _____
13. instead _____
14. bad _____
15. love _____
16. breakfast _____
17. reach _____
18. song _____
19. cupcake _____
20. trunk _____

Sentences:

Comprehends: ☐ a lot ☐ some ☐ none

Form A, Level 3

1. beginning _____
2. thankful _____
3. written _____
4. reason _____
5. bent _____
6. patient _____
7. manage _____
8. arithmetic _____
9. burst _____
10. bush _____
11. gingerbread _____
12. tremble _____
13. planet _____
14. struggle _____
15. museum _____
16. grin _____
17. ill _____
18. alarm _____
19. cool _____
20. engine _____

Sentences:

Comprehends: ☐ a lot ☐ some ☐ none

FORM A

Form A, Level 6

1. seventeen _____
2. annoy _____
3. dwindle _____
4. rival _____
5. hesitation _____
6. navigator _____
7. gorge _____
8. burglar _____
9. construction _____
10. exploration _____
11. technical _____
12. spice _____
13. spike _____
14. prevail _____
15. memorial _____
16. initiation _____
17. undergrowth _____
18. ladle _____
19. walnut _____
20. tributary _____

Sentences: _____

Comprehends: ☐ a lot ☐ some ☐ none

Form A, Level 5

1. abandon _____
2. zigzag _____
3. terrific _____
4. terrify _____
5. plantation _____
6. loaf _____
7. hike _____
8. relative _____
9. available _____
10. grief _____
11. physical _____
12. commander _____
13. error _____
14. woodcutter _____
15. submarine _____
16. ignore _____
17. disappointed _____
18. wrestle _____
19. vehicle _____
20. international _____

Sentences: _____

Comprehends: ☐ a lot ☐ some ☐ none

Form A, Level 4

1. worm _____
2. afford _____
3. player _____
4. scientific _____
5. meek _____
6. rodeo _____
7. festival _____
8. hillside _____
9. coward _____
10. boom _____
11. booth _____
12. freeze _____
13. protest _____
14. nervous _____
15. sparrow _____
16. level _____
17. underground _____
18. oxen _____
19. eighty _____
20. shouldn't _____

Sentences: _____

Comprehends: ☐ a lot ☐ some ☐ none

Cueing Systems

Miscue	Grapho-phonically Similar I M F (word level)	Syntactically Acceptable Unacceptable (sentence level)	Semantic Change in Meaning (CM) No Change in Meaning (NCM) (sentence level)
L I N E #			

Summary

□ Most, □ few, □ no   miscues were graphophonically similar to the word in the passage.

□ Most, □ few, □ no   miscues were syntactically matched.

□ Most, □ few, □ no   miscues maintained the author's meaning.

□ The self-corrections demonstrate that the reader monitors the meaning.

FORM A, LEVEL PREPRIMER   Reader's Passages page 4

Prior Knowledge/Prediction
□ Read the title and predict what the story is about.

□ Read the first two sentences and add more to your prediction.

Prior Knowledge
□ a lot
□ some
□ none

The Lost Candy

		O	I	S	A	Rp	Rv
1	"I lost my candy," said the boy.						
2	"Help me find it."						
3	"I see it," said Mom. "I see it in						
4	your hair! I will pull it out! Don't						
5	cry!"						
	TOTALS						

Number of miscues _____

Number of self-corrections _____

Form A, Level Preprimer

Scoring Guide Summary

WORD RECOGNITION
Independent 0
Instructional 1-2
Frustration .... 3+

COMPREHENSION
Independent 0
Instructional 1-2
Frustration .... 3+

Emotional Status:

Retelling

Note: Indicate any probing with a "P"

Story Elements	All	Some	None
Main Character(s)			
Time and Place			
Problem			
Plot Details in Sequence			
Turning Point			
Resolution			
Reader's Thumbnail Summary:			

Fluency: Does the Reader . . .

☐ read smoothly, accurately, in meaningful phrases?

☐ read word-by-word, choppy, plodding?

☐ use pitch, stress, and intonation to convey meaning of the text?

☐ repeat words and phrases because s/he is monitoring the meaning (self-correcting)?

☐ repeat words and phrases because s/he is trying to sound out words?

☐ use punctuation to divide the text into units of meaning?

☐ ignore the punctuation?

Rating Scale: Circle One
4 = fluent reading / good pace
3 = fairly fluent / reasonable pace
2 = choppy, plodding reading / slow pace
1 = clearly labored, disfluent reading / very slow pace

Retelling Summary: ☐ many details, logical order ☐ some details, some order ☐ few details, disorder

Comprehension Questions and Possible Answers

___ (RIF) 1. Who are the main characters in this story? (a boy and his mom)

___ (CAR) 2. What do you know about the word *lost?* (something can't be found; it's misplaced) What does the word *lost* have to do with the story? (the boy lost his candy)

___ (CAR) 3. What do you know about the word *help?* (to do something for someone who can't do it by himself) What does the word *help* have to do with this story? (the boy asked his mom to help him find his candy)

___ (RIF) 4. Where is the candy? (in the boy's hair)

___ (CAR) 5. What do you know about the phrase *pull it out?* (when something is stuck you have to yank it out) What does the phrase *pull it out* have to do with this story? (the boy's mom is going to pull the candy out of his hair)

___ (EAS) 6. Do you think the boy will cry? You think this because the story said ... (no, mom will be gentle when she pulls it out; yes, it always hurts when candy is stuck in your hair)

Reader Text Relationship (RTR)   From the Text ☐ adequate ☐ not adequate   From Head to Text ☐ adequate ☐ not adequate

Cueing Systems

Miscue	Grapho-phonically Similar I M F (word level)	Syntactically Acceptable Unacceptable (sentence level)	Semantic Change in Meaning (CM) No Change in Meaning (NCM) (sentence level)
L I N E #			

Summary

☐ Most, ☐ few, ☐ no   miscues were graphophonically similar to the word in the passage.

☐ Most, ☐ few, ☐ no   miscues were syntactically matched.

☐ Most, ☐ few, ☐ no   miscues maintained the author's meaning.

☐ The self-corrections demonstrate that the reader monitors the meaning.

FORM A, PRIMER   Reader's Passages page 5

Prior Knowledge/Prediction

☐ Read the title and predict what the story is about.

Prior Knowledge
- ☐ a lot
- ☐ some
- ☐ none

☐ Read the first two sentences and add more to your prediction.

Pat Hides Out

		O	I	S	A	Rp	Rv
1	Pat sat by the tree. "Pat," his mom						
2	called. "I want you to help me," she said.						
3	"I do not want to help her," Pat said to						
4	himself. "I do not want to work. I will hide from						
5	her. I will hide by this big tree! My mom will not						
6	find me."						

Number of miscues _____   TOTALS

Number of self-corrections _____

Scoring Guide Summary

WORD RECOGNITION
Independent.....0-1
Instructional.....2-3
Frustration.....5+

COMPREHENSION
Independent.....0
Instructional.....1-2
Frustration.....3+

Emotional Status:

Retelling

Note: Indicate any probing with a "P"

Story Elements	All	Some	None
Main Character(s)			
Time and Place			
Problem			
Plot Details in Sequence			
Turning Point			
Resolution			

Reader's Thumbnail Summary:

Fluency: Does the Reader . . .

□ read smoothly, accurately, in meaningful phrases?

□ read word-by-word, choppy, plodding?

□ use pitch, stress, and intonation to convey meaning of the text?

□ repeat words and phrases because s/he is monitoring the meaning (self-correcting)?

□ repeat words and phrases because s/he is trying to sound out words?

□ use punctuation to divide the text into units of meaning?

□ ignore the punctuation?

Rating Scale: Circle One
4 = fluent reading / good pace
3 = fairly fluent / reasonable pace
2 = choppy, plodding reading / slow pace
1 = clearly labored, disfluent reading / very slow pace

Retelling Summary: □ many details, logical order □ some details, some order □ few details, disorder

Comprehension Questions and Possible Answers

_____ (RIF) 1. Who are the two characters in this story? (Pat and his mom)

_____ (RIF) 2. Where is Pat sitting? (by the big tree)

_____ (PIT) 3. What is Pat's problem? (Mom wants Pat to work, but Pat doesn't want to help her work)

_____ (CAR) 4. What do you know about the word *work?* (work is a chore like doing dishes) What does the word *work* have to do with this story? (Mom wanted Pat to do some work, probably chores)

_____ (PIT) 5. What did Pat decide to do about the problem? (decided to hide, will hide by the big tree)

_____ (EAS) 6. Do you think mom will find Pat? You think this because . . . (yes, she might know where Pat always hides) (no, she might not see Pat because the tree is too big)

Reader Text Relationship (RTR)   From the Text □ adequate □ not adequate   From Head to Text □ adequate □ not adequate

FORM A

Cueing Systems

LINE #	Miscue	Grapho-phonically Similar I M F (word level)	Syntactically Acceptable Unacceptable (sentence level)	Semantic Change in Meaning (CM) No Change in Meaning (NCM) (sentence level)

Summary

☐ Most, ☐ few, ☐ no miscues were graphophonically similar to the word in the passage.

☐ Most, ☐ few, ☐ no miscues were syntactically matched.

☐ Most, ☐ few, ☐ no miscues maintained the author's meaning.

☐ The self-corrections demonstrate that the reader monitors the meaning.

FORM A, LEVEL 1   Reader's Passages page 6

Prior Knowledge/Prediction

☐ Read the title and predict what the story is about.

Prior Knowledge
☐ a lot
☐ some
☐ none

☐ Read the first two sentences and add more to your prediction.

The Crowded Car

		O	I	S	A	Rp	Rv
1	Terry got into a little car. He had something						
2	for Show and Tell in a big paper bag. Next, Bill got						
3	into the car with his big paper bag.						
4	Then Ann got into the car. She had something						
5	for Show and Tell in a big paper bag, too. Last, Sue						
6	got into the car with her big paper bag. Now, the little						
7	car was ready to go to school. "This little car is getting						
8	fat!" said Terry. The children laughed.						

TOTALS

Number of miscues _____   Number of self-corrections _____

Fluency: Does the Reader . . .

- [ ] read smoothly, accurately, in meaningful phrases?
- [ ] read word-by-word, choppy, plodding?
- [ ] use pitch, stress, and intonation to convey meaning of the text?
- [ ] repeat words and phrases because s/he is monitoring the meaning (self-correcting)?
- [ ] repeat words and phrases because s/he is trying to sound out words?
- [ ] use punctuation to divide the text into units of meaning?
- [ ] ignore the punctuation?

Rating Scale: Circle One

4 = fluent reading / good pace
3 = fairly fluent / reasonable pace
2 = choppy, plodding reading / slow pace
1 = clearly labored, disfluent reading / very slow pace

Retelling

Note: Indicate any probing with a "P"

Story Elements	All	Some	None
Main Character(s)			
Time and Place			
Problem			
Plot Details in Sequence			
Turning Point			
Resolution			
Reader's Thumbnail Summary:			

Retelling Summary: ☐ many details, logical order ☐ some details, some order ☐ few details, disorder

Comprehension Questions and Possible Answers

_____ (RIF) 1. Who is the main character in this story? (Terry)

_____ (RIF) 2. What does each child have? (a big paper bag with something for Show and Tell)

_____ (CAR) 3. What do you know about the phrase **Show and Tell?** (kids take something to school to show and talk about)
What does the phrase **Show and Tell** have to do with this story? (the kids had things for Show and Tell in paper bags)

_____ (PIT) 4. What is the problem in this story? (the little car is crowded; the kids have big paper bags)

_____ (PIT) 5. Why did the children laugh? (Terry made a joke; he said, "The little car is getting fat")

_____ (EAS) 6. Do you think Terry's joke was funny? You think this because . . .
(yes, a car can't really get fat, that's funny) (no, it's silly talking about a car getting fat)

Reader Text Relationship (RTR)   From the Text ☐ adequate ☐ not adequate   From Head to Text ☐ adequate ☐ not adequate

Scoring Guide Summary

WORD RECOGNITION
Independent 0-1
Instructional 3-4
Frustration ..... 8+

COMPREHENSION
Independent 0
Instructional 1-2
Frustration ..... 3+

Emotional Status:

FORM A

Cueing Systems

Miscue	Grapho-phonically Similar I M F (word level)	Syntactically Acceptable Unacceptable (sentence level)	Semantic Change in Meaning (CM) No Change in Meaning (NCM) (sentence level)
L I N E #			

The cueing system grid is continued on the next page.

Prior Knowledge/Prediction

☐ Read the title and predict what the story is about.

Prior Knowledge
☐ a lot
☐ some
☐ none

☐ Read the first two sentences and add more to your prediction.

		O	I	S	A	Rp	Rv
	The Baseball Star						
1	Whiz! The baseball went right by me, and I struck at the						
2	air! "Strike one," called the man. I could feel my legs begin						
3	to shake!						
4	Whiz! The ball went by me again, and I began to feel bad.						
5	"Strike two," screamed the man.						
6	I held the bat back because this time I would smack the ball!						
7	I would hit it right out of the park! I was so scared that I bit						
8	down on my lip. My knees shook and my hands grew wet.						
9	Swish! The ball came right over the plate. Crack! I hit it a						

The text is continued on the next page.

Cueing Systems

		Grapho-phonically Similar I M F (word level)	Syntactically Acceptable Unacceptable (sentence level)	Semantic Change in Meaning (CM) No Change in Meaning (NCM) (sentence level)
Miscue	L I N E #			

Summary

☐ Most, ☐ few, ☐ no   miscues were graphophonically similar to the word in the passage.

☐ Most, ☐ few, ☐ no   miscues were syntactically matched.

☐ Most, ☐ few, ☐ no   miscues maintained the author's meaning.

☐ The self-corrections demonstrate that the reader monitors the meaning.

	O	I	S	A	Rp	Rv
1 0	good one! Then I ran like the wind. Everyone was yelling for me						
1 1	because I was now a baseball star.						

TOTALS

Number of miscues _____ Number of self-corrections _____

Fluency: Does the Reader . . . .

☐ read smoothly, accurately, in meaningful phrases?

☐ read word-by-word, choppy, plodding?

☐ use pitch, stress, and intonation to convey meaning of the text?

☐ repeat words and phrases because s/he is monitoring the meaning (self-correcting)?

☐ repeat words and phrases because s/he is trying to sound out words?

☐ use punctuation to divide the text into units of meaning?   ☐ ignore the punctuation?

Rating Scale: Circle One

4 = fluent reading / good pace   2 = choppy, plodding reading / slow pace

3 = fairly fluent / reasonable pace   1 = clearly labored, disfluent reading / very slow pace

Note: Indicate any probing with a "P"

Story Elements	All	Some	None
Main Character(s)			
Time and Place			
Problem			
Plot Details in Sequence			
Turning Point			
Resolution			

Reader's Thumbnail Summary:

Scoring Guide Summary

WORD RECOGNITION
Independent......... 1
Instructional....... 5-6
Frustration......... 11-12+

COMPREHENSION
Independent......... 0
Instructional....... 1-2
Frustration......... 3+

Emotional Status:

Form A, Level 2

Retelling

Retelling Summary: ☐ many details, logical order ☐ some details, some order ☐ few details, disorder

Comprehension Questions and Possible Answers

____ (RIF) 1. Who is the main character in this story? (the batter)

____ (PIT) 2. After strike one, how do you think the batter felt? (nervous) You think this because . . . (it said his legs began to shake)

____ (RIF) 3. After strike two, what did the batter plan to do? (planned to smack the ball)

____ (CAR) 4. What did it mean when the batter said, "I'll smack the ball"? (hit the ball real hard; try to get a home run)

____ (PIT) 5. Why was the last pitch good? (because it went right over the plate)

____ (EAS) 6. Do you think it was good or bad to hit the ball right out of the park? You think this because . . . (good . . . it's a home run because it will go so far the other team can't get it and the batter can run around the bases and no one can tag him; or bad because it is a run, but if you only have one ball, then it's gone)

____ (EAS) 7. How do you think the batter felt after hitting the ball? (felt good, confident) You think this because . . . (the story said everyone yelled because he/she was a baseball star)

Reader Text Relationship (RTR)   From the Text   ☐ adequate ☐ not adequate   From Head to Text   ☐ adequate ☐ not adequate

Cueing Systems

Miscue	Grapho-phonically Similar I M F (word level)	Syntactically Acceptable Unacceptable (sentence level)	Semantic Change in Meaning (CM) No Change in Meaning (NCM) (sentence level)
LINE #			

The cueing system grid is continued on the next page.

FORM A, LEVEL 3   Reader's Passages page 8

Prior Knowledge/Prediction

☐ Read the title and predict what the story is about.

Prior Knowledge

☐ a lot
☐ some
☐ none

☐ Read the first two sentences and add more to your prediction.

Exploring a Cave

		O	I	S	A	Rp	Rv
1	The sunlight shined into the mouth of the cave so Mark						
2	could see easily at first, but the farther he walked, the darker it						
3	grew. His dog, Boxer, ran off to explore on his own.						
4	Soon it grew so dark that Mark could see nothing, but he						
5	could hear water dripping off the cave walls. He touched a wall						
6	with his hand to find it cold and damp. Mark began to grow fearful,						
7	so he lit his candle and held it high to look around.						
8	Suddenly, the flame went out. He tried to relight the						
9	candle, but the first match went out! Finally, Mark's shaking hand						

The text is continued on the next page.

Cueing Systems

L I N E #	Miscue	Grapho- phonically Similar I M F (word level)	Syntactically Acceptable Unacceptable (sentence level)	Semantic Change in Meaning (CM) No Change in Meaning (NCM) (sentence level)

Summary

- Most, □ few, □ no   miscues were graphophonically similar to the word in the passage.
- Most, □ few, □ no   miscues were syntactically matched.
- Most, □ few, □ no   miscues maintained the author's meaning.
- The self-corrections demonstrate that the reader monitors the meaning.

Form A, Level 3

	O	I	S	A	Rp	Rv
10	held the lighted candle high. He heard a low growl near him and					
11	saw a pair of fierce, green eyes glowing in the dark! "Boxer!" he					
12	shouted. "Now I recognize those green eyes of yours! Let's get out					
13	of here!"					

TOTALS

Number of miscues _____   Number of self-corrections _____

Fluency: Does the Reader . . .

□ read smoothly, accurately, in meaningful phrases?

□ read word-by-word, choppy, plodding?

□ use pitch, stress, and intonation to convey meaning of the text?

□ repeat words and phrases because s/he is monitoring the meaning (self-correcting)?

□ repeat words and phrases because s/he is trying to sound out words?

□ use punctuation to divide the text into units of meaning?   □ ignore the punctuation?

Rating Scale: Circle One

4 = fluent reading / good pace   2 = choppy, plodding reading / slow pace

3 = fairly fluent / reasonable pace   1 = clearly labored, disfluent reading / very slow pace

Retelling

Note: Indicate any probing with a "P"

Story Elements	All	Some	None
Main Character(s)			
Time and Place			
Problem			
Plot Details in Sequence			
Turning Point			
Resolution			
Reader's Thumbnail Summary:			

Retelling Summary: ☐ many details, logical order ☐ some details, some order ☐ few details, disorder

Comprehension Questions and Possible Answers

_____ (RIF) 1. Who are the two main characters in this story?   (a boy named Mark and his dog, Boxer)

_____ (PIT) 2. What is the problem in this story?   (Mark and Boxer walked into a cave that is getting darker and darker)

_____ (RIF) 3. When they first went into the cave, what did Boxer do?   (ran off to explore on his own)

_____ (PIT) 4. Why did Mark light the candle the first time?   (it was dark; he couldn't see; he grew fearful)

_____ (RIF) 5. What did Mark do when the candle went out?   (Mark tried to relight it, but the first match went out)

_____ (EAS) 6. How do you think Mark felt when the candle went out?   (he got scared)
You think this because . . .   (the story said his hand was shaking)

_____ (CAR) 7. Explain what you know about the word *recognize*.   (you know something, maybe you've seen it before)
What does the word *recognize* have to do with this story?   (it said Mark recognized Boxer)

_____ (EAS) 8. Do you think Mark was smart to go into a cave alone?   (no, you'd get scared and fall, get hurt, and no one could find you)   You think this because . . . (Mark got scared; his candle went out)

Reader Text Relationship (RTR)   From the Text ☐ adequate ☐ not adequate   From Head to Text ☐ adequate ☐ not adequate

Scoring Guide Summary

WORD RECOGNITION
Independent 1-2
Instructional 7-8
Frustration ....15+

COMPREHENSION
Independent........0
Instructional........2
Frustration..........4+

Emotional Status:

Form A, Level 3

Cueing Systems

L I N E #	Miscue	Grapho-phonically Similar I M F (word level)	Syntactically Acceptable Unacceptable (sentence level)	Semantic Change in Meaning (CM) No Change in Meaning (NCM) (sentence level)

The cueing system grid is continued on the next page.

FORM A, LEVEL 4	Reader's Passages page 9

Prior Knowledge/Prediction

☐ Read the title and predict what the story is about.

Prior Knowledge
☐ a lot
☐ some
☐ none

☐ Read the first two sentences and add more to your prediction.

	O	I	S	A	Rp	Rv

Crossing the River*

1   The two dogs and the cat were growing tired from their long journey.

2   Now they had to cross a river. It was wide and deep, so they would have to

3   swim across.

4   The younger dog plunged into the icy water, barking for the others to

5   follow him. The older dog jumped into the water. He was weak and suffering

6   from pain, but somehow he managed to struggle to the opposite bank.

7   The poor cat was left alone. He was so afraid that he ran up and down

8   the bank wailing with fear. The younger dog swam back and forth trying to

9   help. Finally, the cat jumped in and began swimming near his friend.

The text is continued on the next page.

*This passage is a retelling from the novel *The Incredible Journey* by Sheila Burnford.

Cueing Systems

Miscue	Grapho-phonically Similar I M F (word level)	Syntactically Acceptable Unacceptable (sentence level)	Semantic Change in Meaning (CM) No Change in Meaning (NCM) (sentence level)
L I N E #			

Summary

- ☐ Most, ☐ few, ☐ no miscues were graphophonically similar to the word in the passage.
- ☐ Most, ☐ few, ☐ no miscues were syntactically matched.
- ☐ Most, ☐ few, ☐ no miscues maintained the author's meaning.
- ☐ The self-corrections demonstrate that the reader monitors the meaning.

	O	I	S	A	Rp	Rv
1 0	At that moment something bad happened. A beaver dam from					
1 1	upstream broke. The water rushed downstream, hurling a large log					
1 2	toward the animals. It struck the cat and swept him helplessly away.					

TOTALS

Number of miscues _____   Number of self-corrections _____

Fluency: Does the Reader . . .

- ☐ read smoothly, accurately, in meaningful phrases?
- ☐ read word-by-word, choppy, plodding?
- ☐ use pitch, stress, and intonation to convey meaning of the text?
- ☐ repeat words and phrases because s/he is monitoring the meaning (self-correcting)?
- ☐ repeat words and phrases because s/he is trying to sound out words?
- ☐ use punctuation to divide the text into units of meaning?   ☐ ignore the punctuation?

Rating Scale: Circle One

4 = fluent reading / good pace   2 = choppy, plodding reading / slow pace

3 = fairly fluent / reasonable pace   1 = clearly labored, disfluent reading / very slow pace

Note: Indicate any probing with a "P"

Story Elements	All	Some	None
Main Character(s)			
Time and Place			
Problem			
Plot Details in Sequence			
Turning Point			
Resolution			

Reader's Thumbnail Summary:

Scoring Guide Summary

WORD RECOGNITION
Independent 1-2
Instructional 7-8
Frustration ...... 15+

COMPREHENSION
Independent 0-1
Instructional 2
Frustration ...... 4+

Emotional Status:

Form A, Level 4

Retelling

Retelling Summary: ☐ many details, logical order ☐ some details, some order ☐ few details, disorder

Comprehension Questions and Possible Answers

_____ (RIF) 1. Who are the characters in this story?　　(older dog, younger dog, and a cat)

_____ (PIT) 2. What is the problem in this story?　　(the animals are tired; they have to swim across a wide, deep river)

_____ (CAR) 3. What do you know about the word *suffering?*　　(to experience pain or injury)
What does *suffering* have to do with this story?　　(the older dog was weak and suffering from pain)

_____ (RIF) 4. Why did the younger dog bark at the older dog and the cat?　　(he wanted them to follow him into the water)

_____ (CAR) 5. Explain what you know about the phrase *wailing with fear.*　　(to cry out in fear)
What does *wailing with fear* have to do with this story?　　(it said the cat ran up and down the bank wailing with fear)

_____ (EAS) 6. How do you think the cat felt?　　(afraid, scared, terrified, panicked)
You think this because . . .　　(the story said the poor cat was left alone; he was afraid he couldn't get across)

_____ (PIT) 7. After the cat jumped in, what happened?　　(an old beaver dam broke; a log came hurling downstream and hit the cat)

_____ (RIF) 8. Why did a large log come hurling downstream?　　(the force of the water from the beaver dam hurled the log, made it go fast)

Reader Text Relationship (RTR)　　From the Text ☐ adequate ☐ not adequate　　From Head to Text ☐ adequate ☐ not adequate

Cueing Systems

Miscue	Grapho-phonically Similar I M F (word level)		Syntactically Acceptable Unacceptable (sentence level)		Semantic Change in Meaning (CM) No Change in Meaning (NCM) (sentence level)
L I N E #					

The cueing system grid is continued on the next page.

FORM A, LEVEL 5 Reader's Passages page 10

Prior Knowledge/Prediction

☐ Read the title and predict what the story is about.

☐ Read the first two sentences and add more to your prediction.

Prior Knowledge
☐ a lot
☐ some
☐ none

The Bicycle Race

		O	I	S	A	Rp	Rv
1	"Look out," Sheila Young thought as she saw her challenger's						
2	bicycle come too close. "Watch out or you will foul me!"						
3	At that moment a horrifying thing happened as she was bumped						
4	by another racer at forty miles an hour. Sheila's bicycle crashed, and she						
5	skidded on the surface of the track. From the wreck she received a						
6	nine-inch gash on her head.						
7	The judges ruled that the race should be run again since a foul						
8	had been made. Sheila would not have enough time to get her wound						
9	stitched; still, she didn't want to quit the race because she could only						

The text is continued on the next page.

FORM A

Cueing Systems

LINE #	Miscue	Grapho-phonically Similar I M F (word level)	Syntactically Acceptable Unacceptable (sentence level)	Semantic Change in Meaning (CM) No Change in Meaning (NCM) (sentence level)

Summary

- ☐ Most, ☐ few, ☐ no miscues were graphophonically similar to the word in the passage.
- ☐ Most, ☐ few, ☐ no miscues were syntactically matched.
- ☐ Most, ☐ few, ☐ no miscues maintained the author's meaning.
- ☐ The self-corrections demonstrate that the reader monitors the meaning.

Form A, Level 5

	O	I	S	A	Rp	Rv

10 think of winning. "Just staple the cut together and bandage it," she told

11 the doctor. "I want to win this race!"

12 The doctor did as Sheila asked, and as she stood in silence while

13 being treated, tears rolled down her face from the intense pain. Then,

14 with a blood-stained bandage on her throbbing head, she pushed on to

15 amaze the crowd with a sensational victory and a gold medal!

TOTALS

Number of miscues _____ Number of self-corrections _____

Fluency: Does the Reader . . .

- ☐ read smoothly, accurately, in meaningful phrases?
- ☐ read word-by-word, choppy, plodding?
- ☐ use pitch, stress, and intonation to convey meaning of the text?
- ☐ repeat words and phrases because s/he is monitoring the meaning (self-correcting)?
- ☐ repeat words and phrases because s/he is trying to sound out words?
- ☐ use punctuation to divide the text into units of meaning?   ☐ ignore the punctuation?

Rating Scale: Circle One

4 = fluent reading / good pace   2 = choppy, plodding reading / slow pace
3 = fairly fluent / reasonable pace   1 = clearly labored, disfluent reading / very slow pace

Scoring Guide Summary

WORD RECOGNITION
Independent......1-2
Instructional......8-9
Frustration......17+

COMPREHENSION
Independent......0-1
Instructional......2
Frustration......4+

Emotional Status:

Retelling

Note: Indicate any probing with a "P"

Story Elements	All	Some	None
Main Character(s)			
Time and Place			
Problem			
Plot Details in Sequence			
Turning Point			
Resolution			
Reader's Thumbnail Summary:			

Retelling Summary: □ many details, logical order □ some details, some order □ few details, disorder

Comprehension Questions and Possible Answers

____(RIF) 1. Who is the main character in this story? (Sheila Young)

____(PIT) 2. What is the problem in this story? (she was bumped by another racer)

____(CAR) 3. What do you know about the word **challenger?** (someone who is racing against you; another competitor)
What does **challenger** have to do with this story? (Sheila saw her challenger's bike come too close)

____(PIT) 4. How do you know the crash was dangerous? (it was horrifying; the crash occurred at forty miles per hour)

____(RIF) 5. What injury did Sheila receive in the crash? (a nine-inch gash on her head)

____(RIF) 6. Why didn't Sheila want to quit the race? (she could only think of winning)

____(CAR) 7. What do you know about the phrase **intense pain?** (strong pain, agony)
What does the phrase **intense pain** have to do with this story? (tears rolled down Sheila's face from the intense pain)

____(EAS) 8. In your opinion, how important was this race to Sheila? (extremely important)
You think this because . . . (the story said even though she was badly hurt, she wanted the gold medal so badly that she raced with a blood-stained bandage on her throbbing head)

Reader Text Relationship (RTR)   From the Text □ adequate □ not adequate   From Head to Text □ adequate □ not adequate

Cueing Systems

Miscue	Grapho-phonically Similar I M F (word level)	Syntactically Acceptable Unacceptable (sentence level)	Semantic Change in Meaning (CM) No Change in Meaning (NCM) (sentence level)
L I N E #			

The cueing system grid is continued on the next page.

FORM A, LEVEL 6

Reader's Passages page 11

Prior Knowledge/Prediction
☐ Read the title and predict what the story is about.

Prior Knowledge
☐ a lot
☐ some
☐ none

☐ Read the first two sentences and add more to your prediction.

Remembering a Surgeon

		O	I	S	A	Rp	Rv
1	It was a dreary April afternoon in 1950. Family, friends,						
2	and physicians from Freedmen's Hospital in Washington, D.C.,						
3	gathered in the cemetery to attend the funeral of Dr. Charles Drew.						
4	After the burial two men stood off to the side talking in low, hushed						
5	voices.						
6	"His research on blood transfusions saved the lives of thousands in						
7	war-torn Europe during World War II," one of the men remarked.						
8	"He was an outstanding surgeon," the second man continued to add						
9	to the list of Drew's many accomplishments.						

The text is continued on the next page.

Cueing Systems

Miscue	Grapho-phonically Similar I M F (word level)	Syntactically Acceptable Unacceptable (sentence level)	Semantic Change in Meaning (CM) No Change in Meaning (NCM) (sentence level)
L I N E #			

Summary

☐ Most, ☐ few, ☐ no   miscues were graphophonically similar to the word in the passage.

☐ Most, ☐ few, ☐ no   miscues were syntactically matched.

☐ Most, ☐ few, ☐ no   miscues maintained the author's meaning.

☐ The self-corrections demonstrate that the reader monitors the meaning.

	O	I	S	A	Rp	Rv
1 0 "Why did he attempt to drive the long distance from Washington to						
1 1 Alabama when he could have traveled by train?" the first man asked in a						
1 2 voice that revealed his deep sorrow.						
1 3 "He had planned to take the train, but chose to drive because some						
1 4 fellow surgeons could not afford to take the train. He had been the						
1 5 honored speaker at a meeting the night before they left for the long car trip						
1 6 to Alabama. No one knew that he'd only had a few hours of sleep before						
1 7 starting out at two o'clock in the morning. No one realized that he						
1 8 was so tired."						

TOTALS

Number of miscues _____   Number of self-corrections _____

Fluency: Does the Reader . . .

☐ read smoothly, accurately, in meaningful phrases?

☐ read word-by-word, choppy, plodding?

☐ use pitch, stress, and intonation to convey meaning of the text?

☐ repeat words and phrases because s/he is monitoring the meaning (self-correcting)?

☐ repeat words and phrases because s/he is trying to sound out words?

☐ use punctuation to divide the text into units of meaning?   ☐ ignore the punctuation?

Rating Scale: Circle One

4 = fluent reading / good pace   2 = choppy, plodding reading / slow pace

3 = fairly fluent / reasonable pace   1 = clearly labored, disfluent reading / very slow pace

FORM A

Note: Indicate any probing with a "P"

Story Elements	All	Some	None
Main Character(s)			
Time and Place			
Problem			
Plot Details in Sequence			
Turning Point			
Resolution			
Reader's Thumbnail Summary:			

Retelling

Retelling Summary: □ many details, logical order □ some details, some order □ few details, disorder

Comprehension Questions and Possible Answers

___(PIT) 1. Where does this story take place?   (at the funeral of Dr. Charles Drew)

___(PIT) 2. What is the problem in this story?   (Dr. Drew died in a car accident)

___(CAR) 3. What do you know about the word **burial?**   (after a death, a person is placed underground) What does the word **burial** have to do with the story?   (it takes place at the cemetery where Dr. Drew was buried)

___(RIF) 4. When does this story take place?   (on a dreary afternoon, April 1950)

___(CAR) 5. What do you know about the phrase **blood transfusions?**   (if you need blood, a doctor can give you another person's blood; to transfer blood from a donor to an injured person) What does the phrase **blood transfusions** have to do with this story?   (Dr. Drew had done important research about blood transfusions)

___(PIT) 6. Why didn't Dr. Drew go on the train?   (he had planned to but changed his plans, choosing to drive because some fellow surgeons could not afford to take the train)

___(PIT) 7. Why was Dr. Drew so tired?   (he had been the honored speaker at a meeting the night before they left, and they had left so early in the morning, at two o'clock in the morning)

___(EAS) 8. Who do you think was driving the car? You think this because the text said . . .   (Dr. Drew must have fallen asleep at the wheel because the text said that he had only had a few hours of sleep; he had been a speaker at an event the night before)

Reader Text Relationship (RTR)   From the Text □ adequate □ not adequate   From Head to Text □ adequate □ not adequate

Form A, Level 6

Cueing Systems

Miscue	Grapho-phonically Similar I M F (word level)	Syntactically Acceptable Unacceptable (sentence level)	Semantic Change in Meaning (CM) No Change in Meaning (NCM) (sentence level)
L I N E #			

The cueing system grid is continued on the next page.

FORM A, LEVEL 7 Reader's Passages page 12

Prior Knowledge/Prediction

☐ Read the title and predict what the story is about.

Prior Knowledge
☐ a lot
☐ some
☐ none

☐ Read the first two sentences and add more to your prediction.

Turning Himself In*

	O	I	S	A	Rp	Rv
1	While he had been hiding out for the past five days, Johnny had given serious					
2	thought to the whole mess. He had decided to return home, turn himself in to the					
3	police, and take the consequences of his crime. Being only sixteen, he was too young					
4	to run away for the rest of his life. He knew the fight had been in self-defense, but					
5	the fact still remained that he had killed another person, and the thought of that					
6	miserable night in the city park sent Johnny into a terrified panic.					
7	He told Dally and Ponyboy of his decision, and now Dally reluctantly began the					
8	long drive home. Dally had gone to jail before, and this was one wretched experience					
9	he did not want his friend to have to endure.					
10	As they reached the top of Jay Mountain, Dally slammed on the brakes! The old					

The text is continued on the next page.

*This passage is a retelling from the novel *The Outsiders* by S. E. Hinton.

FORM A

Cueing Systems

LINE #	Miscue	Grapho-phonically Similar I M F (word level)	Syntactically Acceptable Unacceptable (sentence level)	Semantic Change in Meaning (CM) No Change in Meaning (NCM) (sentence level)

Summary

☐ Most, ☐ few, ☐ no   miscues were graphophonically similar to the word in the passage.

☐ Most, ☐ few, ☐ no   miscues were syntactically matched.

☐ Most, ☐ few, ☐ no   miscues maintained the author's meaning.

☐ The self-corrections demonstrate that the reader monitors the meaning.

Form A, Level 7

	O	I	S	A	Rp	Rv
1 1	church where Johnny and Ponyboy had been hiding was in flames! Ponyboy and						
1 2	Johnny bolted from the car to question a bystander, who explained that they were						
1 3	having a school picnic when the church began to burn.						
1 4	Suddenly, the crowd was shocked to hear desperate cries from inside! Ponyboy						
1 5	and Johnny ran into the burning church, and the boys lifted the children one by one						
1 6	through a window to safety. Chunks of the old roof were already beginning to fall as						
1 7	the last child was taken out. Ponyboy leaped through the window, vaguely hearing						
1 8	the sound of falling timber. Then, as he lay coughing and exhausted on the ground,						
1 9	he heard Johnny's terrifying scream!						

TOTALS

Number of miscues _____   Number of self-corrections _____

Fluency: Does the Reader . . .

☐ read smoothly, accurately, in meaningful phrases?

☐ read word-by-word, choppy, plodding?

☐ use pitch, stress, and intonation to convey meaning of the text?

☐ repeat words and phrases because s/he is monitoring the meaning (self-correcting)?

☐ repeat words and phrases because s/he is trying to sound out words?

☐ use punctuation to divide the text into units of meaning?   ☐ ignore the punctuation?

Rating Scale: Circle One

4 = fluent reading / good pace   2 = choppy, plodding reading / slow pace

3 = fairly fluent / reasonable pace   1 = clearly labored, disfluent reading / very slow pace

Retelling

Note: Indicate any probing with a "P"

Story Elements	All	Some	None
Main Character(s)			
Time and Place			
Problem			
Plot Details in Sequence			
Turning Point			
Resolution			
Reader's Thumbnail Summary:			

Retelling Summary: ☐ many details, logical order ☐ some details, some order ☐ few details, disorder

Scoring Guide Summary

WORD RECOGNITION
Independent 2-3
Instructional 13
Frustration ......26+

COMPREHENSION
Independent 0-1
Instructional 2
Frustration ......4+

Emotional Status:

Form A, Level 7

Comprehension Questions and Possible Answers

____ (RIF) 1. Who are the three characters in this story? (Johnny, Dally, and Ponyboy)

____ (RIF) 2. What is Johnny's problem? (he has committed a crime)

____ (PIT) 3. What did Johnny decide to do? (he decided to return home, turn himself in to the police, and take the consequences of his crime)

____ (CAR) 4. What do you know about the phrase *take the consequences of his crime?* (take the punishment or penalty) What does *take the consequences of his crime* have to do with this story? (Johnny was ready to be punished for his crime)

____ (PIT) 5. What was the crime? (a fight in self-defense; he had killed the person)

____ (RIF) 6. As they reached Jay Mountain, why did Dally slam on the brakes? (he saw a burning church)

____ (PIT) 7. What did Ponyboy and Johnny do? (bolted from the car; questioned a bystander; ran into the burning church)

____ (EAS) 8. What do you think happened to Johnny? (he was injured or killed by falling chunks of old roof) You think this because . . . (Ponyboy heard Johnny's terrifying scream)

Reader Text Relationship (RTR)   From the Text   ☐ adequate ☐ not adequate   From Head to Text   ☐ adequate ☐ not adequate

FORM A

Cueing Systems

Miscue	Grapho-phonically Similar I M F (word level)	Syntactically Acceptable Unacceptable (sentence level)	Semantic Change in Meaning (CM) No Change in Meaning (NCM) (sentence level)
L I N E #			

The cueing system grid is continued on the next page.

FORM A, LEVEL 8 — Reader's Passages page 13

Prior Knowledge/Prediction

☐ Read the title and predict what the story is about.

Prior Knowledge
☐ a lot
☐ some
☐ none

☐ Read the first two sentences and add more to your prediction.

Adjusting to a New School

		O	I	S	A	Rp	Rv
1	Painfully shy, Jeffrey Vargus practically had to force himself off the school bus.						
2	"One step forward," he muttered in an attempt to convince himself to take on this						
3	awesome responsibility, "then eleven steps homeward where I can be stress-free						
4	working on my computer!" The problem of being a new student and having to make						
5	new acquaintances weighed heavily on his mind. Why did his parents have to move						
6	to a new town just as he was entering the eighth grade? Obviously reluctant, he						
7	trudged along at a less than enthusiastic pace toward the front door of Comstock						
8	Middle School.						
9	Other students poured around him as if they were hurrying toward the building						
10	like a bunch of kids scampering toward ice cream and cake. "Every single student in						
11	the school knows everybody else, and nobody knows me, not a solitary soul!" Sweat						
12	began to drip from his forehead, causing his thick, dark-rimmed glasses to slide down						
13	his nose. "I'm returning home this instant," his head bellowed out the words, but						
14	not one came from his mouth. Suddenly, without warning, he spun around, thinking						

The text is continued on the next page.

Cueing Systems

	Miscue	Grapho-phonically Similar I M F (word level)	Syntactically Acceptable Unacceptable (sentence level)	Semantic Change in Meaning (CM) No Change in Meaning (NCM) (sentence level)
L I N E #				

Form A, Level 8

Summary

☐ Most, ☐ few, ☐ no miscues were graphophonically similar to the word in the passage.

☐ Most, ☐ few, ☐ no miscues were syntactically matched.

☐ Most, ☐ few, ☐ no miscues maintained the author's meaning.

☐ The self-corrections demonstrate that the reader monitors the meaning.

		O	I	S	A	Rp	Rv
1 5	perhaps he'd escape into thin air. He dropped the book that had been tucked						
1 6	between his arm and chest like a security blanket. It smacked to the sidewalk, and						
1 7	he leaned forward to capture it from trampling feet.						
1 8	"Hey, New Boy, you dropped your book!" a voice resounded so close to his ear						
1 9	that he stumbled backward. *"Computer Programming Tips for Whiz-Kid Teens!"* the						
2 0	voice read the title in a congenial manner. "Wow, are you interested in computer						
2 1	programming? Our school has the most elaborate computer lab in the entire county!						
2 2	Man, computer programming is my life's passion and challenge, so follow me. I'll						
2 3	show you the layout and introduce you to the other kids!"						

TOTALS

Number of miscues _____   Number of self-corrections _____

Fluency: Does the Reader . . . :

☐ read smoothly, accurately, in meaningful phrases?

☐ read word-by-word, choppy, plodding?

☐ use pitch, stress, and intonation to convey meaning of the text?

☐ repeat words and phrases because s/he is monitoring the meaning (self-correcting)?

☐ repeat words and phrases because s/he is trying to sound out words?

☐ use punctuation to divide the text into units of meaning?   ☐ ignore the punctuat on?

Rating Scale: Circle One

4 = fluent reading / good pace   2 = choppy, plodding reading / slow pace

3 = fairly fluent / reasonable pace   1 = clearly labored, disfluent reading / very slow pace

Note: Indicate any probing with a "P"

Story Elements	All	Some	None
Main Character(s)			
Time and Place			
Problem			
Plot Details in Sequence			
Turning Point			
Resolution			
Reader's Thumbnail Summary:			

Scoring Guide Summary

WORD RECOGNITION

Independent 3
Instructional 15
Frustration .... 30+

COMPREHENSION

Independent 0-1
Instructional 2
Frustration .... 4+

Emotional Status:

Retelling

Retelling Summary: ☐ many details, logical order ☐ some details, some order ☐ few details, disorder

Comprehension Questions and Possible Answers

___ (RIF) 1. Who is the main character in this story? (Jeffrey Vargus)

___ (RIF) 2. Where does this story take place? (at Comstock Middle School)

___ (PIT) 3. What is the problem in this story? (the boy is nervous about being a new student in the school; he doesn't know anyone)

___ (PIT) 4. Why is Jeffrey attending a new school? (his parents moved to a new town)

___ (CAR) 5. What do you know about the phrase *obviously reluctant?* (it can easily be seen that you don't want to do something)
What does the phrase *obviously reluctant* have to do with the story? (it said that obviously reluctant, he trudged along . . .)

___ (EAS) 6. What do you think working on his computer meant to Jeffrey? You think this because. . . (it was his identity, his way of gaining confidence) (it said that he wanted to take 11 steps homeward where he could be stress-free working on his computer; he had his computer book tucked between his arm and chest like a security blanket)

___ (CAR) 7. What do you know about the phrase *congenial manner?* (a friendly way of doing something) What does the phrase *congenial manner* have to do with this story? (it said a person's voice read the title of the book in a congenial manner)

___ (RIF) 8. What kind of computer labs did the new school have? (the most elaborate labs in the entire county)

Reader Text Relationship (RTR)   From the Text   ☐ adequate ☐ not adequate   From Head to Text   ☐ adequate ☐ not adequate

Form A, Level 8

Cueing Systems

LINE #	Miscue	Grapho-phonically Similar I M F (word level)	Syntactically Acceptable Unacceptable (sentence level)	Semantic Change in Meaning (CM) No Change in Meaning (NCM) (sentence level)

The cueing system grid is continued on the next page.

FORM A, LEVEL 9   Reader's Passages page 14

Prior Knowledge/Prediction

☐ Read the title and predict what the story is about.

Prior Knowledge
☐ a lot
☐ some
☐ none

☐ Read the first two sentences and add more to your prediction.

The Crystal Clear Lake

		O	I	S	A	Rp	Rv
1	"This magnificent lake contains treated sewer water!" the old gentleman						
2	murmured to himself as he sat on the park bench as close to the shore as possible.						
3	Leaning forward, his elbows resting on his knees, he looked out over the glistening						
4	water. The breeze across the lake caused the sailboats to glide about effortlessly, and in						
5	the distance he could see children entertaining themselves on the beach.						
6	"We are making great environmental strides," he said quietly. He knew the						
7	history of this remarkable lake nestled in the foothills of southern California. He swelled						
8	with pride to recall the wise choice the Santee citizens had made when they voted not						
9	to support a disposal system that discharged waste directly into the Pacific Ocean.						
10	Rather, the citizens agreed to construct their own sewage facility, one that reclaimed						
11	the sewer water, spared the environment, and created community recreational						
12	opportunities.						
13	"What an ingenious and environmentally conscious plan it was to build a city						
14	park just yards downstream from a sewer plant," the gentleman thought. He leaned						

The text is continued on the next page.

Cueing Systems

L I N E #	Miscue	Grapho-phonically Similar I M F (word level)	Syntactically Acceptable Unacceptable (sentence level)	Semantic Change in Meaning (CM) No Change in Meaning (NCM) (sentence level)

Summary

□ Most, □ few, □ no   miscues were graphophonically similar to the word in the passage.

□ Most, □ few, □ no   miscues were syntactically matched.

□ Most, □ few, □ no   miscues maintained the author's meaning.

□ The self-corrections demonstrate that the reader monitors the meaning.

Form A, Level 9

	O	I	S	A	Rp	Rv
15	forward and scooped up a handful of water. "This lake is more sanitary than many					
16	natural lakes! Inventive foresight and resourcefulness, that's what it took to make this					
17	unprecedented plan possible! Not only do the sewage waste solids furnish marketable					
18	soil conditioners and plant fertilizers, but the pure water provides lucrative recreational					
19	facilities!"					
20	As the old gentleman got up, he saw dirty wrappers and other paper carelessly					
21	strewn over the walkways. "We demand it, use it, and thoughtlessly throw it away!" he					
22	muttered, and his contented expression changed to one of concern. His thoughts raced					
23	on as he bent forward to pick up the mess. "With such needless waste, how long can					
24	the world's resources continue to supply our reckless use? The United States comprises					
25	such a small percent of the world's population, yet we are the world's largest consumer					
26	of raw materials." He thought about this widespread behavior of consumption and					
27	waste, and as he discarded the paper into a nearby trash container, he wondered if					
28	things would ever change.					

TOTALS

Number of miscues _____   Number of self-corrections _____

Fluency: Does the Reader . . .

□ read smoothly, accurately, in meaningful phrases?

□ read word-by-word, choppy, plodding?

□ use pitch, stress, and intonation to convey meaning of the text?

□ repeat words and phrases because s/he is monitoring the meaning (self-correcting)?

□ repeat words and phrases because s/he is trying to sound out words?

□ use punctuation to divide the text into units of meaning?   □ ignore the punctuation?

Rating Scale: Circle One

4 = fluent reading / good pace   2 = choppy, plodding reading / slow pace

3 = fairly fluent / reasonable pace   1 = clearly labored, disfluent reading / very slow pace

Form A, Level 9

Retelling

Note: Indicate any probing with a "P"

Story Elements	All	Some	None
Main Character(s)			
Time and Place			
Problem			
Plot Details in Sequence			
Turning Point			
Resolution			
Reader's Thumbnail Summary:			

Retelling Summary: ☐ many details, logical order ☐ some details, some order ☐ few details, disorder

Scoring Guide Summary

WORD RECOGNITION

Independent 3-4
Instructional 17
Frustration .... 34+

COMPREHENSION

Independent 0-1
Instructional 2
Frustration .... 4+

Emotional Status:

Comprehension Questions and Possible Answers

____ (RIF) 1. Where does this story take place? (Santee, in the foothills of southern California)

____ (PIT) 2. What did the citizens of Santee vote to do? (they voted not to support a disposal system that discharged waste directly into the Pacific Ocean)

____ (EAS) 3. In your opinion, should they have voted to do this? You think this because . . . (yes, they did not pollute the Pacific; they gained recreational opportunities) (no, if they constructed their own the cost might be difficult to pay)

____ (PIT) 4. How did the old gentleman feel about the plan? (he swelled with pride; he called it remarkable, ingenious)

____ (PIT) 5. Why was the Santee plan so significant? (it was ingenious and environmentally conscious)

____ (CAR) 6. What do you know about the phrase **unprecedented plan?** (one that had never been done before)
What does the phrase **unprecedented plan** have to do with this story? (it said the Santee citizens were inventive and resourceful to make this unprecedented plan possible)

____ (CAR) 7. What do you know about the phrase **lucrative recreational facilities?** (that leisure time activities such as sailing will make money) What does the phrase **lucrative recreational facilities** have to do with this story? (the clean water provided lucrative recreational facilities)

____ (PIT) 8. What is so significant about the fact that the United States is the world's largest consumer of raw materials? (the United States comprises a small percent of the world's population, yet it is the world's largest consumer)

Reader Text Relationship (RTR)   From the Text ☐ adequate ☐ not adequate   From Head to Text ☐ adequate ☐ not adequate

◪ FORM B ◪

Word Lists and Narrative Passages, Preprimer—Nine

FORM B

Form B, Primer

1. birthday _____
2. went _____
3. fish _____
4. like _____
5. something _____
6. blue _____
7. that _____
8. they _____
9. train _____
10. what _____
11. mother _____
12. ride _____
13. house _____
14. new _____
15. here _____
16. paint _____
17. work _____
18. stop _____
19. away _____
20. around _____

Sentences:

Comprehends: ☐ a lot ☐ some ☐ none

Form B, Level 1

1. town _____
2. bear _____
3. sound _____
4. party _____
5. there _____
6. these _____
7. don't _____
8. brown _____
9. shoe _____
10. light _____
11. hair _____
12. water _____
13. own _____
14. race _____
15. why _____
16. hear _____
17. fly _____
18. grass _____
19. morning _____
20. animal _____

Sentences:

Comprehends: ☐ a lot ☐ some ☐ none

Form B, Level 2

1. yet _____
2. minute _____
3. act _____
4. bunny _____
5. empty _____
6. inside _____
7. squirrel _____
8. thumb _____
9. grandmother _____
10. dragon _____
11. elephant _____
12. I'd _____
13. threw _____
14. beautiful _____
15. roof _____
16. through _____
17. leave _____
18. unhappy _____
19. garden _____
20. branch _____

Sentences:

Comprehends: ☐ a lot ☐ some ☐ none

Form B, Level 3

1. broom _____
2. hammer _____
3. log _____
4. step _____
5. question _____
6. wrinkle _____
7. invisible _____
8. vegetable _____
9. engineer _____
10. allow _____
11. knee _____
12. excitement _____
13. storm _____
14. repair _____
15. sweep _____
16. swept _____
17. million _____
18. buzz _____
19. doorbell _____
20. you've _____

Sentences:

Comprehends: ☐ a lot ☐ some ☐ none

Form B, Level 4

1. zebra
2. liberty
3. mend
4. dolphin
5. ability
6. compound
7. gentlemen
8. holly
9. swamp
10. swarm
11. chill
12. wreck
13. solid
14. alphabet
15. holiday
16. equal
17. dull
18. shiver
19. they're
20. nonsense

Sentences:

Comprehends: ☐ a lot ☐ some ☐ none

Form B, Level 5

1. splendor
2. mason
3. radiant
4. cease
5. fisherman
6. brief
7. distress
8. fake
9. false
10. gust
11. proceed
12. triumph
13. scuffle
14. operation
15. military
16. hull
17. genius
18. contribution
19. reverse
20. indicate

Sentences:

Comprehends: ☐ a lot ☐ some ☐ none

Form B, Level 6

1. counterclockwise
2. diesel
3. mathematical
4. representative
5. accomplishment
6. extraordinary
7. congratulation
8. daily
9. odor
10. resemble
11. acquire
12. combine
13. opportunity
14. transparent
15. transport
16. cheap
17. fifteenth
18. phase
19. violet
20. woolen

Sentences:

Comprehends: ☐ a lot ☐ some ☐ none

FORM B

FORM B

Cueing Systems

L I N E #	Miscue	Grapho- phonically Similar I M F (word level)	Syntactically Acceptable Unacceptable (sentence level)	Semantic Change in Meaning (CM) No Change in Meaning (NCM) (sentence level)

Summary

- ☐ Most, ☐ few, ☐ no miscues were graphophonically similar to the word in the passage.
- ☐ Most, ☐ few, ☐ no miscues were syntactically matched.
- ☐ Most, ☐ few, ☐ no miscues maintained the author's meaning.
- ☐ The self-corrections demonstrate that the reader monitors the meaning.

FORM B, PREPRIMER   Reader's Passages page 18

Prior Knowledge/Prediction

☐ Read the title and predict what the story is about.

Prior Knowledge
- ☐ a lot
- ☐ some
- ☐ none

☐ Read the first two sentences and add more to your prediction.

Winning the Game

		O	I	S	A	Rp	Rv
1	"Catch the ball!" said the girl.						
2	The boy looked at the ball. It						
3	came right to him. He did catch it.						
4	"You win the game!" she said.						
	TOTALS						

Number of miscues _____   Number of self-corrections _____

FORM B

Scoring Guide Summary

WORD RECOGNITION
Independent 0
Instructional 1-2
Frustration .... 3+

COMPREHENSION
Independent 0
Instructional 1-2
Frustration .... 3+

Emotional Status:

Retelling

Note: Indicate any probing with a "P"

Story Elements	All	Some	None
Main Character(s)			
Time and Place			
Problem			
Plot Details in Sequence			
Turning Point			
Resolution			
Reader's Thumbnail Summary:			

Fluency: Does the Reader . . .

☐ read smoothly, accurately, in meaningful phrases?

☐ read word-by-word, choppy, plodding?

☐ use pitch, stress, and intonation to convey meaning of the text?

☐ repeat words and phrases because s/he is monitoring the meaning (self-correcting)?

☐ repeat words and phrases because s/he is trying to sound out words?

☐ use punctuation to divide the text into units of meaning?

☐ ignore the punctuation?

Rating Scale: Circle One

4 = fluent reading / good pace

3 = fairly fluent / reasonable pace

2 = choppy, plodding reading / slow pace

1 = clearly labored, disfluent reading / very slow pace

Retelling Summary: ☐ many details, logical order ☐ some details, some order ☐ few details, disorder

---

Comprehension Questions and Possible Answers

_____ (RIF) 1. Who is the main character in this story? (a girl)

_____ (EAS) 2. Where do you think the story takes place? You think this because the story said . . .
(inside because you can throw a ball inside; outside because you shouldn't throw a ball inside)

_____ (CAR) 3. What do you know about the word *catch?* (when something is thrown you get it with your hands) What does the word *catch* have to do with this story? (the girl said to catch the ball)

_____ (CAR) 4. What do you know about the word *right?* (in the very spot on the target) What does the word *right* have to do with this story? (the ball came right to the boy)

_____ (PIT) 5. What did the boy do? (he catches the ball and wins the game)

_____ (CAR) 6. What do you know about the phrase *win the game?* (you get the top score; you get there first) What does the phrase *win the game* have to do with this story? (the boy wins the game)

Reader Text Relationship (RTR)   From the Text ☐ adequate ☐ not adequate   From Head to Text ☐ adequate ☐ not adequate

---

Cueing Systems

L I N E #	Miscue	Grapho- phonically Similar I M F (word level)	Syntactically Acceptable Unacceptable (sentence level)	Semantic Change in Meaning (CM) No Change in Meaning (NCM) (sentence level)

Summary

☐ Most, ☐ few, ☐ no   miscues were graphophonically similar to the word in the passage.

☐ Most, ☐ few, ☐ no   miscues were syntactically matched.

☐ Most, ☐ few, ☐ no   miscues maintained the author's meaning.

☐ The self-corrections demonstrate that the reader monitors the meaning.

FORM B, PRIMER   Reader's Passages page 19

Prior Knowledge/Prediction

☐ Read the title and predict what the story is about.

Prior Knowledge
☐ a lot
☐ some
☐ none

☐ Read the first two sentences and add more to your prediction.

Growing Up

		O	I	S	A	Rp	Rv
1	"When I grow up," said Sally, "I will be big!						
2	My legs and arms will grow. My head will grow.						
3	My face will grow. My nose will grow, too.						
4	What if my nose does not grow? Then my nose						
5	would be a little baby nose on my big face! I would						
6	look funny!"						

TOTALS

Number of miscues _____   Number of self-corrections _____

FORM B

Fluency: Does the Reader . . .

- □ read smoothly, accurately, in meaningful phrases?
- □ read word-by-word, choppy, plodding?
- □ use pitch, stress, and intonation to convey meaning of the text?
- □ repeat words and phrases because s/he is monitoring the meaning (self-correcting)?
- □ repeat words and phrases because s/he is trying to sound out words?
- □ use punctuation to divide the text into units of meaning?
- □ ignore the punctuation?

Rating Scale: Circle One

4 = fluent reading / good pace

3 = fairly fluent / reasonable pace

2 = choppy, plodding reading / slow pace

1 = clearly labored, disfluent reading / very slow pace

Retelling

Note: Indicate any probing with a "P"

Story Elements	All	Some	None
Main Character(s)			
Time and Place			
Problem			
Plot Details in Sequence			
Turning Point			
Resolution			
Reader's Thumbnail Summary:			

Retelling Summary: □ many details, logical order □ some details, some order □ few details, disorder

Comprehension Questions and Possible Answers

_____ (RIF) 1. Who is the main character in this story? (a little girl named Sally)

_____ (PIT) 2. What is the problem in the story? (Sally is thinking and perhaps worrying about growing up)

_____ (RIF) 3. Name two body parts that Sally says will grow bigger. (legs, arms, head, face, nose)

_____ (PIT) 4. What did Sally say would happen if her nose didn't grow? (her nose would stay a little baby nose on a big face)

_____ (CAR) 5. What do you know about the phrase *I would look funny?* What does *I would look funny* have to do with this story? (to look or appear different or strange) (Sally said that if her nose didn't grow then she would look funny)

_____ (EAS) 6. How do you think Sally feels about growing up? (she feels okay, but maybe a little worried or sensitive) You think this because . . . (she questioned or worried about her nose not growing. Nobody wants to feel funny, people might laugh at you, then you'd feel bad)

Reader Text Relationship (RTR)   From the Text   □ adequate □ not adequate   From Head to Text   □ adequate □ not adequate

Scoring Guide Summary

WORD RECOGNITION

Independent 0-1

Instructional 2-3

Frustration .... 5+

COMPREHENSION

Independent 0

Instructional 1-2

Frustration .... 3+

Emotional Status:

Form B, Primer

Cueing Systems

L I N E #	Miscue	Grapho-phonically Similar I M F (word level)	Syntactically Acceptable Unacceptable (sentence level)	Semantic Change in Meaning (CM) No Change in Meaning (NCM) (sentence level)

Summary

☐ Most, ☐ few, ☐ no   miscues were graphophonically similar to the word in the passage.

☐ Most, ☐ few, ☐ no   miscues were syntactically matched.

☐ Most, ☐ few, ☐ no   miscues maintained the author's meaning.

☐ The self-corrections demonstrate that the reader monitors the meaning.

FORM B, LEVEL 1   Reader's Passages page 20

Prior Knowledge/Prediction

☐ Read the title and predict what the story is about.

Prior Knowledge
☐ a lot
☐ some
☐ none

☐ Read the first two sentences and add more to your prediction.

The Surprise Party

		O	I	S	A	Rp	Rv
1	"Hurry," Sue called to all her sisters and brothers.						
2	"Hide the balloons and then everybody hide! Don't make						
3	a sound or say a word! Dad will be coming home soon!"						
4	When Mr. Brown came into the house, he didn't see						
5	his children. All was still, so he didn't hear anything. Then						
6	he heard his children laughing, singing, and calling,						
7	"Surprise!" He saw many blue, green, and red balloons						
8	flying in the air! A big smile grew on his face.						

TOTALS

Number of miscues _____   Number of self-corrections _____

Retelling

Note: Indicate any probing with a "P"

Story Elements	All	Some	None
Main Character(s)			
Time and Place			
Problem			
Plot Details in Sequence			
Turning Point			
Resolution			
Reader's Thumbnail Summary:			

Scoring Guide Summary

WORD RECOGNITION

Independent......0-1
Instructional.....3-4
Frustration.......8+

COMPREHENSION

Independent......0
Instructional.....1-2
Frustration.......3+

Emotional Status:

Fluency: Does the Reader . . .

☐ read smoothly, accurately, in meaningful phrases?

☐ read word-by-word, choppy, plodding?

☐ use pitch, stress, and intonation to convey meaning of the text?

☐ repeat words and phrases because s/he is monitoring the meaning (self-correcting)?

☐ repeat words and phrases because s/he is trying to sound out words?

☐ use punctuation to divide the text into units of meaning?

☐ ignore the punctuation?

Rating Scale: Circle One

4 = fluent reading / good pace
3 = fairly fluent / reasonable pace
2 = choppy, plodding reading / slow pace
1 = clearly labored, disfluent reading / very slow pace

Retelling Summary: ☐ many details, logical order ☐ some details, some order ☐ few details, disorder

Comprehension Questions and Possible Answers

____ (RIF) 1. Who are the main characters in this story? (Sue and Mr. Brown)

____ (RIF) 2. What are the children planning for their dad? (a surprise party)

____ (PIT) 3. Why did the children hurry to hide? (because Dad was coming home soon, they wanted to surprise him)

____ (CAR) 4. What do you know about the phrase **all was still?** (nobody was moving or making a sound)
What does **all was still** have to do with this story? (when Mr. Brown came into the house, nobody was moving or making a sound)

____ (EAS) 5. What kind of party do you think this was? (a surprise party for a birthday or a celebration of a special event such as a job promotion or an honor) You think this because the story says . . . (there were balloons, singing, and the children called, "Surprise!")

____ (EAS) 6. How do you think Dad felt about the surprise? (he was happy, pleased)
You think this because the story says . . . (a big smile grew on his face)

Reader Text Relationship (RTR) From the Text ☐ adequate ☐ not adequate From Head to Text ☐ adequate ☐ not adequate

FORM B

Cueing Systems

L I N E #	Miscue	Grapho- phonically Similar I M F (word level)	Syntactically Acceptable Unacceptable (sentence level)	Semantic Change in Meaning (CM) No Change in Meaning (NCM) (sentence level)

The cueing system grid is continued on the next page.

FORM B, LEVEL 2   Reader's Passages page 21

Prior Knowledge/Prediction

☐ Read the title and predict what the story is about.

Prior Knowledge
☐ a lot
☐ some
☐ none

☐ Read the first two sentences and add more to your prediction.

	The Soccer Game	O	I	S	A	Rp	Rv
1	I ran down the soccer field kicking the ball.						
2	I was heading straight for the goal. I was close enough						
3	to score. I felt like a million dollars! Wham! I kicked						
4	the ball into the air. It smacked the top of the goalpost						
5	and landed right behind the goal. I really felt rotten!						
6	So, the other team's player got the ball. He looked						
7	like he was ready to power-kick the ball to the moon. Smack!						
8	The ball flew right toward me. I bent my knees low and then						
9	jumped up with all my might. Whack! I hit the ball with my head.						

The text is continued on the next page.

Cueing Systems

Miscue	Grapho-phonically Similar I M F (word level)	Syntactically Acceptable Unacceptable (sentence level)	Semantic Change in Meaning (CM) No Change in Meaning (NCM) (sentence level)
L I N E #			

Summary

☐ Most, ☐ few, ☐ no   miscues were graphophonically similar to the word in the passage.

☐ Most, ☐ few, ☐ no   miscues were syntactically matched.

☐ Most, ☐ few, ☐ no   miscues maintained the author's meaning.

☐ The self-corrections demonstrate that the reader monitors the meaning.

Form B, Level 2

FORM B

	O	I	S	A	Rp	Rv
1						
0						

It went jetting straight into the goal. I was truly a soccer hero!

TOTALS

Number of miscues _____   Number of self-corrections _____

Fluency: Does the Reader . . .

☐ read smoothly, accurately, in meaningful phrases?

☐ read word-by-word, choppy, plodding?

☐ use pitch, stress, and intonation to convey meaning of the text?

☐ repeat words and phrases because s/he is monitoring the meaning (self-correcting)?

☐ repeat words and phrases because s/he is trying to sound out words?

☐ use punctuation to divide the text into units of meaning?   ☐ ignore the punctuat on?

Rating Scale: Circle One

4 = fluent reading / good pace   2 = choppy, plodding reading / slow pace

3 = fairly fluent / reasonable pace   1 = clearly labored, disfluent reading / very slow pace

FORM B

Note: Indicate any probing with a "P"

Story Elements	All	Some	None
Main Character(s)			
Time and Place			
Problem			
Plot Details in Sequence			
Turning Point			
Resolution			
Reader's Thumbnail Summary:			

Scoring Guide Summary
WORD RECOGNITION
Independent........1
Instructional....5-6
Frustration.......11-12+
COMPREHENSION
Independent........0
Instructional......1-2
Frustration.......3+
Emotional Status:

Form B, Level 2

Retelling

Retelling Summary: □ many details, logical order □ some details, some order □ few details, disorder

Comprehension Questions and Possible Answers

_____ (RIF) 1. Who is the main character in this story? (a soccer player)

_____ (PIT) 2. What is the problem in the story? (at first the player missed the goal)

_____ (CAR) 3. What do you know about the phrase *close enough to score?* (so near the goal that a player could make a point) What does the phrase *close enough to score* have to do with this story? (the player was so near the goal that he or she could have kicked it in)

_____ (CAR) 4. What do you know about the phrase *felt like a million dollars?* (really feel good about something) What does the phrase *felt like a million dollars* have to do with this story? (the player felt really good when he or she was heading straight for the goal)

_____ (EAS) 5. Do you think the player should have bent his knees and jumped? You think this because the story said . . . (yes, he saw the power kick coming toward him and thought he might be able to knock it into the goal; no, he should have been running to get the ball)

_____ (PIT) 6. What two things happened after the player bent his knees and jumped? (hit the ball with his or her head, it went straight into the goal)

Reader Text Relationship (RTR)   From the Text   □ adequate □ not adequate   From Head to Text   □ adequate □ not adequate

Cueing Systems

Miscue	Grapho-phonically Similar I M F (word level)	Syntactically Acceptable Unacceptable (sentence level)	Semantic Change in Meaning (CM) No Change in Meaning (NCM) (sentence level)
L I N E #			

The cueing system grid is continued on the next page.

FORM B, LEVEL 3	Reader's Passages page 22

Prior Knowledge/Prediction

☐ Read the title and predict what the story is about.

Prior Knowledge

☐ a lot
☐ some
☐ none

☐ Read the first two sentences and add more to your prediction.

The Baseball Card

		O	I	S	A	Rp	Rv
1	The boys got together because it was the afternoon of the great						
2	baseball card swap.						
3	"I've got an old timer!" Joe shouted. In his hand he clutched a card						
4	that he secretly thought was a loser. It wasn't a popular one like the						
5	ones the boys had boasted about all week. Everyone stopped to listen.						
6	No sooner had the words left Joe's mouth than he began to have						
7	second thoughts. Like a flash of lightning he remembered when he and						
8	his grandfather had gone to the card shop in search of baseball card						
9	treasures. He remembered how his grandfather had stood close as they						

The text is continued on the next page.

FORM B

	O	I	S	A	Rp	Rv
1 0 looked through the stacks of cards for endless hours. He remembered						
1 1 the feeling of his grandfather's strong hand on his shoulder.						
1 2 Joe's face turned flush. In a quiet voice he said, "Oh, never mind!						
1 3 Nobody wants this card because the edges are worn."						

TOTALS

Number of miscues _____ Number of self-corrections _____

Fluency: Does the Reader . . .

□ read smoothly, accurately, in meaningful phrases?

□ read word-by-word, choppy, plodding?

□ use pitch, stress, and intonation to convey meaning of the text?

□ repeat words and phrases because s/he is monitoring the meaning (self-correcting)?

□ repeat words and phrases because s/he is trying to sound out words?

□ use punctuation to divide the text into units of meaning?   □ ignore the punctuation?

Rating Scale: Circle One

4 = fluent reading / good pace   2 = choppy, plodding reading / slow pace

3 = fairly fluent / reasonable pace   1 = clearly labored, disfluent reading / very slow pace

Cueing Systems

	Miscue	Grapho-phonically Similar I M F (word level)	Syntactically Acceptable / Unacceptable (sentence level)	Semantic Change in Meaning (CM) / No Change in Meaning (NCM) (sentence level)
L I N E #				

Summary

□ Most, □ few, □ no   miscues were graphophonically similar to the word in the passage.

□ Most, □ few, □ no   miscues were syntactically matched.

□ Most, □ few, □ no   miscues maintained the author's meaning.

□ The self-corrections demonstrate that the reader monitors the meaning.

Form B, Level 3

Retelling

Note: Indicate any probing with a "P"

Story Elements	All	Some	None
Main Character(s)			
Time and Place			
Problem			
Plot Details in Sequence			
Turning Point			
Resolution			
Reader's Thumbnail Summary:			

Retelling Summary: ☐ many details, logical order ☐ some details, some order ☐ few details, disorder

Scoring Guide Summary

WORD RECOGNITION
Independent 1-2
Instructional 7
Frustration ..... 14+

COMPREHENSION
Independent 0-1
Instructional 2
Frustration ..... 4+

Emotional Status:

Comprehension Questions and Possible Answers

____ (RIF) 1. Who is the main character in this story? (Joe)

____ (RIF) 2. When did the boys meet? (in the afternoon)

____ (PIT) 3. What is Joe's problem? (he wants to trade his baseball card, but then realizes that he can't give it up because it reminds him of his grandfather)

____ (CAR) 4. What do you know about the phrase *secretly thought it was a loser?* (in your mind you think something is not a winner) What does the phrase *secretly thought it was a loser* have to do with this story? (Joe thought his baseball card was one that no one would want)

____ (CAR) 5. What do you know about the phrase *old timer?* (something that is old fashioned, antique) What does the phrase *old timer* have to do with this story? (Joe said about his baseball card, "I've got an old timer!")

____ (PIT) 6. What did Joe remember? (when his grandfather had gone to the card shop to search for baseball treasures; how his grandfather had stood close as they rummaged through the stacks of cards; the feeling of his grandfather's strong hand on his shoulder)

____ (CAR) 7. What do you know about the phrase *endless hours?* (it's a very long time) What does the phrase *endless hours* have to do with this story? (Joe and grandfather looked through stacks of cards for endless hours)

____ (EAS) 8. Do you think Joe really wanted to trade the card? You think this because the story said ... (no, because the memories about his grandfather caused him to change his mind; yes, he thought it was a loser)

Reader Text Relationship (RTR)   From the Text   ☐ adequate ☐ not adequate   From Head to Text   ☐ adequate ☐ not adequate

FORM B

Form B, Level 3

FORM B

Prior Knowledge/Prediction

☐ Read the title and predict what the story is about.

Prior Knowledge
☐ a lot
☐ some
☐ none

☐ Read the first two sentences and add more to your prediction.

The Small Pony*

		O	I	S	A	Rp	Rv
1	A long time ago a strong horse was important to a farmer,						
2	so it was no surprise that Joel's father was storming mad. Mr. Goss						
3	had sent Joel to a nearby town to collect some money a man owed him.						
4	Joel had returned with a pony instead of the money! The news had						
5	spread that the pony was small. People were already laughing.						
6	What good was a small pony when there was heavy farm work to do?						
7	Joel hoped to calm his father's anger by telling him about the						
8	pony's unusual strength. Mr. Goss would not listen. He pounded						
9	his fist on the table shouting several commands! The pony could not stay						

The text is continued on the next page.

*This passage is a retelling from the novel *Justin Morgan Had a Horse* by M. Henry.

Cueing Systems

LINE#	Miscue	Grapho-phonically Similar I M F (word level)	Syntactically Acceptable Unacceptable (sentence level)	Semantic Change in Meaning (CM) No Change in Meaning (NCM) (sentence level)

The cueing system grid is continued on the next page.

Cueing Systems

LINE #	Miscue	Grapho-phonically Similar I M F (word level)	Syntactically Acceptable Unacceptable (sentence level)	Semantic Change in Meaning (CM) No Change in Meaning (NCM) (sentence level)

Summary

☐ Most, ☐ few, ☐ no   miscues were graphophonically similar to the word in the passage.

☐ Most, ☐ few, ☐ no   miscues were syntactically matched.

☐ Most, ☐ few, ☐ no   miscues maintained the author's meaning.

☐ The self-corrections demonstrate that the reader monitors the meaning.

FORM B

	O	I	S	A	Rp	Rv
1 0	on his land! In the morning he would take his son to the saw mill					
1 1	and ask if Joel could live and work there. Joel felt shocked and hurt.					
1 2	How could he leave his home and also lose the pony he loved?					

TOTALS

Number of miscues _____ Number of self-corrections _____

Fluency: Does the Reader . . .

☐ read smoothly, accurately, in meaningful phrases?

☐ read word-by-word, choppy, plodding?

☐ use pitch, stress, and intonation to convey meaning of the text?

☐ repeat words and phrases because s/he is monitoring the meaning (self-correcting)?

☐ repeat words and phrases because s/he is trying to sound out words?

☐ use punctuation to divide the text into units of meaning? ☐ ignore the punctuation?

Rating Scale: Circle One

4 = fluent reading / good pace   2 = choppy, plodding reading / slow pace

3 = fairly fluent / reasonable pace   1 = clearly labored, disfluent reading / very slow pace

FORM B

Note: Indicate any probing with a "P"

Story Elements	All	Some	None
Main Character(s)			
Time and Place			
Problem			
Plot Details in Sequence			
Turning Point			
Resolution			
Reader's Thumbnail Summary:			

Retelling

Retelling Summary: ☐ many details, logical order ☐ some details, some order ☐ few details, disorder

Comprehension Questions and Possible Answers

____ (RIF) 1. Who are the two main characters in this story?   (Joel and his father, Mr. Goss)

____ (RIF) 2. Where does this story take place?   (on a farm, in the country)

____ (PIT) 3. Why was Joel's father storming mad?   (he had sent Joel to collect a debt and Joel had returned with a small pony)

____ (PIT) 4. Why were people laughing about the pony?   (a farmer needed a strong horse, and a small pony could not do the heavy farm work)

____ (RIF) 5. How had Joel hoped to calm his father's anger?   (by convincing Mr. Goss of the pony's unusual strength)

____ (CAR) 6. What do you know about the phrase *shouting several commands?*   (to yell out many orders one after the other) What does the phrase *shouting several commands* have to do with the story?   (Mr. Goss pounded his fist on the table shouting several commands)

____ (PIT) 7. What did Mr. Goss command?   (the pony could not stay on the property; Joel had to leave his house and get a job working and living at the saw mill)

____ (EAS) 8. Do you think Joel's father's behavior was right? You think this because the text said . . . (no, he should have let his son show how strong the pony was; yes, Joel should not have disobeyed his father by not bringing back the money)

Reader Text Relationship (RTR)   From the Text   ☐ adequate ☐ not adequate   From Head to Text   ☐ adequate ☐ not adequate

Cueing Systems

Miscue	Grapho-phonically Similar I M F (word level)	Syntactically Acceptable Unacceptable (sentence level)	Semantic Change in Meaning (CM) No Change in Meaning (NCM) (sentence level)
L I N E #			

The cueing system grid is continued on the next page.

FORM B, LEVEL 5	Reader's Passages page 24

Prior Knowledge/Prediction

☐ Read the title and predict what the story is about.

Prior Knowledge

☐ a lot
☐ some
☐ none

☐ Read the first two sentences and add more to your prediction.

A Woman Jockey

		O	I	S	A	Rp	Rv
1	"I know that I was last in the race," announced Robyn Smith, "but I						
2	am determined to be the best jockey, even if I am a woman!"						
3	It was a rainy morning in 1969, and as Robyn stood outside talking						
4	to a horse trainer, Frank Wright, she was so dripping wet that water came						
5	running out of the top of her boots. Wright never doubted her ability, and so						
6	he gave her a chance to prove herself. One December afternoon Robyn won						
7	fourth place in a tough race. People noticed that she had a special way with						
8	horses that made them run fast for her.						
9	Then Robyn got another chance. She was to compete against a						

The text is continued on the next page.

Cueing Systems

LINE #	Miscue	Grapho-phonically Similar I M F (word level)	Syntactically Acceptable Unacceptable (sentence level)	Semantic Change in Meaning (CM) No Change in Meaning (NCM) (sentence level)

Summary

☐ Most, ☐ few, ☐ no   miscues were graphophonically similar to the word in the passage.

☐ Most, ☐ few, ☐ no   miscues were syntactically matched.

☐ Most, ☐ few, ☐ no   miscues maintained the author's meaning.

☐ The self-corrections demonstrate that the reader monitors the meaning.

Form B, Level 5

O	I	S	A	Rp	Rv

1 0 famous horse named Onion. At race time Robyn mounted her horse, and he

1 1 nervously pranced back and forth. "Everyone thinks you are wild on the

1 2 track!" she said in a soft voice. "North Star, you and I will defeat Onion," she

1 3 said, and he quickly calmed. Then, to everyone's surprise, she won the race.

1 4 Now the whole world would accept her as an excellent rider.

TOTALS

Number of miscues _____   Number of self-corrections _____

Fluency: Does the Reader . . .

☐ read smoothly, accurately, in meaningful phrases?

☐ read word-by-word, choppy, plodding?

☐ use pitch, stress, and intonation to convey meaning of the text?

☐ repeat words and phrases because s/he is monitoring the meaning (self-correcting)?

☐ repeat words and phrases because s/he is trying to sound out words?

☐ use punctuation to divide the text into units of meaning?   ☐ ignore the punctuation?

Rating Scale: Circle One

4 = fluent reading / good pace   2 = choppy, plodding reading / slow pace

3 = fairly fluent / reasonable pace   1 = clearly labored, disfluent reading / very slow pace

Form B, Level 5

Note: Indicate any probing with a "P"

Story Elements	All	Some	None
Main Character(s)			
Time and Place			
Problem			
Plot Details in Sequence			
Turning Point			
Resolution			
Reader's Thumbnail Summary:			

Scoring Guide Summary

WORD RECOGNITION
Independent....... 2
Instructional...... 9
Frustration ......18+

COMPREHENSION
Independent...... 0-1
Instructional...... 2
Frustration....... 4+

Emotional Status:

Retelling

Retelling Summary: ☐ many details, logical order ☐ some details, some order ☐ few details, disorder

Comprehension Questions and Possible Answers

___(RIF) 1. Who are the two main characters in this story?   (Robyn Smith and Frank Wright)

___(RIF) 2. What is Robyn's goal?   (to be the best jockey, even though she is a woman)

___(PIT) 3. Why was water running out of Robyn's boots?   (she was standing outside talking to Frank Wright, it was raining, she was dripping wet, and her boots filled to the top with water)

___(CAR) 4. What do you know about the phrase **never doubted her ability?**   (never to think someone can't do or accomplish something) What does the phrase **never doubted her ability** have to do with this story?   (Wright never doubted her ability, and so he gave her a chance to prove herself)

___(PIT) 5. What makes you think that Wright thought she could be a good rider?   (the story said that he felt she could be a successful rider, he gave her a chance)

___(CAR) 6. What do you know about the phrase **had a special way with horses?**   (that means you have a unique system for successfully handling something, you can do things in a manner that others cannot do)   What does the phrase **had a special way with horses** have to do with this story?   (Robyn would make horses go fast for her, she could calm a horse that was wild on the track)

___(EAS) 7. In your opinion, what was so unusual about Robyn's career?   (in 1969, and even today, there were not many women jockeys, so she was special)   You think this because . . . (the story said she was determined to be the best jockey even if she was a woman; now, the whole world would accept her as an excellent rider)

___(PIT) 8. What made her victory so special?   (Onion was a winning horse, and North Star was supposed to be wild on the track, so Robyn succeeded at two difficult things)

Reader Text Relationship (RTR)   From the Text   ☐ adequate ☐ not adequate   From Head to Text   ☐ adequate ☐ not adequate

Cueing Systems

LINE #	Miscue	Grapho-phonically Similar I M F (word level)	Syntactically Acceptable Unacceptable (sentence level)	Semantic Change in Meaning (CM) No Change in Meaning (NCM) (sentence level)

The cueing system grid is continued on the next page.

FORM B, LEVEL 6   Reader's Passages page 25.

Prior Knowledge/Prediction

☐ Read the title and predict what the story is about.

Prior Knowledge
☐ a lot
☐ some
☐ none

☐ Read the first two sentences and add more to your prediction.

The First Gas Mask

		O	I	S	A	Rp	Rv
1	The explosion was horrible that tragic day in Cleveland, Ohio, in						
2	1916. Thirty-two men were trapped in a tunnel 250 feet below Lake Erie, and						
3	no one could enter the smoke-filled atmosphere. "Someone get Garrett						
4	Morgan to help!" shouted a man. "Morgan's breathing device is the only						
5	thing that can help to rescue the survivors!"						
6	Garrett Morgan and his brother quickly volunteered to assist.						
7	"My breathing device will save those victims' lives," Morgan announced with						
8	confidence. "I invented it so firemen can breathe when they enter a burning						
9	house filled with suffocating gases. We tested my device in an air-tight tent						

The text is continued on the next page.

Cueing Systems

Miscue	Grapho-phonically Similar I M F (word level)	Syntactically Acceptable Unacceptable (sentence level)	Semantic Change in Meaning (CM) No Change in Meaning (NCM) (sentence level)
L I N E #			

Summary

☐ Most, ☐ few, ☐ no   miscues were graphophonically similar to the word in the passage.

☐ Most, ☐ few, ☐ no   miscues were syntactically matched.

☐ Most, ☐ few, ☐ no   miscues maintained the author's meaning.

☐ The self-corrections demonstrate that the reader monitors the meaning.

	O	I	S	A	Rp	Rv
10	that was filled with the foulest, thickest smoke. A man put my diver's					
11	helmet-like device with long breathing tubes running to the floor over his					
12	head, went into the tent, stayed twenty minutes, and emerged unharmed!"					
13	Then, Morgan and his brother placed the devices over their heads					
14	and rushed into the death-trap tunnel. One by one they carried each man to					
15	the surface. Although not every life was spared, it was Morgan's invention,					
16	the first gas mask, that saved lives that day and in the years to come.					

TOTALS

Number of miscues _____   Number of self-corrections _____

Fluency: Does the Reader . . .

☐ read smoothly, accurately, in meaningful phrases?

☐ read word-by-word, choppy, plodding?

☐ use pitch, stress, and intonation to convey meaning of the text?

☐ repeat words and phrases because s/he is monitoring the meaning (self-correcting)?

☐ repeat words and phrases because s/he is trying to sound out words?

☐ use punctuation to divide the text into units of meaning?   ☐ ignore the punctuation?

Rating Scale: Circle One

4 = fluent reading / good pace   2 = choppy, plodding reading / slow pace

3 = fairly fluent / reasonable pace   1 = clearly labored, disfluent reading / very slow pace

FORM B

Retelling

Note: Indicate any probing with a "P"

Story Elements	All	Some	None
Main Character(s)			
Time and Place			
Problem			
Plot Details in Sequence			
Turning Point			
Resolution			
Reader's Thumbnail Summary:			

Retelling Summary: ☐ many details, logical order ☐ some details, some order ☐ few details, disorder

Comprehension Questions and Possible Answers

____ (RIF) 1. Who is the main character in the story? (Garrett Morgan)

____ (RIF) 2. Where does this story take place? (Cleveland, Ohio, on Lake Erie)

____ (PIT) 3. Why was it difficult to save the thirty-two men trapped under Lake Erie? (the tunnel was filled with smoke)

____ (CAR) 4. Why did the man ask for Garrett Morgan's help in rescuing the trapped men? (Garrett Morgan had invented a breathing device so people could breathe in smoke)

____ (PIT) 5. What do you know about the phrase ***announced with confidence?*** (to talk to others and be sure of one's self and one's abilities) What does the phrase ***announced with confidence*** have to do with the story? (Garrett Morgan announced with confidence that his breathing device would save the victims' lives)

____ (RIF) 6. Why did Garrett Morgan invent the breathing device? (to help firemen breathe when they enter a burning house filled with suffocating gases)

____ (EAS) 7. How did Garrett Morgan test his breathing device? (a man stayed twenty minutes in a smoke-filled tent and emerged unharmed)

____ (EAS) 8. Do you think that Garrett Morgan had confidence that his invention would work? You think this because . . . (yes, he and his brother volunteered to wear the masks in the foul smoke in order to save lives)

Reader Text Relationship (RTR)   From the Text   ☐ adequate   ☐ not adequate   From Head to Text   ☐ adequate   ☐ not adequate

Scoring Guide Summary

WORD RECOGNITION

Independent.....2
Instructional.....9
Frustration.......19+

COMPREHENSION

Independent......0-1
Instructional......2
Frustration........4+

Emotional Status:

Form B, Level 6

FORM B, LEVEL 7 — Reader's Passages page 26

Prior Knowledge/Prediction

☐ Read the title and predict what the story is about.

☐ Read the first two sentences and add more to your prediction.

Prior Knowledge
☐ a lot
☐ some
☐ none

	Dating a Loner*	O	I	S	A	Rp	Rv
1	Kate sat in her senior biology class, but she wasn't hearing a single word the						
2	teacher was saying because her mind was thoroughly preoccupied. She could think						
3	only about Dave and her date with him last Friday night. The entire thing was so						
4	confusing and distracting that she kept glancing sideways to where he was sitting						
5	near the windows.						
6	He was by far the most handsome boy at Tylerton High. He was tall and strong,						
7	with shaggy hair and brilliant blue eyes, but there was something very different about						
8	Dave Burdick which she found difficult to accept. She knew that he was independent,						
9	and at times actually seemed defiant. She found this disturbing. He always neglected						
10	his appearance as if he didn't care what others thought. He was an excellent football						

The text is continued on the next page.

*This passage is a retelling from the novel *Dave's Song* by Robert McKay.

Cueing Systems

LINE #	Miscue	Grapho-phonically Similar I M F (word level)	Syntactically Acceptable Unacceptable (sentence level)	Semantic Change in Meaning (CM) No Change in Meaning (NCM) (sentence level)

The cueing system grid is continued on the next page.

FORM B

	O	I	S	A	RpRv
1 1	player, probably the best in the entire school, but he quit the team. Sometimes he could				
1 2	be stubborn and belligerent, and would argue with anyone over anything.				
1 3	He never hung around the other kids, so it seemed to her that he was a loner.				
1 4	He drove an old Ford pickup, which had chicken feathers and farm tools scattered all				
1 5	over the floor. Kate felt that he was more interested in raising chickens than in having				
1 6	friends. Yet, even knowing all of these things, she was sure he was a good and decent				
1 7	person. Something crazy was going on in her mind; Dave Burdick was fascinating.				

TOTALS

Number of miscues _____   Number of self-corrections _____

Fluency: Does the Reader . . .

- ☐ read smoothly, accurately, in meaningful phrases?
- ☐ read word-by-word, choppy, plodding?
- ☐ use pitch, stress, and intonation to convey meaning of the text?
- ☐ repeat words and phrases because s/he is monitoring the meaning (self-correcting)?
- ☐ repeat words and phrases because s/he is trying to sound out words?
- ☐ use punctuation to divide the text into units of meaning?   ☐ ignore the punctuation?

Rating Scale: Circle One

4 = fluent reading / good pace   2 = choppy, plodding reading / slow pace
3 = fairly fluent / reasonable pace   1 = clearly labored, disfluent reading / very slow pace

Cueing Systems

Miscue	Graphophonically Similar I M F (word level)	Syntactically Acceptable Unacceptable (sentence level)	Semantic Change in Meaning (CM) No Change in Meaning (NCM) (sentence level)
L I N E #			

Summary

- ☐ Most, ☐ few, ☐ no   miscues were graphophonically similar to the word in the passage.
- ☐ Most, ☐ few, ☐ no   miscues were syntactically matched.
- ☐ Most, ☐ few, ☐ no   miscues maintained the author's meaning.
- ☐ The self-corrections demonstrate that the reader monitors the meaning.

Form B, Level 7

Retelling

Note: Indicate any probing with a "P"

Story Elements	All	Some	None
Main Character(s)			
Time and Place			
Problem			
Plot Details in Sequence			
Turning Point			
Resolution			
Reader's Thumbnail Summary:			

Retelling Summary: ☐ many details, logical order ☐ some details, some order ☐ few details, disorder

Comprehension Questions and Possible Answers

____ (RIF) 1. Who is the main character in this story? (Kate)

____ (PIT) 2. What is the problem in this story? (Dave was different from all of her other friends but she still liked him)

____ (PIT) 3. Why didn't Kate hear a single word the teacher was saying? (her mind was thoroughly preoccupied, she could only think about Dave and her date with him)

____ (CAR) 4. What do you know about the word *independent?* (not dependent on others, self-sufficient) What does the word *independent* have to do with this story? (Dave was independent and sometimes defiant)

____ (RIF) 5. What did Kate find disturbing about Dave? (he had a defiant attitude)

____ (RIF) 6. List two things you know about Dave. (he neglected his appearance; he was an excellent football player, but he quit the team; he was stubborn and belligerent; he would argue with anyone; he never hung around other kids; he drove an old Ford pickup with chicken feathers scattered all over the floor)

____ (EAS) 7. Do you think Dave had a negative attitude? You think this because . . . (Yes. He neglected his appearance; he was an excellent football player, but he quit the team; he was stubborn and belligerent; he would argue with anyone; he never hung around other kids; he drove an old Ford pickup with chicken feathers scattered all over the floor)

____ (PIT) 8. Why did Kate think Dave was a loner? (he never hung around other kids)

Reader Text Relationship (RTR)   From the Text   ☐ adequate   ☐ not adequate   From Head to Text   ☐ adequate   ☐ not adequate

FORM B

Form B, Level 7

FORM B

FORM B, LEVEL 8 — Reader's Passages page 27

Prior Knowledge/Prediction

☐ Read the title and predict what the story is about.

☐ Read the first two sentences and add more to your prediction.

Prior Knowledge
☐ a lot
☐ some
☐ none

	First Day of High School Jitters	O	I	S	A	Rp	Rv
1	"Most ninth graders are a bundle of nerves on the first day of high school,						
2	but not me!" Jack Gaither boasted to a group of fellow ninth graders. "I plan on						
3	being calm, cool, and collected!" he continued as he thumped his chest. "By the end						
4	of day one at Wheaten High School, I will be the most notorious ninth grader!"						
5	The week before school started, Jack meticulously planned each detail. First,						
6	he imagined the casual stroll from the school bus; with his head held up, he invented						
7	a composed appearance. The most difficult assignment, however, would be to get						
8	from his locker to class within three minutes. Dealing with the combination lock had						
9	to go flawlessly, so Jack rehearsed how to efficiently spin the knob forward,						
10	backward, forward, then smugly lift the latch, and gently swing the door open. "The						
11	mission can be accomplished in a minute and a half, leaving plenty of time to						
12	nonchalantly saunter into class!" He knew his plan was absolutely comprehensive!						
13	On the first day of school, as Jack emerged from the bus, he tripped over his						
14	own feet and propelled forward, knocking three students into each other. Once						

The text is continued on the next page.

Cueing Systems

LINE #	Miscue	Grapho-phonically Similar I M F (word level)	Syntactically Acceptable Unacceptable (sentence level)	Semantic Change in Meaning (CM) No Change in Meaning (NCM) (sentence level)

The cueing system grid is continued on the next page.

Cueing Systems

Miscue	Grapho-phonically Similar I M F (word level)	Syntactically Acceptable / Unacceptable (sentence level)	Semantic Change in Meaning (CM) No Change in Meaning (NCM) (sentence level)
L I N E #			

Summary

☐ Most, ☐ few, ☐ no   miscues were graphophonically similar to the word in the passage.

☐ Most, ☐ few, ☐ no   miscues were syntactically matched.

☐ Most, ☐ few, ☐ no   miscues maintained the author's meaning.

☐ The self-corrections demonstrate that the reader monitors the meaning.

Form B, Level 8

	O	I	S	A	Rp	Rv
1 5	inside, he lunged toward his locker, twirling the knob so fast that he absentmindedly					
1 6	forgot the combination. Finally, as he yanked the door open, it smacked him in the					
1 7	head. He hustled down the hallway, lowering his head to prevent anyone from					
1 8	noticing the lump that was welling up on his forehead. He edged through the					
1 9	classroom doorway and settled into a seat in the back row.					
2 0	Abruptly, the bell began clanging, resounding in rhythm with his throbbing					
2 1	head. "This is *Senior English, College Preparation*," the teacher's voice attached itself					
2 2	to the final vibration of the bell. "Well, I recognize all of you except for one student!"					

TOTALS

Number of miscues _____   Number of self-corrections _____

Fluency: Does the Reader . . .

☐ read smoothly, accurately, in meaningful phrases?

☐ read word-by-word, choppy, plodding?

☐ use pitch, stress, and intonation to convey meaning of the text?

☐ repeat words and phrases because s/he is monitoring the meaning (self-correcting)?

☐ repeat words and phrases because s/he is trying to sound out words?

☐ use punctuation to divide the text into units of meaning?   ☐ ignore the punctuation?

Rating Scale: Circle One

4 = fluent reading / good pace   2 = choppy, plodding reading / slow pace

3 = fairly fluent / reasonable pace   1 = clearly labored, disfluent reading / very slow pace

FORM B

FORM B

Story Elements	All	Some	None
Main Character(s)			
Time and Place			
Problem			
Plot Details in Sequence			
Turning Point			
Resolution			
Reader's Thumbnail Summary:			

Scoring Guide Summary

WORD RECOGNITION

Independent 3
Instructional 15
Frustration ......30+

COMPREHENSION

Independent 0-1
Instructional 2
Frustration ......4+

Emotional Status:

Form B, Level 8

Retelling

Retelling Summary: □ many details, logical order □ some details, some order □ few details, disorder

Comprehension Questions and Possible Answers

_____ (RIF)   1. Who is the main character in this story?   (Jack Gaither)

_____ (RIF)   2. Where does this story take place?   (at Wheaten High School)

_____ (PIT)   3. What is the problem in this story? (Jack wants to impress everyone by knowing how to handle his first day of high school; he wants to look like he knows what he is doing)

_____ (PIT)   4. What did Jack do before school started?   (he practiced getting off the bus, working the combination lock, and walking to class)

_____ (CAR)   5. What do you know about the phrase *meticulously planned?* (to pay close attention to every detail about something you are going to do) What does the phrase *meticulously planned* have to do with this story?   (it said before school started Jack meticulously planned every detail)

_____ (CAR)   6. What do you know about the phrase *nonchalantly saunter?* (in an off-hand way, to walk leisurely)   What does the phrase *nonchalantly saunter* have to do with this story?   (it said Jack planned to nonchalantly saunter into class)

_____ (PIT)   7. Why did Jack hustle down the hallway? (he didn't want anyone to notice the lump that was welling up on his forehead; he was embarrassed)

_____ (EAS)   8. In your opinion do you think Jack's plan went well? You think this because . . . (no, everything went wrong) (it said that he tripped when he got off the bus; he forgot the combination to the lock and smacked the door into his head; went into the wrong classroom)

Reader Text Relationship (RTR)   From the Text   □ adequate □ not adequate   From Head to Text   □ adequate □ not adequate

Cueing Systems

Miscue	L I N E #	Grapho-phonically Similar I M F (word level)	Syntactically Acceptable Unacceptable (sentence level)	Semantic Change in Meaning (CM) No Change in Meaning (NCM) (sentence level)

The cueing system grid is continued on the next page.

FORM B, LEVEL 9	Reader's Passages page 28

Prior Knowledge/Prediction

☐ Read the title and predict what the story is about.

Prior Knowledge
☐ a lot
☐ some
☐ none

☐ Read the first two sentences and add more to your prediction.

	Restoring Pigeon Creek	O	I	S	A	Rp	Rv
1	Some time ago Pigeon Creek flowed with transparent, unpolluted water and						
2	was a prolific spawning ground for salmon. Then Everett, Washington's population						
3	flourished, and for decades to follow, members of the community thoughtlessly dumped						
4	debris into the stream. Bottles, aluminum cans, styrofoam cups, old tires, smashed						
5	cardboard, rusted bedsprings, ruined refrigerators, and other contaminants choked the						
6	once unpolluted water. Erosion occurred from the cutting of trees, causing silt to slide						
7	down the embankments. The water turned from transparent to murky, consequently						
8	threatening the lives of the fish. Eventually, the fish disappeared; not one had been						
9	sighted for twenty years.						
10	The creek's final half-mile runs below Jackson Elementary School and then						
11	meanders toward Puget Sound through a culvert, under a railroad track, and finally						
12	across a sandy beach as it flows toward the sea. The students and their teachers had						
13	studied environmental issues and decided to take a stand. "We want to adopt Pigeon						
14	Creek and work to restore its clean water," the president of the student council						

The text is continued on the next page.

Cueing Systems

Miscue	Grapho-phonically Similar I M F (word level)	Syntactically Acceptable Unacceptable (sentence level)	Semantic Change in Meaning (CM) No Change in Meaning (NCM) (sentence level)
L I N E #			

	O	I	S	A	Rp	Rv
15	announced.					
16	"Pigeon Creek is past saving! Maybe you should just forget it!" advised many					
17	adults.					
18	Undaunted, the elementary students began working, and "Operation Pigeon					
19	Creek" became the slogan for their mission. Guided by their teachers, the students					
20	began to extricate the rubbish and to patrol the creek-side to discourage new dumping.					
21	They made signs and placed them throughout the community, reminding people not to					
22	dump refuse in the creek. Eventually, the students garnered so much public attention					
23	that they brought political pressure on the city council and stopped the construction of					
24	a storage facility that would have been built near the mouth of the creek.					
25	Then, the school set up an aquarium and stocked it with salmon eggs, and the					
26	students accepted the responsibility for maintaining the tank and caring for the eggs.					
27	They watched in wonder as the eggs hatched and grew; shortly, they released the					
28	young salmon into the creek for their migration to the sea. "Will some eventually					
29	return to Pigeon Creek to begin the life-cycle over again?" one student asked as the					
30	young salmon wiggled into the water.					

TOTALS

Number of miscues _____ Number of self-corrections _____

Fluency: Does the Reader . . . .

□ read smoothly, accurately, in meaningful phrases?
□ read word-by-word, choppy, plodding?
□ use pitch, stress, and intonation to convey meaning of the text?
□ repeat words and phrases because s/he is monitoring the meaning (self-correcting)?
□ repeat words and phrases because s/he is trying to sound out words?
□ use punctuation to divide the text into units of meaning?   □ ignore the punctuation?

Rating Scale: Circle One

4 = fluent reading / good pace   2 = choppy, plodding reading / slow pace
3 = fairly fluent / reasonable pace   1 = clearly labored, disfluent reading / very slow pace

Summary

□ Most, □ few, □ no   miscues were graphophonically similar to the word in the passage.

□ Most, □ few, □ no   miscues were syntactically matched.

□ Most, □ few, □ no   miscues maintained the author's meaning.

□ The self-corrections demonstrate that the reader monitors the meaning.

Form B, Level 9

Retelling

Note: Indicate any probing with a "P"

Story Elements	All	Some	None
Main Character(s)			
Time and Place			
Problem			
Plot Details in Sequence			
Turning Point			
Resolution			
Reader's Thumbnail Summary:			

Retelling Summary: ☐ many details, logical order ☐ some details, some order ☐ few details, disorder

Comprehension Questions and Possible Answers

___(RIF) 1. Where does this story take place? (on Pigeon Creek, Everett, Washington)

___(PIT) 2. What is the problem in this story? (the creek is polluted; the students want to clean it up)

___(PIT) 3. How did the creek become polluted? (as the city's population increased, people discarded trash into the creek; erosion caused silt to slide down the embankment)

___(RIF) 4. Name three items that were trashed in the creek. (bottles, aluminum cans, styrofoam cups, old tires, smashed cardboard, rusted bedsprings, ruined refrigerators, and other contaminants)

___(EAS) 5. In your opinion, could the pollution have been prevented? You think this because . . . (yes, the items trashed in the creek were ones that people could have recycled or reused or disposed of properly)

___(CAR) 6. What do you know about the word **undaunted?** (not intimidated, not filled with dismay) What does the word **undaunted** have to do with this story? (the students were undaunted by the adults' comments telling them to give up)

___(PIT) 7. After the aquarium was stocked, what responsibility did the students assume? (maintaining the fish tank and caring for the eggs)

___(PIT) 8. What did they do with the young salmon? (released them in the creek so they would migrate to the sea)

Reader Text Relationship (RTR)   From the Text ☐ adequate ☐ not adequate   From Head to Text ☐ adequate ☐ not adequate

FORM B

Form B, Level 9

◼ FORM C ◼

Word Lists and Narrative Passages, Preprimer—Nine

FORM C

Form C, Primer

1. about _____
2. can _____
3. who _____
4. with _____
5. some _____
6. goat _____
7. out _____
8. trees _____
9. father _____
10. red _____
11. green _____
12. make _____
13. is _____
14. yes _____
15. saw _____
16. get _____
17. ball _____
18. and _____
19. down _____
20. are _____

Sentences:

Comprehends: ☐ a lot ☐ some ☐ none

Form C, Level 1

1. ice _____
2. before _____
3. another _____
4. children _____
5. stopped _____
6. hurry _____
7. drop _____
8. friend _____
9. balloon _____
10. when _____
11. where _____
12. those _____
13. picnic _____
14. laugh _____
15. farm _____
16. airplane _____
17. tomorrow _____
18. wagon _____
19. made _____
20. surprise _____

Sentences:

Comprehends: ☐ a lot ☐ some ☐ none

Form C, Level 2

1. goose _____
2. mouse _____
3. library _____
4. teacher _____
5. kite _____
6. cart _____
7. different _____
8. anyone _____
9. feather _____
10. pie _____
11. sidewalk _____
12. straight _____
13. telephone _____
14. clean _____
15. remember _____
16. wood _____
17. summer _____
18. bell _____
19. gun _____
20. matter _____

Sentences:

Comprehends: ☐ a lot ☐ some ☐ none

Form C, Level 3

1. clap _____
2. fright _____
3. diamond _____
4. silence _____
5. nurse _____
6. wiggle _____
7. precious _____
8. salt _____
9. bread _____
10. breath _____
11. fellow _____
12. several _____
13. unusual _____
14. overhead _____
15. driven _____
16. fool _____
17. darkness _____
18. honor _____
19. screen _____
20. they'll _____

Sentences:

Comprehends: ☐ a lot ☐ some ☐ none

Form C, Level 4

1. canoe
2. hasn't
3. dozen
4. motion
5. pride
6. vicious
7. concern
8. harvest
9. sample
10. official
11. windshield
12. human
13. humor
14. decorate
15. slender
16. seventh
17. parachute
18. good-bye
19. dignity
20. trudge

Sentences:

Comprehends: ☐ a lot ☐ some ☐ none

Form C, Level 5

1. prevent
2. kindle
3. grease
4. typical
5. foam
6. blur
7. mumps
8. telegram
9. vision
10. sandal
11. argument
12. hail
13. halt
14. region
15. manager
16. sleet
17. yarn
18. parallel
19. coconut
20. dissolve

Sentences:

Comprehends: ☐ a lot ☐ some ☐ none

Form C, Level 6

1. midstream
2. lens
3. bail
4. college
5. failure
6. falter
7. width
8. graceful
9. somewhat
10. privacy
11. microphone
12. particle
13. clutter
14. applaud
15. vapor
16. reluctant
17. contract
18. nephew
19. insurance
20. fund

Sentences:

Comprehends: ☐ a lot ☐ some ☐ none

FORM C

FORM C

FORM C, PREPRIMER   Reader's Passages page 32

Prior Knowledge/Prediction

☐ Read the title and predict what the story is about.

Prior Knowledge
☐ a lot
☐ some
☐ none

☐ Read the first two sentences and add more to your prediction.

The Runaway Dog

		O	I	S	A	Rp	Rv
1	"I see the dog!" said Dad.						
2	"The dog is running. Now I do not see her.						
3	Where is the dog? Here she is. She has						
4	come back home."						

TOTALS

Number of miscues _____   Number of self-corrections _____

Cueing Systems

L I N E #	Miscue	Grapho-phonically Similar I M F (word level)	Syntactically Acceptable Unacceptable (sentence level)	Semantic Change in Meaning (CM) No Change in Meaning (NCM) (sentence level)

Summary

☐ Most, ☐ few, ☐ no   miscues were graphophonically similar to the word in the passage.

☐ Most, ☐ few, ☐ no   miscues were syntactically matched.

☐ Most, ☐ few, ☐ no   miscues maintained the author's meaning.

☐ The self-corrections demonstrate that the reader monitors the meaning.

FORM C

Fluency: Does the Reader . . .

☐ read smoothly, accurately, in meaningful phrases?

☐ read word-by-word, choppy, plodding?

☐ use pitch, stress, and intonation to convey meaning of the text?

☐ repeat words and phrases because s/he is monitoring the meaning (self-correcting)?

☐ repeat words and phrases because s/he is trying to sound out words?

☐ use punctuation to divide the text into units of meaning?

☐ ignore the punctuation?

Rating Scale: Circle One

4 = fluent reading / good pace

3 = fairly fluent / reasonable pace

2 = choppy, plodding reading / slow pace

1 = clearly labored, disfluent reading / very slow pace

Retelling

Note: Indicate any probing with a "P"

Story Elements	All	Some	None
Main Character(s)			
Time and Place			
Problem			
Plot Details in Sequence			
Turning Point			
Resolution			
Reader's Thumbnail Summary:			

Scoring Guide Summary

WORD RECOGNITION

Independent 0
Instructional 1-2
Frustration .... 3+

COMPREHENSION

Independent 0
Instructional 1-2
Frustration .... 3+

Emotional Status:

Form C, Preprimer

Retelling Summary: ☐ many details, logical order ☐ some details, some order ☐ few details, disorder

Comprehension Questions and Possible Answers

_____ (RIF) 1. Who is the main character in this story? (Dad)

_____ (EAS) 2. Where do you think this story takes place? You think this because the story said . . . . (outside at Dad's house because it said that the dog was running and that she came home)

_____ (CAR) 3. What do you know about the word *running?* (to go faster than a walk) What does the word *running* have to do with this story? (the dog is running)

_____ (CAR) 4. What do you know about the word *now?* (right in this moment or minute) What does the word *now* have to do with this story? (Dad said now I do not see the dog)

_____ (PIT) 5. What did the dog do? (ran around then came back home)

_____ (CAR) 6. What do you know about the phrase *has come back?* to go back where you started) What does the phrase *has come back* have to do with this story? (the dog ran around then came back home)

Reader Text Relationship (RTR)   From the Text ☐ adequate ☐ not adequate   From Head to Text ☐ adequate ☐ not adequate

169

FORM C

Prior Knowledge/Prediction

☐ Read the title and predict what the story is about.

Prior Knowledge
- ☐ a lot
- ☐ some
- ☐ none

☐ Read the first two sentences and add more to your prediction.

Too Many Animals

		O	I	S	A	Rp	Rv
1	I found a lost baby turtle. I took him home to						
2	live with me. A friend gave me his rabbit, and I took						
3	it home. I found a lost duck. I took her home. Then						
4	I saw a cow who looked so sad. I took her home!						
5	Then Mom said, "No, no, not a cow!"						

TOTALS

Number of miscues _____   Number of self-corrections _____

Cueing Systems

L I N E #	Miscue	Grapho-phonically Similar I M F (word level)	Syntactically Acceptable Unacceptable (sentence level)	Semantic Change in Meaning (CM) No Change in Meaning (NCM) (sentence level)

Summary

- ☐ Most, ☐ few, ☐ no   miscues were graphophonically similar to the word in the passage.
- ☐ Most, ☐ few, ☐ no   miscues were syntactically matched.
- ☐ Most, ☐ few, ☐ no   miscues maintained the author's meaning.
- ☐ The self-corrections demonstrate that the reader monitors the meaning.

Retelling

Note: Indicate any probing with a "P"

Story Elements	All	Some	None
Main Character(s)			
Time and Place			
Problem			
Plot Details in Sequence			
Turning Point			
Resolution			

Reader's Thumbnail Summary:

Scoring Guide Summary

WORD RECOGNITION
Independent 0-1
Instructional 2-3
Frustration ..... 5+

COMPREHENSION
Independent 0
Instructional 1-2
Frustration ..... 3+

Emotional Status:

Form C, Primer

Fluency: Does the Reader . . .

☐ read smoothly, accurately, in meaningful phrases?

☐ read word-by-word, choppy, plodding?

☐ use pitch, stress, and intonation to convey meaning of the text?

☐ repeat words and phrases because s/he is monitoring the meaning (self-correcting)?

☐ repeat words and phrases because s/he is trying to sound out words?

☐ use punctuation to divide the text into units of meaning?

☐ ignore the punctuation?

Rating Scale: Circle One
4 = fluent reading / good pace
3 = fairly fluent / reasonable pace
2 = choppy, plodding reading / slow pace
1 = clearly labored, disfluent reading / very slow pace

Retelling Summary: ☐ many details, logical order ☐ some details, some order ☐ few details, disorder

Comprehension Questions and Possible Answers

_____ (RIF) 1. Who is the main character in this story? (a child)

_____ (PIT) 2. What is the child doing? (collecting animals)

_____ (RIF) 3. What animal did the child find first? (a lost baby turtle)

_____ (CAR) 4. What do you know about the word *lost?* (you can't find your home or way somewhere)
What does the word *lost* have to do with this story? (there is a lost baby turtle)

_____ (PIT) 5. Name two other animals the child found. (duck and a cow)

_____ (EAS) 6. How do you think mom feels about the cow? (she is upset, maybe mad)
You think this because the story said . . . (Mom said, "No, no, not a cow!")

Reader Text Relationship (RTR)   From the Text ☐ adequate ☐ not adequate   From Head to Text ☐ adequate ☐ not adequate

Cueing Systems

L I N E #	Miscue	Grapho-phonically Similar I M F (word level)	Syntactically Acceptable Unacceptable (sentence level)	Semantic Change in Meaning (CM) No Change in Meaning (NCM) (sentence level)

Summary

☐ Most, ☐ few, ☐ no   miscues were graphophonically similar to the word in the passage.

☐ Most, ☐ few, ☐ no   miscues were syntactically matched.

☐ Most, ☐ few, ☐ no   miscues maintained the author's meaning.

☐ The self-corrections demonstrate that the reader monitors the meaning.

FORM C, LEVEL 1   Reader's Passages page 34

Prior Knowledge/Prediction

☐ Read the title and predict what the story is about.

Prior Knowledge
☐ a lot
☐ some
☐ none

☐ Read the first two sentences and add more to your prediction.

The Show-Off

		O	I	S	A	Rp	Rv
1	Jake was playing all by himself outside his house. He						
2	saw a friend from school walk by his yard.						
3	He yelled to him, "Look at me! I can run as fast as a						
4	wild horse! I can jump so high! I can jump over a big,						
5	tall tree! I can ride my bike as fast as a speeding train!						
6	Watch me! I can do it all! I am great. Do you want to						
7	play with me?"						

Note: Indicate any probing with a "P"

Story Elements	All	Some	None
Main Character(s)			
Time and Place			
Problem			
Plot Details in Sequence			
Turning Point			
Resolution			
Reader's Thumbnail Summary:			

Scoring Guide Summary

WORD RECOGNITION
Independent 0-1
Instructional 3-4
Frustration .... 7-8+

COMPREHENSION
Independent 0
Instructional 1-2
Frustration ...... 3+

Emotional Status:

Retelling

Fluency: Does the Reader . . .

☐ read smoothly, accurately, in meaningful phrases?

☐ read word-by-word, choppy, plodding?

☐ use pitch, stress, and intonation to convey meaning of the text?

☐ repeat words and phrases because s/he is monitoring the meaning (self-correcting)?

☐ repeat words and phrases because s/he is trying to sound out words?

☐ use punctuation to divide the text into units of meaning?

☐ ignore the punctuation?

Rating Scale: Circle One

4 = fluent reading / good pace
3 = fairly fluent / reasonable pace
2 = choppy, plodding reading / slow pace
1 = clearly labored, disfluent reading / very slow pace

Retelling Summary: ☐ many details, logical order ☐ some details, some order ☐ few details, disorder

Comprehension Questions and Possible Answers

____ (RIF)   1. Who is the main character in this story?   (Jake)

____ (PIT)   2. Where was Jake?   (outside, in his yard)

____ (CAR)   3. What do you know about the phrase *all by himself*?   (you are alone or can do something alone)
             What does the phrase *all by himself* have to do with this story?   (Jake was playing all by himself)

____ (RIF)   4. How high does Jake say he can jump?   (over a big, tall tree)

____ (CAR)   5. What do you know about the phrase *as fast as a speeding train*?   (someone who can run very fast)
             What does the phrase *as fast as a speeding train* have to do with this story?   (Jake said that he can ride his
             bike as fast as a speeding train)

____ (EAS)   6. How do you think Jake feels about himself?   You think this because the story said ...   (great, he is
             confident because he said, "I am great. I can do it all."; no: so great and he just says all of those things
             because he really needs a friend)

Reader Text Relationship (RTR)   From the Text ☐ adequate ☐ not adequate   From Head to Text ☐ adequate ☐ not adequate

FORM C

FORM C, LEVEL 2 Reader's Passages page 35

Prior Knowledge/Prediction
☐ Read the title and predict what the story is about.

☐ Read the first two sentences and add more to your prediction.

Prior Knowledge
☐ a lot
☐ some
☐ none

The Busy Road

	O	I	S	A	Rp	Rv
1	"Look out, you'll get hit!" I yelled as my dog ran across the					
2	busy road. *Thud* was the noise I heard, and then I saw my pup					
3	lying in the street. "Oh, no!" I shouted. I felt scared inside. "Rex is					
4	my best friend!" I wanted to cry out. I knew that he was hurt, but					
5	he'd be all right if I could get help fast. I knew I had to be brave.					
6	"Mom! Dad!" I yelled as I ran straight home. I tried to fight					
7	back the tears. They started rolling down my face anyway as I					
8	blasted through the door. "Rex has been hit, and he needs help					

The text is continued on the next page.

Cueing Systems

LINE #	Miscue	Graphophonically Similar I M F (word level)	Syntactically Acceptable Unacceptable (sentence level)	Semantic Change in Meaning (CM) No Change in Meaning (NCM) (sentence level)

The cueing system grid is continued on the next page.

	O	I	S	A	Rp	Rv
9	now!" I cried out. "Please hurry so we can save him!"					

TOTALS

Number of miscues _____ Number of self-corrections _____

Fluency: Does the Reader . . .

☐ read smoothly, accurately, in meaningful phrases?

☐ read word-by-word, choppy, plodding?

☐ use pitch, stress, and intonation to convey meaning of the text?

☐ repeat words and phrases because s/he is monitoring the meaning (self-correcting)?

☐ repeat words and phrases because s/he is trying to sound out words?

☐ use punctuation to divide the text into units of meaning?　　☐ ignore the punctuation?

Rating Scale: Circle One

4 = fluent reading / good pace　　2 = choppy, plodding reading / slow pace

3 = fairly fluent / reasonable pace　　1 = clearly labored, disfluent reading / very slow pace

Cueing Systems

	Miscue	Grapho-phonically Similar I M F (word level)	Syntactically Acceptable Unacceptable (sentence level)	Semantic Change in Meaning (CM) No Change in Meaning (NCM) (sentence level)
L I N E #				

Summary

☐ Most, ☐ few, ☐ no　miscues were graphophonically similar to the word in the passage.

☐ Most, ☐ few, ☐ no　miscues were syntactically matched.

☐ Most, ☐ few, ☐ no　miscues maintained the author's meaning.

☐ The self-corrections demonstrate that the reader monitors the meaning.

Form C, Level 2

FORM C

FORM C

Retelling

Note: Indicate any probing with a "P"

Story Elements	All	Some	None
Main Character(s)			
Time and Place			
Problem			
Plot Details in Sequence			
Turning Point			
Resolution			
Reader's Thumbnail Summary:			

Retelling Summary: ☐ many details, logical order ☐ some details, some order ☐ few details, disorder

Scoring Guide Summary

WORD RECOGNITION
Independent 1
Instructional 6
Frustration ...... 12+

COMPREHENSION
Independent 0
Instructional 1-2
Frustration ...... 3+

Emotional Status:

Comprehension Questions and Possible Answers

____ (RIF) 1. Who is the main character in this story?   (a child, boy or girl)

____ (PIT) 2. What is the problem in the story?   (the dog ran across a busy street and got hit)

____ (PIT) 3. Do you think the dog is an old dog or a young one?   (a young dog, the child calls the dog a pup)

____ (CAR) 4. What do you know about the phrase *fight back the tears?*   (you try not to cry, you try to be brave, you try to keep the tears from rolling down your cheeks) What does the phrase *fight back the tears* have to do with this story? (when the child ran home to get mom and dad, he/she tried to fight back the tears)

____ (PIT) 5. Why did the child run home?   (to get help fast so he/she could save the dog)

____ (EAS) 6. Do you think the dog will be all right? You think this because . . . (yes, the child is getting help fast; no, maybe they can't hurry fast enough)

Reader Text Relationship (RTR)   From the Text ☐ adequate ☐ not adequate   From Head to Text ☐ adequate ☐ not adequate

Form C, Level 2

176   SECTION IV ▪ Examiner's Records

FORM C, LEVEL 3	Reader's Passages page 36

Prior Knowledge/Prediction

☐ Read the title and predict what the story is about.

☐ Read the first two sentences and add more to your prediction.

Prior Knowledge

☐ a lot
☐ some
☐ none

	Belonging to the Club	O	I	S	A	Rp	Rv
1	This was the sign that Jack read as he stood outside the						
2	neighborhood kids' clubhouse.						
3	FOR NEIGHBORHOOD TIGERS ONLY!						
4	KNOCK ONE HUNDRED TIMES						
5	AND SAY THE SECRET WORD						
6	BEFORE ENTERING!						
7	Jack was a new boy, and he really wanted to belong to the club.						
8	"How can I get the kids to agree to let me belong?" he thought.						
9	Suddenly, he dashed home and soon returned with a bucket of						

The text is continued on the next page.

Cueing Systems

LINE #	Miscue	Grapho-phonically Similar I M F (word level)	Syntactically Acceptable Unacceptable (sentence level)	Semantic Change in Meaning (CM) No Change in Meaning (NCM) (sentence level)

The cueing system grid is continued on the next page.

FORM C

FORM C

Cueing Systems

Miscue	Grapho-phonically Similar I M F (word level)	Syntactically Acceptable Unacceptable (sentence level)	Semantic Change in Meaning (CM) No Change in Meaning (NCM) (sentence level)
L I N E #			

Summary

☐ Most, ☐ few, ☐ no   miscues were graphophonically similar to the word in the passage.

☐ Most, ☐ few, ☐ no   miscues were syntactically matched.

☐ Most, ☐ few, ☐ no   miscues maintained the author's meaning.

☐ The self-corrections demonstrate that the reader monitors the meaning.

	O	I	S	A	Rp	Rv
1 0	yellow paint, one of black, and several brushes. He began pounding					
1 1	on the clubhouse door.					
1 2	"I'm knocking one hundred times!" he shouted. "I don't know					
1 3	the secret word," he declared, "but I have something important to tell					
1 4	everyone! I'm the new boy," he explained. "Since the name of your club					
1 5	is *Tigers,* I thought you might want to paint your clubhouse					
1 6	yellow with black stripes!" All the kids thought this was a great idea					
1 7	and quickly invited Jack to belong!					

TOTALS

Number of miscues _____   Number of self-corrections _____

Fluency: Does the Reader . . . .

☐ read smoothly, accurately, in meaningful phrases?

☐ read word-by-word, choppy, plodding?

☐ use pitch, stress, and intonation to convey meaning of the text?

☐ repeat words and phrases because s/he is monitoring the meaning (self-correcting)?

☐ repeat words and phrases because s/he is trying to sound out words?

☐ use punctuation to divide the text into units of meaning?   ☐ ignore the punctuation?

Rating Scale: Circle One

4 = fluent reading / good pace   2 = choppy, plodding reading / slow pace

3 = fairly fluent / reasonable pace   1 = clearly labored, disfluent reading / very slow pace

Retelling

Story Elements	All	Some	None
Main Character(s)			
Time and Place			
Problem			
Plot Details in Sequence			
Turning Point			
Resolution			
Reader's Thumbnail Summary:			

Retelling Summary: ☐ many details, logical order ☐ some details, some order ☐ few details, disorder

Comprehension Questions and Possible Answers

____ (RIF) 1. Who is the main character in this story?   (Jack)

____ (PIT) 2. Why does Jack want to belong to the club?   (he is the new boy and wants to make new friends)

____ (CAR) 3. What do you know about the word **belong?**   (to be a member, to have a rightful place)
What does the word **belong** have to do with this story?   (Jack wants to get the kids to agree to let him belong to the club)

____ (RIF) 4. What did Jack dash home to get?   (bucket of yellow paint, one of black, and several brushes)

____ (PIT) 5. Why did Jack knock one hundred times on the clubhouse door?   (the sign said to do that; he has something important to tell the club members)

____ (CAR) 6. What do you know about the phrase **secret word?**   (clubs have a secret password, only members know the word)
What does the phrase **secret word** have to do with this story?   (Jack says he doesn't know the secret word)

____ (PIT) 7. What was Jack's clever idea?   (because the club's name is Tigers, Jack thought they might want to paint the clubhouse yellow with black stripes)

____ (EAS) 8. In your opinion did it take courage to do what Jack did? (yes, it's hard to be the new kid and try to make friends)
You think this because . . . (he wanted to belong so bad that he thought of a clever idea to get the kids to like him)

Reader Text Relationship (RTR)   From the Text ☐ adequate ☐ not adequate   From Head to Text ☐ adequate ☐ not adequate

Scoring Guide Summary

WORD RECOGNITION

Independent 1-2
Instructional 7-8
Frustration .... 15+

COMPREHENSION

Independent 0-1
Instructional 2
Frustration .... 4+

Emotional Status:

FORM C

Form C, Level 3

FORM C

Prior Knowledge/Prediction

□ Read the title and predict what the story is about.

Prior Knowledge
□ a lot
□ some
□ none

□ Read the first two sentences and add more to your prediction.

The Beloved Horse

	O	I	S	A	Rp	Rv
1	Jody was so worried that she had stayed in the barn all day					
2	to take care of her sick horse, Gabe. She thought his condition					
3	seemed to be growing worse. His breathing grew louder and harder.					
4	At nightfall, Jody brought a blanket from the house so she could sleep					
5	near her beloved animal. In the middle of the night the wind whipped around					
6	the barn, rattling windows, and the barn door shook as if it would break into					
7	splinters. She had been so exhausted that she slept through all the noise.					
8	When the dawn light poured through the windows, Jody stirred. Bits of					
9	straw stuck in her hair and onto her wrinkled clothes. Where was the sound of					

The text is continued on the next page.

Cueing Systems

Miscue	Grapho- phonically Similar I M F (word level)	Syntactically Acceptable Unacceptable (sentence level)	Semantic Change in Meaning (CM) No Change in Meaning (NCM) (sentence level)
L I N E #			

The cueing system grid is continued on the next page.

Cueing Systems

Miscue	Grapho-phonically Similar I M F (word level)	Syntactically Acceptable Unacceptable (sentence level)	Semantic Change in Meaning (CM) No Change in Meaning (NCM) (sentence level)
L I N E #			

Summary

- ☐ Most, ☐ few, ☐ no   miscues were graphophonically similar to the word in the passage.
- ☐ Most, ☐ few, ☐ no   miscues were syntactically matched.
- ☐ Most, ☐ few, ☐ no   miscues maintained the author's meaning.
- ☐ The self-corrections demonstrate that the reader monitors the meaning.

FORM C

		O	I	S	A	Rp	Rv
1 0	the sickly breathing? She sat up with a jolt! Then she saw Gabe, healthy and						
1 1	strong, standing by the open door. To her surprise it looked like he was saying,						
1 2	"Let's go for a run!"						

TOTALS

Number of miscues _____   Number of self-corrections _____

Fluency: Does the Reader . . .

- ☐ read smoothly, accurately, in meaningful phrases?
- ☐ read word-by-word, choppy, plodding?
- ☐ use pitch, stress, and intonation to convey meaning of the text?
- ☐ repeat words and phrases because s/he is monitoring the meaning (self-correcting)?
- ☐ repeat words and phrases because s/he is trying to sound out words?
- ☐ use punctuation to divide the text into units of meaning?   ☐ ignore the punctuation?

Rating Scale: Circle One

4 = fluent reading / good pace   2 = choppy, plodding reading / slow pace
3 = fairly fluent / reasonable pace   1 = clearly labored, disfluent reading / very slow pace

FORM C

Retelling

Retelling Summary: ☐ many details, logical order ☐ some details, some order ☐ few details, disorder

Note: Indicate any probing with a "P"

Story Elements	All	Some	None
Main Character(s)			
Time and Place			
Problem			
Plot Details in Sequence			
Turning Point			
Resolution			
Reader's Thumbnail Summary:			

Comprehension Questions and Possible Answers

___ (RIF) 1. Who is the main character in this story?   (Jody)

___ (RIF) 2. Where does this story take place?   (in a barn; in the country)

___ (PIT) 3. What is the problem in this story?   (Jody's horse is sick)

___ (CAR) 4. What do you know about the phrase *his condition seemed to be growing worse?*   (state of health; his health was poor)
What does the phrase *his condition seemed to be growing worse* have to do with this story? (his condition seemed to be growing worse; his breathing grew louder and harder)

___ (RIF) 5. Why did Jody take a blanket to the barn?   (so she could sleep near her sick horse)

___ (RIF) 6. Why did the windows rattle and the barn door shake?   (in the middle of the night the wind whipped around the barn)

___ (CAR) 7. What do you know about the word *dawn?*   (sunrise, start of the day)   What does the word *dawn* have to do with this story?   (the dawn light poured through the windows of the barn)

___ (EAS) 8. Do you think Jody's horse will be all right? You think this because the text said . . .   (yes, Gabe stood healthy and strong by the barn door; no, he just looks healthy and strong, he's still sick)

Reader Text Relationship (RTR)   From the Text   ☐ adequate ☐ not adequate   From Head to Text   ☐ adequate ☐ not adequate

Scoring Guide Summary

WORD RECOGNITION
  Independent 2
  Instructional 7-8
  Frustration .... 15+

COMPREHENSION
  Independent 0-1
  Instructional 2
  Frustration .... 4+

Emotional Status:

Form C, Level 4

Cueing Systems

Miscue	Grapho-phonically Similar I M F (word level)	Syntactically Acceptable Unacceptable (sentence level)	Semantic Change in Meaning (CM) No Change in Meaning (NCM) (sentence level)
L I N E #			

The cueing system grid is continued on the next page.

FORM C, LEVEL 5	Reader's Passages page 38

Prior Knowledge/Prediction

☐ Read the title and predict what the story is about.

Prior Knowledge
☐ a lot
☐ some
☐ none

☐ Read the first two sentences and add more to your prediction.

		O	I	S	A	Rp	Rv
	A Woman Race Car Driver						
1	"I want to be the fastest woman top fuel car driver in the world,"						
2	stated Shirley Muldowney. "I want to go 500 miles per hour!" In those						
3	days, top fuel cars were the fastest, the most powerful, and the most carefully						
4	built machines in the car racing sport.						
5	At last the day of Shirley's big race arrived. The engines roared and						
6	Shirley blasted forward just like she was the top challenger in the						
7	country! It wasn't long before the speedometer read 220 miles per hour,						
8	and as Shirley's determination kicked in, the car seemed to propel forward.						
9	Her mind raced as she whizzed around the track. "I can accomplish						

The text is continued on the next page.

Cueing Systems

Miscue	Grapho-phonically Similar I M F (word level)	Syntactically Acceptable Unacceptable (sentence level)	Semantic Change in Meaning (CM) No Change in Meaning (NCM) (sentence level)
L I N E #			

Summary

□ Most, □ few, □ no   miscues were graphophonically similar to the word in the passage.

□ Most, □ few, □ no   miscues were syntactically matched.

□ Most, □ few, □ no   miscues maintained the author's meaning.

□ The self-corrections demonstrate that the reader monitors the meaning.

Form C, Level 5

	O	I	S	A	Rp	Rv
10	anything I set out to do!" At 230 miles per hour her confidence and					
11	her nerves of steel began to push the car faster.					
12	Then, at 242 miles per hour, she established a record speed that no					
13	other top fuel driver had reached. Seconds later, her car rushed over the					
14	victory line! "Finally," she thought as she pulled into Victory Lane, "now people					
15	will think of me as a top race car driver and not just as a woman who					
16	drives a race car!"					

TOTALS

Number of miscues _____   Number of self-corrections _____

Fluency: Does the Reader . . . .

□ read smoothly, accurately, in meaningful phrases?

□ read word-by-word, choppy, plodding?

□ use pitch, stress, and intonation to convey meaning of the text?

□ repeat words and phrases because s/he is monitoring the meaning (self-correcting)?

□ repeat words and phrases because s/he is trying to sound out words?

□ use punctuation to divide the text into units of meaning?   □ ignore the punctuation?

Rating Scale: Circle One

4 = fluent reading / good pace   2 = choppy, plodding reading / slow pace

3 = fairly fluent / reasonable pace   1 = clearly labored, disfluent reading / very slow pace

Retelling

Note: Indicate any probing with a "P"

Story Elements	All	Some	None
Main Character(s)			
Time and Place			
Problem			
Plot Details in Sequence			
Turning Point			
Resolution			
Reader's Thumbnail Summary:			

Retelling Summary: ☐ many details, logical order ☐ some details, some order ☐ few details, disorder

Scoring Guide Summary

WORD RECOGNITION

Independent 2
Instructional 9-10
Frustration .... 19+

COMPREHENSION

Independent 0-1
Instructional 2
Frustration ...... 4+

Emotional Status:

Comprehension Questions and Possible Answers

_____ (RIF) 1. Who is the main character in this story?   (Shirley Muldowney)

_____ (RIF) 2. What is Shirley's goal?   (she wants to be the fastest woman driver in the world; to go 500 miles per hour)

_____ (PIT) 3. What were top fuel cars like?   (fastest, most powerful, and among the most carefully built machines)

_____ (CAR) 4. What do you know about the phrase **top challenger?**   (someone who competes against someone else and is the best, the top one)   What does the phrase **top challenger** have to do with the story?   (Shirley started the race like she was the top challenger in the whole country)

_____ (CAR) 5. What do you know about the word **speedometer?**   (it is the instrument that measures the speed of a car, how fast it is going)   What does **speedometer** have to do with the story?   (the speedometer reached 242 miles per hour)

_____ (PIT) 6. What happened when Shirley's determination kicked in?   (the car seemed to propel forward)

_____ (EAS) 7. In your opinion, what was so unusual about Shirley being a top fuel driver?   (in the story, she said, "Finally, now people will think of me as a top race car driver and not just as a woman who drives a race car!")

_____ (PIT) 8. Why won't people think of her "just as a woman who drives a race car"?   (she wins races; she has confidence and nerves of steel, she is a top fuel driver)

Reader Text Relationship (RTR)   From the Text ☐ adequate ☐ not adequate   From Head to Text ☐ adequate ☐ not adequate

Form C, Level 5

FORM C

FORM C, LEVEL 6 — Reader's Passages page 39

Prior Knowledge/Prediction

☐ Read the title and predict what the story is about.

☐ Read the first two sentences and add more to your prediction.

Prior Knowledge

☐ a lot
☐ some
☐ none

	Open Heart Surgery	O	I	S	A	Rp	Rv
1	It was a hot and humid July day in Chicago in 1893. Tempers flared, and a						
2	fight in a saloon ended in a stabbing. "James Cornish has been stabbed in the						
3	chest!" shouted one horrified bystander. "Rush him to Provident Hospital,						
4	immediately!"						
5	Cornish arrived at the hospital with a one-inch knife wound dangerously						
6	near his heart. Dr. Daniel Hale Williams was called in to operate. After an						
7	examination, Williams found that the knife had indeed cut the heart as well as the						
8	sac around the heart, so he knew he had to work swiftly. In those days chest						
9	surgery was rarely attempted because blood transfusions and antibiotics were						

The text is continued on the next page.

Cueing Systems

LINE #	Miscue	Grapho-phonically Similar I M F (word level)	Syntactically Acceptable Unacceptable (sentence level)	Semantic Change in Meaning (CM) No Change in Meaning (NCM) (sentence level)

The cueing system grid is continued on the next page.

Cueing Systems

Miscue	Grapho-phonically Similar I M F (word level)	Syntactically Acceptable Unacceptable (sentence level)	Semantic Change in Meaning (CM) No Change in Meaning (NCM) (sentence level)
LINE #			

Summary

☐ Most, ☐ few, ☐ no   miscues were graphophonically similar to the word in the passage.

☐ Most, ☐ few, ☐ no   miscues were syntactically matched.

☐ Most, ☐ few, ☐ no   miscues maintained the author's meaning.

☐ The self-corrections demonstrate that the reader monitors the meaning.

	O	I	S	A	Rp	Rv
1 0	unknown. Open heart surgery was an invitation to death. "Would infection set in					
1 1	and kill the patient? Should I risk my reputation?" Williams must have been					
1 2	thinking. The atmosphere in the operating room was tense as six other physicians					
1 3	prepared to observe this daring surgery.					
1 4	Fifty-one days after Cornish came to the hospital a dying man, he was					
1 5	discharged a well man! In fact, he lived for fifty years after his surgery and even					
1 6	outlived Dr. Daniel Hale Williams by twelve years.					

TOTALS

Number of miscues _____   Number of self-corrections _____

Fluency: Does the Reader . . .

☐ read smoothly, accurately, in meaningful phrases?

☐ read word-by-word, choppy, plodding?

☐ use pitch, stress, and intonation to convey meaning of the text?

☐ repeat words and phrases because s/he is monitoring the meaning (self-correcting)?

☐ repeat words and phrases because s/he is trying to sound out words?

☐ use punctuation to divide the text into units of meaning?   ☐ ignore the punctuation?

Rating Scale: Circle One

4 = fluent reading / good pace   2 = choppy, plodding reading / slow pace

3 = fairly fluent / reasonable pace   1 = clearly labored, disfluent reading / very slow pace

FORM C

FORM C

Retelling

Note: Indicate any probing with a "P"

Story Elements	All	Some	None
Main Character(s)			
Time and Place			
Problem			
Plot Details in Sequence			
Turning Point			
Resolution			
Reader's Thumbnail Summary:			

Retelling Summary: ☐ many details, logical order ☐ some details, some order ☐ few details, disorder

Comprehension Questions and Possible Answers

____ (RIF) 1. Where does this story take place? (Chicago)

____ (RIF) 2. When did it take place? (1893)

____ (PIT) 3. What is the problem in this story? (James Cornish has been stabbed in the chest)

____ (PIT) 4. What did Dr. Williams find out about the wound? (it was a one-inch knife wound in his chest, dangerously near his heart; it had cut the heart and the sac around the heart)

____ (PIT) 5. Why was chest surgery rarely attempted? (in those days blood transfusions and antibiotics were unknown; it was an invitation to death)

____ (EAS) 6. In your opinion, how do you think Dr. Williams felt about doing the first heart surgery? (he was probably very worried, scared, uncertain, not sure if he should do it) You think this because . . . (he thought, "Should I risk my reputation?")

____ (CAR) 7. What do you know about the sentence *Should I risk my reputation?* (other people have an opinion about you, bad or good; sometimes we worry what other people think about what we do) What does *Should I risk my reputation?* have to do with this story? (Dr. Williams worried about risking his reputation. He was a successful doctor, if he failed, would other people say he wasn't a good doctor any more?)

____ (PIT) 8. What happened to James Cornish? (he got well; he was discharged fifty-one days after the surgery)

Reader Text Relationship (RTR)   From the Text ☐ adequate ☐ not adequate   From Head to Text ☐ adequate ☐ not adequate

Form C, Level 6

FORM C, LEVEL 7 — Reader's Passages page 40

Prior Knowledge/Prediction

☐ Read the title and predict what the story is about.

☐ Read the first two sentences and add more to your prediction.

Prior Knowledge

☐ a lot
☐ some
☐ none

	Broken Friendship	O	I	S	A	Rp	Rv
1	Jim was sixteen years old, and he thought more of his older brother Kevin than						
2	anyone else. In Jim's opinion, Kevin was the greatest guy in the entire world. He was						
3	certain it would be a terrific summer because he believed it would be an opportunity for						
4	a genuine brother-to-brother reunion. He had informed all his friends that he was going						
5	to spend the total summer with Kevin.						
6	When Kevin arrived home from his first year at college, he was a different person.						
7	He had new friends, attitudes, and interests that gave Jim an uneasy feeling. Kevin						
8	wasn't interested in talking to Jim about old times. When Jim tried to talk to him, Kevin						
9	seemed disinterested, making Jim feel like he was talking to a brick wall. When the						
10	phone rang, Kevin rushed to answer it, then strolled down the hallway, closing the door						

The text is continued on the next page.

Cueing Systems

LINE #	Miscue	Grapho-phonically Similar I M F (word level)	Syntactically Acceptable Unacceptable (sentence level)	Semantic Change in Meaning (CM) No Change in Meaning (NCM) (sentence level)

The cueing system grid is continued on the next page.

FORM C

FORM C

	O	S	I	A	Rp	Rv
1 1	behind him. It wasn't long before Jim felt rejected like an outcast being shoved away.					
1 2	Before Kevin went away, they had a tight relationship. As far back as Jim could					
1 3	remember, they drove the long fifteen miles from the farm to school together. When					
1 4	Jim was a freshman in high school, Kevin was a senior, and they attended every sport					
1 5	event as a pair—no one could separate them. They told each other jokes and laughed					
1 6	just like super buddies. Jim could still feel Kevin's brotherly smack on his shoulder that					
1 7	always went with these words, "Well, okay, Little Brother, as partners we make up a					
1 8	superior team!" Now, Jim felt like a side liner. Was he going to be an outsider forever?					

TOTALS

Number of miscues _____ Number of self-corrections _____

Cueing Systems

LINE #	Miscue	Grapho-phonically Similar I M F (word level)	Syntactically Acceptable Unacceptable (sentence level)	Semantic Change in Meaning (CM) No Change in Meaning (NCM) (sentence level)

Summary

☐ Most, ☐ few, ☐ no   miscues were graphophonically similar to the word in the passage.

☐ Most, ☐ few, ☐ no   miscues were syntactically matched.

☐ Most, ☐ few, ☐ no   miscues maintained the author's meaning.

☐ The self-corrections demonstrate that the reader monitors the meaning.

Form C, Level 7

Fluency: Does the Reader . . .

☐ read smoothly, accurately, in meaningful phrases?

☐ read word-by-word, choppy, plodding?

☐ use pitch, stress, and intonation to convey meaning of the text?

☐ repeat words and phrases because s/he is monitoring the meaning (self-correcting)?

☐ repeat words and phrases because s/he is trying to sound out words?

☐ use punctuation to divide the text into units of meaning?   ☐ ignore the punctuation?

Rating Scale: Circle One

4 = fluent reading / good pace   2 = choppy, plodding reading / slow pace

3 = fairly fluent / reasonable pace   1 = clearly labored, disfluent reading / very slow pace

Retelling

Note: Indicate any probing with a "P"

Story Elements	All	Some	None
Main Character(s)			
Time and Place			
Problem			
Plot Details in Sequence			
Turning Point			
Resolution			
Reader's Thumbnail Summary:			

Retelling Summary: ☐ many details, logical order ☐ some details, some order ☐ few details, disorder

Scoring Guide Summary

WORD RECOGNITION
Independent 2-3
Instructional 12
Frustration ...... 24+

COMPREHENSION
Independent 0-1
Instructional 2
Frustration ...... 4+

Emotional Status:

Form C, Level 7

FORM C

Comprehension Questions and Possible Answers

_____ (RIF) 1. Who are the two characters in this story?   (Jim and his brother Kevin)

_____ (RIF) 2. Where does this story take place?   (at home on the farm)

_____ (PIT) 3. What is the problem in this story?   (Jim feels left out because his college-age brother doesn't pay attention to him)

_____ (CAR) 4. What do you know about the phrase *rejected like an outcast?*   (feeling sad or low like someone thrown out of the group) What does *rejected like an outcast* have to do with this story?   (Jim felt like Kevin had turned away from him; Kevin wasn't paying any attention to him)

_____ (CAR) 5. What do you know about the phrase *tight relationship?*   (true friends or buddies) What does the phrase *tight relationship* have to do with this story?   (before Kevin went to college the brothers had a tight relationship)

_____ (EAS) 6. In your opinion, why was Kevin acting so unfriendly toward Jim?   (he wanted to be a big college boy and Jim reminded him of his high school days) You think this because the text said . . .   (he had new friends, attitudes, and interests; he shut his door when talking on the phone)

_____ (PIT) 7. Can you tell how Jim felt?   (rejected, like a side liner, like talking to a brick wall, like an outsider)

_____ (PIT) 8. What tells you that Jim and Kevin grew up in a rural, country setting?   (as far back as Jim could remember they drove the long fifteen miles from the farm to school together)

Reader Text Relationship (RTR)   From the Text ☐ adequate ☐ not adequate   From Head to Text ☐ adequate ☐ not adequate

FORM C

FORM C, LEVEL 8 — Reader's Passages page 41

Prior Knowledge/Prediction

☐ Read the title and predict what the story is about.

☐ Read the first two sentences and add more to your prediction.

Prior Knowledge

☐ a lot
☐ some
☐ none

	The Science Project	O	I	S	A	Rp	Rv
1	Janice Cornwell was a top-notch student, so when the eighth grade science						
2	projects were assigned, all the other students in the class glowered at Janice because						
3	they knew her grade would be an A+. Jason Crawford often heckled, "Janice is						
4	going to get an A+++!"						
5	Janice wanted to do research on nutrition. She planned to purchase three						
6	guinea pigs and over a two-month period prepare meals containing different						
7	amounts of protein. One guinea pig would get a diet with protein-rich foods, another						
8	got the same food plus protein supplements, and the last guinea pig would get minimal						
9	amounts of protein. She named the three laboratory animals after famous scholars:						
10	Plato, Socrates, and Da Vinci. "I'll gather data by observing the quality of their fur and						
11	the energy level of each research guinea pig. The procedure is sound and everything is						
12	scientifically factual!"						
13	After two weeks something happened that didn't figure on the data chart.						
14	Plato, whose coat was getting thick and fluffy, liked to be petted; Socrates, whose						

The text is continued on the next page.

Cueing Systems

LINE #	Miscue	Grapho-phonically Similar I M F (word level)	Syntactically Acceptable Unacceptable (sentence level)	Semantic Change in Meaning (CM) No Change in Meaning (NCM) (sentence level)

The cueing system grid is continued on the next page.

Cueing Systems

L I N E #	Miscue	Grapho-phonically Similar I M F (word level)	Syntactically Acceptable Unacceptable (sentence level)	Semantic Change in Meaning (CM) No Change in Meaning (NCM) (sentence level)

Summary

☐ Most, ☐ few, ☐ no   miscues were graphophonically similar to the word in the passage.

☐ Most, ☐ few, ☐ no   miscues were syntactically matched.

☐ Most, ☐ few, ☐ no   miscues maintained the author's meaning.

☐ The self-corrections demonstrate that the reader monitors the meaning.

Form C, Level 8

	O	I	S	A	Rp	Rv
15	coat was less thick and less fluffy, liked to cuddle; and poor little Da Vinci, whose					
16	coat was getting scraggly, liked his stomach scratched. Unexpectedly, this scientific					
17	experiment was turning from a data-gathering event into a labor of love.					
18	On the day the projects were due, students came to school carrying cages,					
19	large charts, and final reports. The science teacher told everyone to set their projects					
20	on the counters in alphabetical order. Janice refused to set her cage on the					
21	counter. She wasn't about to place it near Jason Crawford's boa constrictor					
22	experiment. "I don't have any data and I don't have a final report!" she announced.					
23	Stunned, everyone turned toward Janice. "How can I experiment on my pets?"					

TOTALS

Number of miscues _____   Number of self-corrections _____

Fluency: Does the Reader . . .

☐ read smoothly, accurately, in meaningful phrases?

☐ read word-by-word, choppy, plodding?

☐ use pitch, stress, and intonation to convey meaning of the text?

☐ repeat words and phrases because s/he is monitoring the meaning (self-correcting)?

☐ repeat words and phrases because s/he is trying to sound out words?

☐ use punctuation to divide the text into units of meaning?   ☐ ignore the punctuation?

Rating Scale: Circle One
4 = fluent reading / good pace   2 = choppy, plodding reading / slow pace
3 = fairly fluent / reasonable pace   1 = clearly labored, disfluent reading / very slow pace

FORM C

FORM C

Story Elements	All	Some	None
Main Character(s)			
Time and Place			
Problem			
Plot Details in Sequence			
Turning Point			
Resolution			
Reader's Thumbnail Summary:			

Scoring Guide Summary

WORD RECOGNITION
Independent 3
Instructional 14
Frustration .... 29+

COMPREHENSION
Independent 0-1
Instructional 2
Frustration .... 4+

Emotional Status:

Form C, Level 8

Retelling

Retelling Summary: ☐ many details, logical order ☐ some details, some order ☐ few details, disorder

Comprehension Questions and Possible Answers

_____ (RIF) 1. Who is the main character in this story? (Janice Cornwell)

_____ (RIF) 2. Where does this story take place? (at school and at Janice's home)

_____ (PIT) 3. What is the problem in this story? (Janice grows attached to the animals in her science experiment and can't mistreat them; she gives up her A+ grade because she is attached to her pets)

_____ (PIT) 4. What was the content of Janice's science project? (a study of nutrition, specifically the effects of a protein-rich diet)

_____ (CAR) 5. What do you know about the phrase **the procedure was sound?** (the manner in which something is done is reliable) What does the phrase **the procedure was sound** have to do with this story? (it said the procedure she planned to use to conduct her science experiment was sound)

_____ (EAS) 6. In your opinion, how did Janice feel about the animals? (she grew very attached, fond of them) You think this because . . . (it said she didn't get any data which means she fed them all the same diet; because there was no data, she didn't have a final report)

_____ (PIT) 7. Why wouldn't Janice put the guinea pigs next to Jason Crawford's boa? (boas eat rodents; she didn't want to risk hurting her pets)

_____ (EAS) 8. Do you think Janice planned not to complete her science project? You think this because . . . (no, it said unexpectedly this science experiment turned from a data-gathering experiment into a labor of love)

Reader Text Relationship (RTR) From the Text ☐ adequate ☐ not adequate From Head to Text ☐ adequate ☐ not adequate

FORM C, LEVEL 9 — Reader's Passages page 42

Prior Knowledge/Prediction

☐ Read the title and predict what the story is about.

☐ Read the first two sentences and add more to your prediction.

Prior Knowledge

☐ a lot
☐ some
☐ none

	The Urban Garden	O	I	S	A	Rp	Rv
1	"Once this corner was the neighborhood garbage dump!" Malinda Futrell said						
2	as she briskly swung open the chain-link gate leading to an urban garden situated on the						
3	corner of Sixth Street and Avenue B in New York City. To a passerby this luscious corner						
4	of green, thriving amid city air laden with exhaust fumes, cement dust, and general						
5	urban pollution, is an unexpected sight. Yet the sunlight that squeezes between the						
6	towering apartment buildings casts the gift of light on flourishing plots of						
7	vegetables, flowers, and fruit. Here, 105 enthusiastic neighborhood urban gardeners						
8	cultivate the soil and create a touch of rural life amid the noise and bustle of city life.						
9	Several years ago, Joanee Freedom, now one of the neighborhood's avid						
10	gardeners, noticed a tomato plant growing amid the mounds of trash. "How could a						
11	small plant survive those wretched conditions?" she wondered. "I was so intrigued that						
12	I trudged through the rubbish, brushed the debris from the remarkable specimen, and						
13	built a small protective brick wall around it! Then within a short period of time,						
14	another neighbor noticed the extraordinary plant. The next thing I knew, he'd cleared						

The text is continued on the next page.

Cueing Systems

LINE #	Miscue	Grapho-phonically Similar I M F (word level)	Syntactically Acceptable Unacceptable (sentence level)	Semantic Change in Meaning (CM) No Change in Meaning (NCM) (sentence level)

The cueing system grid is continued on the next page.

FORM C

FORM C

	O	I	S	A	Rp	Rv
1 5	a small plot and planted his own garden."					
1 6	The small garden looked conspicuous in contrast to the surrounding litter, and					
1 7	it was this little expression of individuality that launched Malinda Futrell into a plan					
1 8	that eventually grew into the Sixth Street and Avenue B Garden Project. A native of					
1 9	North Carolina, Malinda had moved to the city only to find herself yearning for the land					
2 0	she'd left behind. "What was I doing here with all this noise and cement and no soil to					
2 1	dig my hands into?" she pined. Within a matter of days after seeing the small garden,					
2 2	Malinda secured permission from the city government to create a neighborhood Victory					
2 3	Garden. She promptly began clearing the rubble and cultivating the soil. Now, as a					
2 4	city dweller hustles past the corner of Sixth Street and Avenue B, plots of vegetables,					
2 5	meadows of wildflowers, and corners of fragrant herbs fill the sight and other senses.					
	TOTALS _____					

Number of miscues _____   Number of self-corrections _____

Cueing Systems

L I N E #	Miscue	Grapho-phonically Similar I M F (word level)	Syntactically Acceptable Unacceptable (sentence level)	Semantic Change in Meaning (CM) No Change in Meaning (NCM) (sentence level)

Summary

☐ Most, ☐ few, ☐ no   miscues were graphophonically similar to the word in the passage.

☐ Most, ☐ few, ☐ no   miscues were syntactically matched.

☐ Most, ☐ few, ☐ no   miscues maintained the author's meaning.

☐ The self-corrections demonstrate that the reader monitors the meaning.

Form C, Level 9

Fluency: Does the Reader . . .

☐ read smoothly, accurately, in meaningful phrases?

☐ read word-by-word, choppy, plodding?

☐ use pitch, stress, and intonation to convey meaning of the text?

☐ repeat words and phrases because s/he is monitoring the meaning (self-correcting)?

☐ repeat words and phrases because s/he is trying to sound out words?

☐ use punctuation to divide the text into units of meaning?   ☐ ignore the punctuation?

Rating Scale: Circle One
4 = fluent reading / good pace   2 = choppy, plodding reading / slow pace
3 = fairly fluent / reasonable pace   1 = clearly labored, disfluent reading / very slow pace

Retelling

Note: Indicate any probing with a "P"

Story Elements	All	Some	None
Main Character(s)			
Time and Place			
Problem			
Plot Details in Sequence			
Turning Point			
Resolution			
Reader's Thumbnail Summary:			

Retelling Summary: ☐ many details, logical order ☐ some details, some order ☐ few details, disorder

Comprehension Questions and Possible Answers

_____ (RIF) 1. Where does this story take place? (Sixth Street and Avenue B in New York City)

_____ (RIF) 2. What did Joanee Freedom notice? (a tomato plant growing amid the mounds of trash)

_____ (CAR) 3. What do you know about the word **debris?** (the remnants of something broken to pieces) What does the word **debris** have to do with this story? (she brushed away the debris from the remarkable specimen)

_____ (PIT) 4. What did another neighbor do? (he saw the tomato plant cleared a small plot, and planted his own garden)

_____ (PIT) 5. What did Malinda Futrell do? (she secured permission from the city government to create a neighborhood Victory Garden)

_____ (EAS) 6. In your opinion was Malinda Futrell truly committed to the garden? You think this because . . . (yes, she yearned for her rural home in North Carolina where she could dig in the soil with her hands; she was feeling that New York had noise and cement and not much soil)

_____ (CAR) 7. What do you know about the phrase **cultivating the soil?** (to prepare the land for crops) What does the phrase **cultivating the soil** have to do with this story? (she began cultivating the soil, preparing it for the garden)

_____ (RIF) 8. Name two plants a city dweller sees when hustling by the garden. (vegetables, wildflowers, herbs)

Reader Text Relationship (RTR)   From the Text ☐ adequate ☐ not adequate   From Head to Text ☐ adequate ☐ not adequate

Scoring Guide Summary

WORD RECOGNITION

Independent..... 3-4
Instructional 17
Frustration.......34+

COMPREHENSION

Independent 0-1
Instructional 2
Frustration.......4+

Emotional Status:

Form C, Level 9

FORM C

197

◪ FORM S ◪

Expository Science Passages, One—Nine

FORM S

FORM S, LEVEL 1 — Reader's Passages page 44

Prior Knowledge/Prediction

☐ Read the title and predict what the text is about.

Prior Knowledge
- ☐ a lot
- ☐ some
- ☐ none

☐ Read the first two sentences and add more to your prediction.

The Five Senses

	O I S A Rp Rv
1	We have five senses. They help us learn. We can
2	learn about color if we can see. We can hear our name
3	called out if we can hear. We can feel a soft, warm
4	kitten if we can touch it with our hands. We can smell
5	good things if we can smell. We can taste the salt in the
6	sea if we can taste. Our lives would change if we did not
7	have all five senses. It would be a lot harder to learn.

TOTALS

Number of miscues _____   Number of self-corrections _____

Cueing Systems

L I N E #	Miscue	Grapho-phonically Similar I M F (word level)	Syntactically Acceptable Unacceptable (sentence level)	Semantic Change in Meaning (CM) No Change in Meaning (NCM) (sentence level)

Summary

☐ Most, ☐ few, ☐ no   miscues were graphophonically similar to the word in the passage.

☐ Most, ☐ few, ☐ no   miscues were syntactically matched.

☐ Most, ☐ few, ☐ no   miscues maintained the author's meaning.

☐ The self-corrections demonstrate that the reader monitors the meaning.

Note: Indicate any probing with a "P"

Expository Elements	All	Some	None
Description			
Collection			
Causation			
Problem / Solution			
Comparison			

Reader's Thumbnail Summary:

Scoring Guide Summary

WORD RECOGNITION
Independent 0-1
Instructional 3-4
Frustration ...... 8+

COMPREHENSION
Independent 0
Instructional 1-2
Frustration ...... 3+

Emotional Status:

Retelling

Fluency: Does the Reader . . .

□ read smoothly, accurately, in meaningful phrases?

□ read word-by-word, choppy, plodding?

□ use pitch, stress, and intonation to convey meaning of the text?

□ repeat words and phrases because s/he is monitoring the meaning (self-correcting)?

□ repeat words and phrases because s/he is trying to sound out words?

□ use punctuation to divide the text into units of meaning?

□ ignore the punctuation?

Rating Scale: Circle One
4 = fluent reading / good pace
3 = fairly fluent / reasonable pace
2 = choppy, plodding reading / slow pace
1 = clearly labored, disfluent reading / very slow pace

Retelling Summary: □ many details, logical order □ some details, some order □ few details, disorder

Comprehension Questions and Possible Answers

_____ (RIF)   1. How many senses do we have?   (five)

_____ (CAR)   2. What do you know about the phrase **the five senses?**   (the organs in the body that receive outside stimulus: sight, hearing, touch, smell, taste)   What does the phrase **the five senses** have to do with this text?   (it said we have five senses; they help us learn)

_____ (RIF)   3. What did the text say we can learn about when we see?   (color)

_____ (PIT)   4. Why can we hear our name called out?   (we have the sense of hearing, we can hear with our ears and eardrums)

_____ (RIF)   5. What sense helps us know how soft a kitten feels?   (the sense of touch, we touch it with our hands)

_____ (EAS)   6. In your opinion, what would life be like without all five senses?   (not easy, difficult, different) You think this because . . .   (it said our lives would change, it would be harder to learn)

Reader Text Relationship (RTR)   From the Text   □ adequate □ not adequate   From Head to Text   □ adequate □ not adequate

FORM S

FORM S

FORM S, LEVEL 2 — Reader's Passages page 45

Prior Knowledge/Prediction

☐ Read the title and predict what the text is about.

☐ Read the first two sentences and add more to your prediction.

Prior Knowledge

☐ a lot
☐ some
☐ none

	Hearing Sounds	O	I	S	A	Rp	Rv
1	Sounds can be made in many ways. Sound is made if						
2	someone hits a drum or shakes a paper.						
3	We say something vibrates when it moves back and forth.						
4	As something vibrates back and forth, it makes the air around it						
5	move. The moving air is called a sound wave. Sound waves						
6	move through the air. Ears can hear sound waves.						
7	A bell begins to vibrate if someone hits the bell. The air						
8	around the bell vibrates, too. The sound waves go through						
9	the air. Small parts inside the ears begin to vibrate. The ears						

The text is continued on the next page.

Cueing Systems

LINE #	Miscue	Grapho-phonically Similar I M F (word level)	Syntactically Acceptable Unacceptable (sentence level)	Semantic Change in Meaning (CM) No Change in Meaning (NCM) (sentence level)

The cueing system grid is continued on the next page.

Cueing Systems

	Miscue	Grapho-phonically Similar I M F (word level)	Syntactically Acceptable Unacceptable (sentence level)	Semantic Change in Meaning (CM) No Change in Meaning (NCM) (sentence level)
L I N E #				

Summary

☐ Most, ☐ few, ☐ no   miscues were graphophonically similar to the word in the passage.

☐ Most, ☐ few, ☐ no   miscues were syntactically matched.

☐ Most, ☐ few, ☐ no   miscues maintained the author's meaning.

☐ The self-corrections demonstrate that the reader monitors the meaning.

	O	I	S	A	Rp	Rv
1 0	hear the sound. Ears can hear soft or loud sounds. Ears can					
1 1	hear high or low sounds, and they can hear fuzzy or clear sounds.					

TOTALS

Number of miscues _____   Number of self-corrections _____

Fluency: Does the Reader . . .

☐ read smoothly, accurately, in meaningful phrases?

☐ read word-by-word, choppy, plodding?

☐ use pitch, stress, and intonation to convey meaning of the text?

☐ repeat words and phrases because s/he is monitoring the meaning (self-correcting)?

☐ repeat words and phrases because s/he is trying to sound out words?

☐ use punctuation to divide the text into units of meaning?   ☐ ignore the punctuation?

Rating Scale: Circle One

4 = fluent reading / good pace   2 = choppy, plodding reading / slow pace

3 = fairly fluent / reasonable pace   1 = clearly labored, disfluent reading / very slow pace

FORM S

FORM S

Note: Indicate any probing with a "P"

Expository Elements	All	Some	None
Description			
Collection			
Causation			
Problem / Solution			
Comparison			

Reader's Thumbnail Summary:

Scoring Guide Summary

WORD RECOGNITION
Independent......1
Instructional......6
Frustration........12+

COMPREHENSION
Independent......0
Instructional......1-2
Frustration........3+

Emotional Status:

Form S, Level 2

Retelling

Retelling Summary: □ many details, logical order □ some details, some order □ few details, disorder

Comprehension Questions and Possible Answers

____(RIF) 1. What part of the body detects sounds?   (the ears hear them)

____(CAR) 2. What do you know about the phrase *something vibrates?*   (it moves back and forth like a tuning fork or a bell)
What does the phrase *something vibrates* have to do with this text?   (it said something vibrates when it moves back and forth)

____(PIT) 3. What happens to the air when something vibrates?   (as the object moves back and forth the air around it moves)

____(CAR) 4. What do you know about the phrase *sound wave?*   (when something vibrates like a tuning fork or a bell, it causes the air around it to move in a wave, the wave makes sound)   What does the phrase *sound wave* have to do with this text?   (it said moving air caused from a vibration is a sound wave)

____(PIT) 5. How can a bell make a sound wave?   (someone hits it, it vibrates, the air around it moves and makes a sound wave go through the air)

____(EAS) 6. Why do you think ears can hear different kinds of sounds?   (small parts inside the ear vibrate and pick up different sound waves)   You think this because . . . (it said the ear can hear sounds that are soft and loud, high and low, fuzzy and clear)

Reader Text Relationship (RTR)   From the Text   □ adequate □ not adequate   From Head to Text   □ adequate □ not adequate

Cueing Systems

Miscue	Grapho-phonically Similar I M F (word level)	Syntactically Acceptable Unacceptable (sentence level)	Semantic Change in Meaning (CM) No Change in Meaning (NCM) (sentence level)
L I N E #			

The cueing system grid is continued on the next page.

FORM S, LEVEL 3   Reader's Passages page 46

Prior Knowledge/Prediction

☐ Read the title and predict what the text is about.

Prior Knowledge
☐ a lot
☐ some
☐ none

☐ Read the first two sentences and add more to your prediction.

Changing Matter

	O	I	S	A	Rp	Rv
1	We call an object matter if it takes up space. All things					
2	around you are called matter because they have size, shape, and					
3	weight. Houses, school desks, flowers, and kangaroos are all					
4	matter. People are matter, too.					
5	A rock, milk, and air are matter. Each one is different even					
6	though each is matter. Each has its own size, shape, and weight.					
7	A rock is a solid. Milk is a liquid. Air is a gas. Matter can take					
8	different forms. It can be a solid, a liquid, or a gas.					
9	Matter can change from one form to another. Ice is a solid.					

The text is continued on the next page.

FORM S

		O	I	S	A	Rp	Rv
1 0	Ice can become a liquid called water if it is heated. Water can						
1 1	become a gas called steam if it is heated. Steam can become a						
1 2	liquid if it is cooled. Water can become a solid called ice if it is						
1 3	cooled.						

TOTALS

Number of miscues _____   Number of self-corrections _____

Fluency: Does the Reader . . .

☐ read smoothly, accurately, in meaningful phrases?

☐ read word-by-word, choppy, plodding?

☐ use pitch, stress, and intonation to convey meaning of the text?

☐ repeat words and phrases because s/he is monitoring the meaning (self-correcting)?

☐ repeat words and phrases because s/he is trying to sound out words?

☐ use punctuation to divide the text into units of meaning?   ☐ ignore the punctuation?

Rating Scale: Circle One

4 = fluent reading / good pace   2 = choppy, plodding reading / slow pace
3 = fairly fluent / reasonable pace   1 = clearly labored, disfluent reading / very slow pace

Cueing Systems

LINE #	Miscue	Graphophonically Similar I M F (word level)	Syntactically Acceptable Unacceptable (sentence level)	Semantic Change in Meaning (CM) No Change in Meaning (NCM) (sentence level)

Summary

☐ Most, ☐ few, ☐ no   miscues were graphophonically similar to the word in the passage.

☐ Most, ☐ few, ☐ no   miscues were syntactically matched.

☐ Most, ☐ few, ☐ no   miscues maintained the author's meaning.

☐ The self-corrections demonstrate that the reader monitors the meaning.

Form S, Level 3

Note: Indicate any probing with a "P"

Expository Elements	All	Some	None
Description			
Collection			
Causation			
Problem / Solution			
Comparison			
Reader's Thumbnail Summary:			

Scoring Guide Summary

WORD RECOGNITION
Independent......1-2
Instructional......7
Frustration......14+

COMPREHENSION
Independent......0-1
Instructional......2
Frustration......4+

Emotional Status:

Retelling

Retelling Summary: ☐ many details, logical order ☐ some details, some order ☐ few details, disorder

Comprehension Questions and Possible Answers

____ (RIF) 1. Is matter set, or can it change? (matter can change to a solid, a liquid, or a gas)

____ (PIT) 2. What makes something have matter? (it takes up space; it has size, shape, and weight)

____ (RIF) 3. Name three things in the text that are described as matter. (house, school desk, flower, kangaroo, people)

____ (PIT) 4. How are a rock, milk, and air different? (even though they are all matter they each have their own size, shape, and weight; one is a solid, one a liquid, one a gas)

____ (RIF) 5. Name three forms of matter. (solid, liquid, gas)

____ (CAR) 6. What do you know about the phrase *can change from one form to the other?* (something can change its size, shape, and weight like ice can change to water) What does the phrase *can change from one form to the other* have to do with this text? (it said that matter can change from one form to another like ice to water to steam . . .)

____ (PIT) 7. What happens to ice when it changes form? (if it is heated, it becomes a liquid called water)

____ (EAS) 8. What do you think causes matter to change form? (heat or cold, maybe like weather conditions) You think this because . . . (it said ice becomes water when heated, water becomes gas when heated, steam becomes liquid when cooled, water becomes solid when cooled)

Reader Text Relationship (RTR)   From the Text   ☐ adequate ☐ not adequate   From Head to Text   ☐ adequate ☐ not adequate

FORM S

Form S, Level 3

FORM S

Cueing Systems

# LINE	Miscue	Grapho-phonically Similar I M F (word level)	Syntactically Acceptable Unacceptable (sentence level)	Semantic Change in Meaning (CM) No Change in Meaning (NCM) (sentence level)

The cueing system grid is continued on the next page.

Prior Knowledge/Prediction

☐ Read the title and predict what the text is about.

Prior Knowledge
☐ a lot
☐ some
☐ none

☐ Read the first two sentences and add more to your prediction.

	A Comet	O	I	S	A	Rp	Rv
1	A long time ago people became frightened when they saw a comet.						
2	They thought a comet was a sign that unpleasant events, such as an						
3	earthquake, would take place. Scientists now know that these ideas are not						
4	correct.						
5	A comet is a space object made up of ice particles mixed with dust.						
6	Comets probably come from the far, outer edge of our solar system. Comets						
7	can be seen only when they are close enough to the sun to reflect its light.						
8	A comet has two parts: the head and the tail. The tail is present only						
9	when the comet is heated by the sun. The tail is made of fine dust and gas.						

The text is continued on the next page.

Cueing Systems

Miscue	Grapho-phonically Similar I M F (word level)	Syntactically Acceptable Unacceptable (sentence level)	Semantic Change in Meaning (CM) No Change in Meaning (NCM) (sentence level)
L I N E #			

Summary

☐ Most, ☐ few, ☐ no   miscues were graphophonically similar to the word in the passage.

☐ Most, ☐ few, ☐ no   miscues were syntactically matched.

☐ Most, ☐ few, ☐ no   miscues maintained the author's meaning.

☐ The self-corrections demonstrate that the reader monitors the meaning.

	O	I	S	A	Rp	Rv
10	A comet's tail always points away from the sun. It can be millions of kilometers					
11	long. The head is made of ice, frozen gases, and particles of rock and metal.					
12	It could be described as a dirty snowball. The heads of most comets are only a					
13	few kilometers wide. As they near the sun, reflected sunlight makes them					
14	appear large.					

TOTALS

Number of miscues _____   Number of self-corrections _____

Fluency: Does the Reader . . . .

☐ read smoothly, accurately, in meaningful phrases?

☐ read word-by-word, choppy, plodding?

☐ use pitch, stress, and intonation to convey meaning of the text?

☐ repeat words and phrases because s/he is monitoring the meaning (self-correcting)?

☐ repeat words and phrases because s/he is trying to sound out words?

☐ use punctuation to divide the text into units of meaning?   ☐ ignore the punctuation?

Rating Scale: Circle One

4 = fluent reading / good pace   2 = choppy, plodding reading / slow pace

3 = fairly fluent / reasonable pace   1 = clearly labored, disfluent reading / very slow pace

FORM S

FORM S

Note: Indicate any probing with a "P"

Expository Elements	All	Some	None
Description			
Collection			
Causation			
Problem / Solution			
Comparison			
Reader's Thumbnail Summary:			

Retelling

Retelling Summary: ☐ many details, logical order ☐ some details, some order ☐ few details, disorder

Comprehension Questions and Possible Answers

____ (RIF) 1. In relation to the sun, where does a comet's tail always point?   (away from the sun)

____ (PIT) 2. What happened a long time ago when people saw comets?
(they became frightened because they thought comets were signs of unpleasant events)

____ (EAS) 3. In your opinion, why did people a long time ago become frightened of a comet?   (a long time ago, before telescopes were invented, people didn't know what a comet was; they were superstitious) You think this because . . . (the text said scientists now know these fears were not correct)

____ (RIF) 4. What is a comet?   (a space object made of ice particles with dust)

____ (RIF) 5. Where do comets come from?   (probably come from the outer edge of our solar system)

____ (PIT) 6. When can you see the comet?   (when it is close enough to the sun to reflect the sun's light)

____ (CAR) 7. What do you know about the phrase **reflect the sun's light?**   (when the sun shines on something like a glass car window, the light bounces off of it)   What does the phrase **reflect the sun's light** have to do with this text? (the text said the sun shines on the comet and the light bounces off of it and then we can see it)

____ (PIT) 8. Why is a comet described as a dirty snowball?   (the tail is made from dust and gas; the head is ice, frozen gases, and particles of rock and metal)

Reader Text Relationship (RTR)   From the Text   ☐ adequate ☐ not adequate   From Head to Text   ☐ adequate ☐ not adequate

Form S, Level 4

Cueing Systems

Miscue	Grapho-phonically Similar I M F (word level)	Syntactically Acceptable Unacceptable (sentence level)	Semantic Change in Meaning (CM) No Change in Meaning (NCM) (sentence level)
L I N E #			

The cueing system grid is continued on the next page.

FORM S, LEVEL 5   Reader's Passages page 48

Prior Knowledge/Prediction

☐ Read the title and predict what the text is about.

Prior Knowledge
☐ a lot
☐ some
☐ none

☐ Read the first two sentences and add more to your prediction.

	O	I	S	A	Rp	Rv
Worms: Parasites and Scavengers						
1 Worms that live inside the bodies of other animals are parasites.						
2 Parasites are living things that feed on other living things. When some meat,						
3 such as pork, is not cooked long enough, even people can get worms by eating						
4 the meat. The worms attach themselves to the intestines, where they absorb						
5 food. Soon people who have parasites may lose weight and become weak. It						
6 is important to cook meat well.						
7 Flatworms are the simplest worms. They have one body opening and						
8 a digestive system with intestines. Some flatworms are scavengers.						
9 Scavengers are animals that eat dead animals. The flatworm planarian is a						

The text is continued on the next page.

FORM S

		O	I	S	A	Rp	Rv
1 0	scavenger. Other flatworms are parasites.						
1 1	Roundworms are more complex than flatworms. They have two body						
1 2	openings, not one. The openings are connected by a long intestine. Food						
1 3	enters the mouth and wastes leave from the opposite opening.						
1 4	Segmented worms are the most complex type of worm. Their bodies						
1 5	are divided into small parts, or segments. Two body openings are connected						
1 6	by a long intestine. They have a heart-like organ. It pumps blood through						
1 7	blood vessels. They have a small brain in the front part of their bodies. A						
1 8	nerve cord runs the length of their bodies.						
	TOTALS						
	Number of miscues _____ Number of self-corrections _____						

Cueing Systems

LINE #	Miscue	Grapho-phonically Similar I M F (word level)	Syntactically Acceptable Unacceptable (sentence level)	Semantic Change in Meaning (CM) No Change in Meaning (NCM) (sentence level)

Form S, Level 5

Fluency: Does the Reader . . .

□ read smoothly, accurately, in meaningful phrases?

□ read word-by-word, choppy, plodding?

□ use pitch, stress, and intonation to convey meaning of the text?

□ repeat words and phrases because s/he is monitoring the meaning (self-correcting)?

□ repeat words and phrases because s/he is trying to sound out words?

□ use punctuation to divide the text into units of meaning? □ ignore the punctuation?

Rating Scale: Circle One

4 = fluent reading / good pace   2 = choppy, plodding reading / slow pace

3 = fairly fluent / reasonable pace   1 = clearly labored, disfluent reading / very slow pace

Summary

□ Most, □ few, □ no miscues were graphophonically similar to the word in the passage.

□ Most, □ few, □ no miscues were syntactically matched.

□ Most, □ few, □ no miscues maintained the author's meaning.

□ The self-corrections demonstrate that the reader monitors the meaning.

Note: Indicate any probing with a "P"

Expository Elements	All	Some	None
Description			
Collection			
Causation			
Problem / Solution			
Comparison			
Reader's Thumbnail Summary:			

Retelling

Retelling Summary: ☐ many details, logical order ☐ some details, some order ☐ few details, disorder

Comprehension Questions and Possible Answers

_____ (RIF) 1. Name an example of an animal that is a parasite.   (worm)

_____ (CAR) 2. What do you know about the word **parasite?**   (it's a living organism that gets its food from another living organism)
What does the word **parasite** have to do with this text?   (it said worms that live inside the bodies of other animals are parasites)

_____ (PIT) 3. How can a person get a parasite worm?   (by not properly cooking pork and then eating it)

_____ (EAS) 4. In your opinion, is it dangerous when meat is not cooked enough?   (yes, a person can get sick)   You think this because . . .
(it said that some people who have parasites lose weight and become weak)

_____ (PIT) 5. Why does a person who has parasites lose weight?   (the parasites absorb the person's food and cause weight loss and weakness)

_____ (CAR) 6. What do you know about the word **scavenger?**   (it's an animal that feeds on dead animals or other decaying matter)
What does the word **scavenger** have to do with this text?   (it said scavengers are animals that eat dead animals)

_____ (RIF) 7. Name a flatworm that is a scavenger.   (a planarian)

_____ (PIT) 8. What is the difference between a parasite and a scavenger?   (a parasite feeds on living organisms, a scavenger feeds on dead matter)

Reader Text Relationship (RTR)   From the Text ☐ adequate ☐ not adequate   From Head to Text   ☐ adequate ☐ not adequate

Scoring Guide Summary

WORD RECOGNITION

Independent......... 2
Instructional...... 10
Frustration....... 20+

COMPREHENSION

Independent........ 0-1
Instructional...... 2
Frustration....... 4+

Emotional Status:

FORM S

Form S, Level 5

FORM S

FORM S, LEVEL 6 — Reader's Passages page 49

Prior Knowledge/Prediction

☐ Read the title and predict what the text is about.

☐ Read the first two sentences and add more to your prediction.

Prior Knowledge

☐ a lot
☐ some
☐ none

	Disease Microbes and Antibodies	O	I	S	A	Rp	Rv
1	Your body has many natural ways to prevent disease microbes from						
2	causing infections. For instance, your skin is a barrier for microbes. They seldom						
3	pass through unbroken skin. The hairs in your nose filter some microbes out of						
4	the air you breathe. Also, there are some other ways disease microbes are kept						
5	from entering your body.						
6	Sometimes disease microbes do enter your body. Often when you have						
7	an infection caused by disease microbes, your body makes antibodies. An						
8	antibody is a chemical produced in your blood to destroy certain microbes. Your						
9	body makes a different kind of antibody for each kind of disease microbe.						

The text is continued on the next page.

Cueing Systems

LINE #	Miscue	Grapho-phonically Similar I M F (word level)	Syntactically Acceptable Unacceptable (sentence level)	Semantic Change in Meaning (CM) No Change in Meaning (NCM) (sentence level)

The cueing system grid is continued on the next page.

FORMS

Form S, Level 6

Cueing Systems

LINE #	Miscue	Grapho-phonically Similar I M F (word level)	Syntactically Acceptable Unacceptable (sentence level)	Semantic Change in Meaning (CM) No Change in Meaning (NCM) (sentence level)

Summary

☐ Most, ☐ few, ☐ no   miscues were graphophonically similar to the word in the passage.

☐ Most, ☐ few, ☐ no   miscues were syntactically matched.

☐ Most, ☐ few, ☐ no   miscues maintained the author's meaning.

☐ The self-corrections demonstrate that the reader monitors the meaning.

	O	I	S	A	Rp	Rv
10 Perhaps you have been sick with chicken pox. Chicken pox is caused by a						
11 microbe infection. When you got chicken pox, your body began making						
12 antibodies to destroy the microbes. As the microbes were destroyed by the						
13 antibodies, you began to get well. Antibodies stay in your blood even after you						
14 no longer have the disease. They keep you from getting that disease again. For						
15 this reason most people have a disease like chicken pox only once.						
16 Vaccines are used to help your body make certain antibodies. A vaccine						
17 is made of dead or weak microbes that cause a certain disease. When a vaccine						
18 is put into your body, you do not get the disease.						

TOTALS

Number of miscues _____   Number of self-corrections _____

Fluency: Does the Reader . . .

☐ read smoothly, accurately, in meaningful phrases?

☐ read word-by-word, choppy, plodding?

☐ use pitch, stress, and intonation to convey meaning of the text?

☐ repeat words and phrases because s/he is monitoring the meaning (self-correcting)?

☐ repeat words and phrases because s/he is trying to sound out words?

☐ use punctuation to divide the text into units of meaning?   ☐ ignore the punctuation?

Rating Scale: Circle One

4 = fluent reading / good pace   2 = choppy, plodding reading / slow pace

3 = fairly fluent / reasonable pace   1 = clearly labored, disfluent reading / very slow pace

FORM S

Retelling

Note: Indicate any probing with a "P"

Expository Elements	All	Some	None
Description			
Collection			
Causation			
Problem / Solution			
Comparison			
Reader's Thumbnail Summary:			

Retelling Summary: ☐ many details, logical order ☐ some details, some order ☐ few details, disorder

Comprehension Questions and Possible Answers

_____ (RIF) 1. What does a disease microbe cause when it enters your body?   (infection)

_____ (CAR) 2. What do you know about the phrase **to prevent disease microbes from causing infections?**   (the body has ways to keep bad microbes from making you sick)   What does the phrase **to prevent disease microbes from causing infections** have to do with this text?   (it said your body has many ways to prevent disease microbes from causing infections)

_____ (RIF) 3. Name one natural body barrier against disease microbes.   (the skin or hairs in the nose)

_____ (EAS) 4. Do you think the body can protect itself when disease microbes get into it?   (yes, with medicine and natural antibodies)   You think this because . . .   (it said your body makes antibodies)

_____ (CAR) 5. What do you know about the word **antibody?**   (it's a chemical made in the blood to destroy microbes)   What does the word **antibody** have to do with this text?   (it said your body makes a different kind of antibody for each kind of disease microbe)

_____ (RIF) 6. What causes chicken pox?   (a microbe infection)

_____ (PIT) 7. How does your body react when you get chicken pox?   (your body makes antibodies to destroy the microbes; as the microbes are destroyed, you begin to get well)

_____ (PIT) 8. Why do most people have chicken pox only once?   (antibodies stay in your blood even after you no longer have the disease; they keep you from getting the disease again)

Reader Text Relationship (RTR)   From the Text   ☐ adequate   ☐ not adequate   From Head to Text   ☐ adequate   ☐ not adequate

Form S, Level 6

Cueing Systems

Miscue	Grapho-phonically Similar I M F (word level)	Syntactically Acceptable Unacceptable (sentence level)	Semantic Change in Meaning (CM) No Change in Meaning (NCM) (sentence level)
L I N E #			

The cueing system grid is continued on the next page.

Prior Knowledge/Prediction
☐ Read the title and predict what the text is about.

Prior Knowledge
☐ a lot
☐ some
☐ none

☐ Read the first two sentences and add more to your prediction.

		O	I	S	A	Rp	Rv
	Moving Forces and Inertia						
1	Without motion the hands of a clock would not indicate the time of day. For						
2	every motion there is a force that causes it. A force is needed to start something moving						
3	or to change its direction. A force is also needed to stop motion. The tendency of						
4	matter to stay at rest or in motion unless acted on by a force is called inertia.						
5	A person riding in a car has inertia. Think of a car moving at a speed of 50						
6	kilometers per hour. How fast is the person inside going? The person is moving with						
7	the car and is not left behind; therefore, the person must also be moving at 50						
8	kilometers per hour. If the brakes are applied suddenly, what happens to the person in						
9	the car? The person continues to move forward even though the car is stopping. If the						
10	seatbelt is unfastened, the dashboard or windshield may stop this forward motion.						

The text is continued on the next page.

FORM S

FORM S

	O	I	S	A	Rp	Rv
1 1	If you are standing in a bus, you may be thrown off balance when the bus					
1 2	starts to move. Your body has inertia. It tends to remain in place as the bus begins to					
1 3	move. If the bus goes forward too fast, you may fall backward.					
1 4	All matter has inertia. Inertia is a property of matter. The amount of inertia an					
1 5	object has depends on its mass. The greater the mass of an object, the greater its					
1 6	inertia. A sofa of large mass has more inertia than a kitchen chair. It takes more force					
1 7	to move a sofa than to move a kitchen chair. It takes a larger force to start and stop a					
1 8	bus than to start and stop a small sports car.					
	TOTALS					

Number of miscues _____   Number of self-corrections _____

Fluency: Does the Reader . . .

- ☐ read smoothly, accurately, in meaningful phrases?
- ☐ read word-by-word, choppy, plodding?
- ☐ use pitch, stress, and intonation to convey meaning of the text?
- ☐ repeat words and phrases because s/he is monitoring the meaning (self-correcting)?
- ☐ repeat words and phrases because s/he is trying to sound out words?
- ☐ use punctuation to divide the text into units of meaning?   ☐ ignore the punctuation?

Rating Scale: Circle One

4 = fluent reading / good pace   2 = choppy, plodding reading / slow pace
3 = fairly fluent / reasonable pace   1 = clearly labored, disfluent reading / very slow pace

Cueing Systems

L I N E #	Miscue	Grapho-phonically Similar I M F (word level)	Syntactically Acceptable Unacceptable (sentence level)	Semantic Change in Meaning (CM) No Change in Meaning (NCM) (sentence level)

Summary

- ☐ Most, ☐ few, ☐ no   miscues were graphophonically similar to the word in the passage.
- ☐ Most, ☐ few, ☐ no   miscues were syntactically matched.
- ☐ Most, ☐ few, ☐ no   miscues maintained the author's meaning.
- ☐ The self-corrections demonstrate that the reader monitors the meaning.

Form S, Level 7

Expository Elements	All	Some	None
Description			
Collection			
Causation			
Problem / Solution			
Comparison			
Reader's Thumbnail Summary:			

Scoring Guide Summary

WORD RECOGNITION
Independent 3
Instructional 14
Frustration .... 28+

COMPREHENSION
Independent 0-1
Instructional 2
Frustration .... 4+

Emotional Status:

Form S, Level 7

Retelling

Retelling Summary: □ many details, logical order □ some details, some order □ few details, disorder

Comprehension Questions and Possible Answers

_____ (RIF) 1. What causes a motion?   (a force)

_____ (RIF) 2. What couldn't happen without motion?   (nothing would be able to move)

_____ (PIT) 3. What does a force do to matter?   (it starts something moving, changes its direction, or stops its movement)

_____ (CAR) 4. What do you know about the word *inertia?* (inertia is the tendency for an object to stay in motion or at rest unless acted on by some force)   What does *inertia* have to do with this text? (it said all matter has inertia, inertia is a property of matter)

_____ (PIT) 5. Why is a person who is riding in a car going 50 kilometers per hour also going 50 kilometers per hour?   (the person is sitting on the car seat, which is connected to the car, so the force propelling the car is also propelling the person)

_____ (EAS) 6. In your opinion, is it wise or unwise to wear a seatbelt? You think this because . . .   (wise, because if the brakes are applied to a car going 50 kilometers per hour, the force will stop the car but not the person; a seatbelt serves as a force to stop the person)

_____ (PIT) 7. Why are you thrown off balance when a bus begins to move forward?   (because your body has inertia, it remains standing still while a force has moved the bus forward)

_____ (PIT) 8. What does the amount of inertia an object has depend on?   (its mass, size)

Reader Text Relationship (RTR)   From the Text □ adequate □ not adequate   From Head to Text □ adequate □ not adequate

FORMS

FORM S

Cueing Systems

Miscue	Grapho-phonically Similar I M F (word level)	Syntactically Acceptable Unacceptable (sentence level)	Semantic Change in Meaning (CM) No Change in Meaning (NCM) (sentence level)
L I N E #			

The cueing system grid is continued on the next page.

FORM S, LEVEL 8   Reader's Passages page 51

Prior Knowledge/Prediction

☐ Read the title and predict what the text is about.

Prior Knowledge
☐ a lot
☐ some
☐ none

☐ Read the first two sentences and add more to your prediction.

		O	I	S	A	Rp	Rv
	Cancer						
1	Cancer is a disease in which there is abnormal cell division and a rapid increase						
2	in certain body cells. Cancer can occur in any plant or animal. Dogs, cats, fruit flies,						
3	and horses, as well as humans, can develop various types of cancer. What causes the						
4	abnormal rapid growth of body cells? The DNA of a cell nucleus controls the growth						
5	and division of the cell. Normal cells grow to a certain size. For some unknown						
6	reason, some cells may continue to grow and divide. This rapid growth of cells leads						
7	to a formation of a clump of tissue called a tumor. A benign, non-life-threatening						
8	tumor will grow to a certain size and stop. Most moles and warts are benign tumors.						
9	All malignant tumors are cancers. They can cause death if they are not removed or						
10	destroyed. Cancer cells, unlike normal cells, may separate from a tumor and be						
11	carried through the blood or lymph to other organs of the body. They can invade a						
12	new body tissue and form new tumors.						
13	Cancer in many animals is known to be caused by viruses. Chickens are						
14	affected by a cancer of the connective tissue. Epstein–Barr viruses cause cancer of the						

The text is continued on the next page.

Cueing Systems

Miscue	Grapho-phonically Similar I M F (word level)	Syntactically Acceptable Unacceptable (sentence level)	Semantic Change in Meaning (CM) No Change in Meaning (NCM) (sentence level)
L I N E #			

Summary

- ☐ Most, ☐ few, ☐ no   miscues were graphophonically similar to the word in the passage.
- ☐ Most, ☐ few, ☐ no   miscues were syntactically matched.
- ☐ Most, ☐ few, ☐ no   miscues maintained the author's meaning.
- ☐ The self-corrections demonstrate that the reader monitors the meaning.

		O	I	S	A	Rp	Rv
15	lymph system in humans. Scientists are working to discover how viruses cause cancer.						
16	A carcinogen is a cancer-causing substance. Many different chemicals are						
17	known to be carcinogens. Certain chemicals in the environment can cause cancer.						
18	Nitrosamines, reaction products of sodium nitrate, are carcinogens. Sodium nitrate						
19	is used to preserve meat. The nitrosamines are produced during the digestive						
20	process. Too much sunlight and overexposure to X-rays and other radiation can be						
21	physical causes of cancer.						

TOTALS

Number of miscues _____   Number of self-corrections _____

Fluency: Does the Reader . . .

- ☐ read smoothly, accurately, in meaningful phrases?
- ☐ read word-by-word, choppy, plodding?
- ☐ use pitch, stress, and intonation to convey meaning of the text?
- ☐ repeat words and phrases because s/he is monitoring the meaning (self-correcting)?
- ☐ repeat words and phrases because s/he is trying to sound out words?
- ☐ use punctuation to divide the text into units of meaning?   ☐ ignore the punctuation?

Rating Scale: Circle One

4 = fluent reading / good pace   2 = choppy, plodding reading / slow pace

3 = fairly fluent / reasonable pace   1 = clearly labored, disfluent reading / very slow pace

FORM S

Retelling

Note: Indicate any probing with a "P"

Expository Elements	All	Some	None
Description			
Collection			
Causation			
Problem / Solution			
Comparison			
Reader's Thumbnail Summary:			

Retelling Summary: ☐ many details, logical order ☐ some details, some order ☐ few details, disorder

Comprehension Questions and Possible Answers

____ (RIF) 1. In which organisms can cancer occur?   (all plants and animals, dogs, cats, fruit flies, horses, humans)

____ (CAR) 2. What do you know about the word *cancer?*   (it's a disease that sometimes kills people and animals)   What does the word *cancer* have to do with this text?   (it said it's a disease that causes abnormal cell division and rapid increase in certain body cells)

____ (PIT) 3. What controls the growth and division of normal cells?   (the DNA of a cell nucleus; normal cells grow to a certain size and stop)

____ (RIF) 4. What causes the abnormal growth and division of some cells?   (the reason is unknown)

____ (PIT) 5. What is the difference between a benign and a malignant tumor?   (a benign tumor is a non-life-threatening clump of cells that grows to a certain size and stops; a malignant tumor continues to grow and may cause death if not destroyed or removed)

____ (EAS) 6. In your opinion, how uniquely dangerous are cancer cells?   You think this because . . .   (they are extremely dangerous because, unlike normal cells, they may separate from a tumor and be carried through the blood or lymph to other parts of the body)

____ (RIF) 7. What causes cancer in the lymph system?   (Epstein-Barr viruses)

____ (RIF) 8. Name one carcinogen.   (nitrosamines, or too much sunlight, overexposure to X-rays and other radiation)

Reader Text Relationship (RTR)   From the Text   ☐ adequate ☐ not adequate   From Head to Text   ☐ adequate ☐ not adequate

FORM S, LEVEL 9 — Reader's Passages page 52

Prior Knowledge/Prediction

☐ Read the title and predict what the text is about.

☐ Read the first two sentences and add more to your prediction.

Prior Knowledge
☐ a lot
☐ some
☐ none

	Knowing the Atom	O	I	S	A	Rp	Rv
1	About 2,300 years ago, the Greek philosopher Democritus proposed the idea						
2	that matter is composed of atoms. Democritus reasoned that an apple could be cut						
3	into smaller and smaller pieces. Eventually he would have particles that could no						
4	longer be cut and still be an apple. He called these small particles "atoms," which						
5	is Greek for "unable to cut."						
6	Democritus never saw an atom. Atoms are too small for anyone to view						
7	directly. For example, one drop of water contains millions of atoms. Scientists often						
8	propose models to help them visualize things that they cannot see directly. These						
9	models are based on scientific theories. Much of the early work in atomic theory was						
10	done in England. The Cavendish Laboratory at the University of Cambridge was the						
11	site of many important discoveries about atomic structure. As more information was						
12	gathered by scientists about atoms, the atomic theory was revised. Scientists are still						
13	learning about atoms and atomic structure.						
14	According to current atomic theory, the atom consists of a small, dense						

The text is continued on the next page.

Cueing Systems

LINE #	Miscue	Grapho-phonically Similar I M F (word level)	Syntactically Acceptable Unacceptable (sentence level)	Semantic Change in Meaning (CM) No Change in Meaning (NCM) (sentence level)

The cueing system grid is continued on the next page.

FORM S

	O	I	S	A	Rp	Rv
1 5	nucleus surrounded by mostly empty space in which electrons move at high speeds.					
1 6	Most of an atom's volume is empty space. The average diameter of a nucleus is about					
1 7	5×10^{-13} centimeters. The average diameter of an atom is about 2×10^{-8} centimeters.					
1 8	The difference in these two sizes means an atom is about 40,000 times larger than its					
1 9	nucleus. Consider an example of this relative difference. If the nucleus were the size					
2 0	of an orange, the whole atom would measure twenty-four city blocks across.					
2 1	Even though an atomic nucleus is relatively small, it makes up over 99.9 percent					
2 2	of an atom's mass. The nucleus of an atom contains protons. A proton is a relatively					
2 3	massive particle with a positive electric charge. The nucleus of a helium atom contains					
2 4	two protons. The mass of a helium atom is about twice the mass of two protons. The					
2 5	additional mass is due to neutrons found in the nuclei of the helium atoms. A					
2 6	neutron is a nuclear particle that has no electric charge. A neutron has about the same					
2 7	mass as a proton. Most atomic nuclei contain neutrons.					

TOTALS

Number of miscues ———   Number of self-corrections ———

Fluency: Does the Reader . . .

□ read smoothly, accurately, in meaningful phrases?

□ read word-by-word, choppy, plodding?

□ use pitch, stress, and intonation to convey meaning of the text?

□ repeat words and phrases because s/he is monitoring the meaning (self-correcting)?

□ repeat words and phrases because s/he is trying to sound out words?

□ use punctuation to divide the text into units of meaning?   □ ignore the punctuation?

Rating Scale: Circle One

4 = fluent reading / good pace   2 = choppy, plodding reading / slow pace

3 = fairly fluent / reasonable pace   1 = clearly labored, disfluent reading / very slow pace

Cueing Systems

Miscue	Graphophonically Similar I M F (word level)	Syntactically Acceptable Unacceptable (sentence level)	Semantic Change in Meaning (CM) No Change in Meaning (NCM) (sentence level)
L I N E #			

Summary

□ Most, □ few, □ no   miscues were graphophonically similar to the word in the passage.

□ Most, □ few, □ no   miscues were syntactically matched.

□ Most, □ few, □ no   miscues maintained the author's meaning.

□ The self-corrections demonstrate that the reader monitors the meaning.

Form S, Level 9

Retelling

Note: Indicate any probing with a "P"

Expository Elements	All	Some	None
Description			
Collection			
Causation			
Problem / Solution			
Comparison			
Reader's Thumbnail Summary:			

Scoring Guide Summary

WORD RECOGNITION
Independent.....3-4
Instructional....17-18
Frustration.......35+

COMPREHENSION
Independent.....0-1
Instructional....2
Frustration.......4+

Emotional Status:

Retelling Summary: □ many details, logical order □ some details, some order □ few details, disorder

Comprehension Questions and Possible Answers

___ (RIF) 1. Can we see an atom with our eyes? (no, they are too small; there are millions of atoms in a drop of water)

___ (PIT) 2. What did Democritus reason? (an apple could be cut into smaller and smaller pieces until the particles could no longer be cut and still be an apple)

___ (EAS) 3. Do you think Democritus' proposal was remarkable? You think this because . . . (yes, it was made 2,300 years ago, long before modern science; he never saw an atom but he proposed it existed and named it)

___ (RIF) 4. How does the text define the word *atom* ? (it's Greek for "unable to cut")

___ (RIF) 5. Where is the University of Cambridge? (in England)

___ (RIF) 6. According to current atomic theory, what makes up an atom? (a small dense nucleus surrounded by mostly empty space in which electrons move at high speeds)

___ (EAS) 7. What do you think is remarkable about the difference in size between an atom and its nucleus? You think this because . . . (it's quite remarkable because it said an atom is about 40,000 times larger than its nucleus and still an atom is so small you can't even see it)

___ (CAR) 8. What do you know about the phrase ***relative difference?*** (a distinction between two objects with a comparison or example) What does the phrase ***relative difference*** have to do with this text? (it said if a nucleus were the size of an orange, the whole atom would measure a distance of twenty-four blocks)

Reader Text Relationship (RTR)   From the Text □ adequate □ not adequate   From Head to Text □ adequate □ not adequate

FORMS

▣ FORM SS ▣

Expository Social Studies Passages, One—Nine

Cueing Systems

L I N E #	Miscue	Grapho-phonically Similar I M F (word level)	Syntactically Acceptable Unacceptable (sentence level)	Semantic Change in Meaning (CM) No Change in Meaning (NCM) (sentence level)

Summary

☐ Most, ☐ few, ☐ no   miscues were graphophonically similar to the word in the passage.

☐ Most, ☐ few, ☐ no   miscues were syntactically matched.

☐ Most, ☐ few, ☐ no   miscues maintained the author's meaning.

☐ The self-corrections demonstrate that the reader monitors the meaning.

FORM SS, LEVEL 1   Reader's Passages page 54

Prior Knowledge/Prediction

☐ Read the title and predict what the text is about.

Prior Knowledge
☐ a lot
☐ some
☐ none

☐ Read the first two sentences and add more to your prediction.

	Our Country's Flag	O	I	S	A	Rp	Rv
1	Our country's flag is red, white, and blue.						
2	The colors come from the flag of England. The stars and						
3	stripes on our flag have a special meaning. The thirteen red and						
4	white stripes stand for our first thirteen states. Each star stands						
5	for one of our fifty states.						
6	Our flag stands for the past. Our flag also stands						
7	for the present. It stands for a free nation. It stands for our						
8	country. It stands for the United States of America.						

TOTALS

Number of miscues _____   Number of self-corrections _____

Note: Indicate any probing with a "P"

Expository Elements	All	Some	None
Description			
Collection			
Causation			
Problem / Solution			
Comparison			

Reader's Thumbnail Summary:

Scoring Guide Summary

WORD RECOGNITION

Independent 0-1
Instructional 3-4
Frustration ...... 8+

COMPREHENSION

Independent 0
Instructional 1-2
Frustration ...... 3+

Emotional Status:

Fluency: Does the Reader . . .

Retelling

☐ read smoothly, accurately, in meaningful phrases?

☐ read word-by-word, choppy, plodding?

☐ use pitch, stress, and intonation to convey meaning of the text?

☐ repeat words and phrases because s/he is monitoring the meaning (self-correcting)?

☐ repeat words and phrases because s/he is trying to sound out words?

☐ use punctuation to divide the text into units of meaning?

☐ ignore the punctuation?

Rating Scale: Circle One

4 = fluent reading / good pace

3 = fairly fluent / reasonable pace

2 = choppy, plodding reading / slow pace

1 = clearly labored, disfluent reading / very slow pace

Retelling Summary: ☐ many details, logical order ☐ some details, some order ☐ few details, disorder

Comprehension Questions and Possible Answers

____ (RIF)   1. Where does this text take place?   (United States)

____ (RIF)   2. Where did the colors of the flag come from?   (England)

____ (RIF)   3. What do the stripes on our flag mean?   (thirteen red and white stripes stand for the first thirteen states)

____ (CAR)   4. What do you know about the phrase *our flag stands for the present?*   (our flag tells about our country now) What does the phrase *our flag stands for the present* have to do with this text?   (it says our flag stands for the present)

____ (PIT)   5. Name two other things our flag stands for.   (for our country in the past and for a free nation)

____ (EAS)   6. In your opinion could our flag ever change in the future?   You think this because. . . (yes, we can add more states; it said that each star stands for one of our fifty states)

Reader Text Relationship (RTR)   From the Text ☐ adequate ☐ not adequate   From Head to Text ☐ adequate ☐ not adequate

FORM SS

FORM SS, LEVEL 2 Reader's Passages page 55

Prior Knowledge/Prediction

☐ Read the title and predict what the text is about.

Prior Knowledge
☐ a lot
☐ some
☐ none

☐ Read the first two sentences and add more to your prediction.

The First Thirteen States

		O	I	S	A	Rp	Rv
1	Over 300 years ago, the English started thirteen colonies. Later,						
2	the colonies became the first states in the United States of America.						
3	The people in the first states had difficult lives. For transportation						
4	they often walked. Sometimes they rode horses. It was hard for						
5	the people to travel very far from home because there were no						
6	cars.						
7	The people's houses were much different from our houses						
8	today. The houses had one large room with a fireplace. This room						
9	was used as a kitchen, a dining room, and a living room. Also, it was						

The text is continued on the next page.

Cueing Systems

LINE #	Miscue	Grapho-phonically Similar I M F (word level)	Syntactically Acceptable Unacceptable (sentence level)	Semantic Change in Meaning (CM) No Change in Meaning (NCM) (sentence level)

The cueing system grid is continued on the next page.

Cueing Systems

L I N E #	Miscue	Grapho-phonically Similar I M F (word level)	Syntactically Acceptable Unacceptable (sentence level)	Semantic Change in Meaning (CM) No Change in Meaning (NCM) (sentence level)

Summary

☐ Most, ☐ few, ☐ no   miscues were graphophonically similar to the word in the passage.

☐ Most, ☐ few, ☐ no   miscues were syntactically matched.

☐ Most, ☐ few, ☐ no   miscues maintained the author's meaning.

☐ The self-corrections demonstrate that the reader monitors the meaning.

Form SS, Level 2

	O	I	S	A	Rp	Rv
1 0	often used as a bedroom because of the fireplace. There were no					
1 1	electric lights. Water had to be carried into the house. Even though					
1 2	life was very difficult, the people worked hard because they loved					
1 3	their new land.					

TOTALS

Number of miscues _____   Number of self-corrections _____

Fluency: Does the Reader . . . :

☐ read smoothly, accurately, in meaningful phrases?

☐ read word-by-word, choppy, plodding?

☐ use pitch, stress, and intonation to convey meaning of the text?

☐ repeat words and phrases because s/he is monitoring the meaning (self-correcting)?

☐ repeat words and phrases because s/he is trying to sound out words?

☐ use punctuation to divide the text into units of meaning?   ☐ ignore the punctuation?

Rating Scale: Circle One

4 = fluent reading / good pace   2 = choppy, plodding reading / slow pace
3 = fairly fluent / reasonable pace   1 = clearly labored, disfluent reading / very slow pace

FORM SS

Retelling

Note: Indicate any probing with a "P"

Expository Elements	All	Some	None
Description			
Collection			
Causation			
Problem / Solution			
Comparison			

Reader's Thumbnail Summary:

Retelling Summary: ☐ many details, logical order ☐ some details, some order ☐ few details, disorder

Comprehension Questions and Possible Answers

_____ (RIF) 1. Where does this text take place? (thirteen colonies or first states in the United States)

_____ (RIF) 2. Who started the thirteen colonies? (English people)

_____ (PIT) 3. Why did the people have difficult lives? (they had to walk instead of driving in a car; they couldn't travel very far)

_____ (RIF) 4. Name two ways the people's houses were different from ours today. (only one large room with a fireplace; no electric lights; no running water)

_____ (CAR) 5. What do you know about the word **transportation?** (a way to travel from one place to another)
What does the word **transportation** have to do with this text? (it said for transportation they often walked)

_____ (EAS) 6. In your opinion was the fireplace important to the people? You think this because. . . (yes, the houses had one room which was a kitchen, a dining room, and a living room; the fireplace kept them warm, was a place to cook the food, and provided some light)

Reader Text Relationship (RTR)   From the Text   ☐ adequate ☐ not adequate   From Head to Text   ☐ adequate ☐ not adequate

Scoring Guide Summary

WORD RECOGNITION

Independent........ 1-2
Instructional....... 6-7
Frustration........ 13+

COMPREHENSION

Independent........ 0
Instructional....... 1-2
Frustration........ 3+

Emotional Status:

Form SS, Level 2

Cueing Systems

LINE #	Miscue	Grapho-phonically Similar I M F (word level)	Syntactically Acceptable Unacceptable (sentence level)	Semantic Change in Meaning (CM) No Change in Meaning (NCM) (sentence level)

The cueing system grid is continued on the next page.

FORM SS, LEVEL 3   Reader's Passages page 56

Prior Knowledge/Prediction

☐ Read the title and predict what the text is about.

Prior Knowledge

☐ a lot
☐ some
☐ none

☐ Read the first two sentences and add more to your prediction.

	Writing the *Declaration of Independence*	O	I	S	A	Rp	Rv
1	During the middle 1760s, American colonists became more						
2	and more unhappy with the king of England. They were unhappy						
3	because he took away their right to freedom. They were						
4	unhappy because he took so much of their money for taxes.						
5	In 1776, men from the thirteen colonies met in Philadelphia.						
6	Some men believed that the colonies should separate from England.						
7	These men thought the colonies should be free, even if it meant war.						
8	One of the men at the meeting was Thomas Jefferson.						

The text is continued on the next page.

	O	I	S	A	Rp	Rv
9 Jefferson had read many books about government and law. He did						
10 not speak much during the meeting, but he listened carefully. He						
11 thought about the reasons for freedom.						
12 Later, Jefferson wrote something that told why the colonists						
13 should be free. The other men liked what Jefferson had written. On						
14 July 4th, the men voted to accept Jefferson's work. They called it						
15 the *Declaration of Independence*, and then the war for freedom						
16 became fierce.						

TOTALS

Number of miscues _____   Number of self-corrections _____

Fluency: Does the Reader . . .

☐ read smoothly, accurately, in meaningful phrases?

☐ read word-by-word, choppy, plodding?

☐ use pitch, stress, and intonation to convey meaning of the text?

☐ repeat words and phrases because s/he is monitoring the meaning (self-correcting)?

☐ repeat words and phrases because s/he is trying to sound out words?

☐ use punctuation to divide the text into units of meaning?   ☐ ignore the punctuation?

Rating Scale: Circle One

4 = fluent reading / good pace   2 = choppy, plodding reading / slow pace

3 = fairly fluent / reasonable pace   1 = clearly labored, disfluent reading / very slow pace

Cueing Systems

Miscue	Graphophonically Similar I M F (word level)	Syntactically Acceptable Unacceptable (sentence level)	Semantic Change in Meaning (CM) No Change in Meaning (NCM) (sentence level)
L I N E #			

Summary

☐ Most, ☐ few, ☐ no   miscues were graphophonically similar to the word in the passage.

☐ Most, ☐ few, ☐ no   miscues were syntactically matched.

☐ Most, ☐ few, ☐ no   miscues maintained the author's meaning.

☐ The self-corrections demonstrate that the reader monitors the meaning.

Form SS, Level 3

Note: Indicate any probing with a "P"

Expository Elements	All	Some	None
Description			
Collection			
Causation			
Problem / Solution			
Comparison			

Reader's Thumbnail Summary:

Scoring Guide Summary

WORD RECOGNITION
Independent 1-2
Instructional 7-8
Frustration ....16+

COMPREHENSION
Independent 0
Instructional 2
Frustration ....4+

Emotional Status:

Retelling

Retelling Summary: □ many details, logical order □ some details, some order □ few details, disorder

Comprehension Questions and Possible Answers

____ (RIF) 1. Where does this text take place?   (in the American colonies)

____ (PIT) 2. Why were the colonists unhappy with the King of England?   (he took away their right to freedom, and their money for taxes)

____ (RIF) 3. In what year did the men meet?   (1776)

____ (CAR) 4. What do you know about the phrase *separate from England?*   (the colonists should break away from England) What does the phrase *separate from England* have to do with this text?   (it said that at the meeting in Philadelphia in 1776, the men suggested that the colonies separate from England)

____ (PIT) 5. Why did the men believe that the colonies should separate from England?   (they thought the colonies should be free from English rule)

____ (RIF) 6. Who was one of the men at the meeting?   (Thomas Jefferson)

____ (CAR) 7. What do you know about the phrase *Declaration of Independence?* (it's a document that declares that the American colonies should be free from England)   What does the phrase *Declaration of Independence* have to do with this text?   (on July 4, 1776, the men voted to accept Jefferson's *Declaration of Independence*)

____ (EAS) 8. In your opinion, do you think the colonists should have declared independence, even though it meant war? You think this because . . . (yes, England was taking away their right to freedom and their money) (no, war kills too many people)

Reader Text Relationship (RTR)   From the Text   □ adequate □ not adequate   From Head to Text   □ adequate □ not adequate

FORM SS

Cueing Systems

Miscue	Grapho-phonically Similar I M F (word level)	Syntactically Acceptable Unacceptable (sentence level)	Semantic Change in Meaning (CM) No Change in Meaning (NCM) (sentence level)
L I N E #			

The cueing system grid is continued on the next page.

FORM SS, LEVEL 4   Reader's Passages page 57

Prior Knowledge/Prediction

☐ Read the title and predict what the text is about.

Prior Knowledge
☐ a lot
☐ some
☐ none

☐ Read the first two sentences and add more to your prediction.

	O	I	S	A	Rp	Rv
French Explorers in North America						
1 During the 1600s, the French settled much of eastern Canada. They						
2 called this land New France. They had heard stories about a large body of						
3 water to the west. The French thought it might be the Pacific Ocean. They						
4 wanted more land to add to the French Empire. Soon they began to look for						
5 the great body of water. This journey took them to regions that are now part						
6 of the United States. Some went south instead of west.						
7 In 1679, a Frenchman, La Salle, began a second journey to explore						
8 the Great Lakes region. He started at the south end of Lake Michigan. He						
9 followed the Illinois River to the place where it met the Mississippi River.						

The text is continued on the next page.

Cueing Systems

LINE #	Miscue	Grapho-phonically Similar I M F (word level)	Syntactically Acceptable Unacceptable (sentence level)	Semantic Change in Meaning (CM) No Change in Meaning (NCM) (sentence level)

Summary

☐ Most, ☐ few, ☐ no   miscues were graphophonically similar to the word in the passage.

☐ Most, ☐ few, ☐ no   miscues were syntactically matched.

☐ Most, ☐ few, ☐ no   miscues maintained the author's meaning.

☐ The self-corrections demonstrate that the reader monitors the meaning.

Form SS, Level 4

	O	I	S	A	Rp	Rv
1 0	By 1682, he had gone all the way down the Mississippi to where it flowed into					
1 1	the Gulf of Mexico. He claimed the lands on both sides of the river. He also					
1 2	claimed the rivers that flowed into the land. He named the region Louisiana in					
1 3	honor of Louis XIV, the French king.					

TOTALS

Number of miscues _____   Number of self-corrections _____

Fluency: Does the Reader . . .

☐ read smoothly, accurately, in meaningful phrases?

☐ read word-by-word, choppy, plodding?

☐ use pitch, stress, and intonation to convey meaning of the text?

☐ repeat words and phrases because s/he is monitoring the meaning (self-correcting)?

☐ repeat words and phrases because s/he is trying to sound out words?

☐ use punctuation to divide the text into units of meaning?   ☐ ignore the punctuation?

Rating Scale: Circle One

4 = fluent reading / good pace   2 = choppy, plodding reading / slow pace

3 = fairly fluent / reasonable pace   1 = clearly labored, disfluent reading / very slow pace

FORM SS

Note: Indicate any probing with a "P"

Expository Elements	All	Some	None
Description			
Collection			
Causation			
Problem / Solution			
Comparison			

Reader's Thumbnail Summary:

Scoring Guide Summary

WORD RECOGNITION
Independent 2
Instructional 8-9
Frustration ...... 17+

COMPREHENSION
Independent 0-1
Instructional 2
Frustration ...... 4+

Emotional Status:

Retelling

Retelling Summary: ☐ many details, logical order ☐ some details, some order ☐ few details, disorder

Comprehension Questions and Possible Answers

____ (PIT) 1. What did the French do during the 1600s?   (they explored and settled most of eastern Canada)

____ (CAR) 2. What do you know about the word **settled?**   (to take permanent residence, to stay and live in one spot)
What does the word **settled** have to do with the text?   (they settled eastern Canada)

____ (RIF) 3. What did the French call eastern Canada?   (New France)

____ (RIF) 4. What did the French think the large body of water to the west was?   (the Pacific Ocean)

____ (PIT) 5. Why were the French so eager to explore farther west?   (they wanted more land to add to the French Empire)

____ (RIF) 6. Where did La Salle's second journey take him?   (Great Lakes region; Lake Michigan all the way down the
Mississippi River to the Gulf of Mexico)

____ (CAR) 7. What do you know about the phrase **claimed the lands?**   (he said the land belonged to France, took ownership
of the land)   What does the phrase **claimed the lands** have to do with the text?   (La Salle claimed the land on both
sides of the Mississippi River)

____ (EAS) 8. In your opinion was La Salle loyal to his country and his king?   You think this because . . .   (yes, his journeys
were dangerous and he probably risked his life; he always claimed the land in the name of the French Empire;
he named the land near the Gulf of Mexico Louisiana in honor of the French king)

Reader Text Relationship (RTR)   From the Text   ☐ adequate ☐ not adequate   From Head to Text   ☐ adequate ☐ not adequate

Form SS, Level 4

Prior Knowledge/Prediction

□ Read the title and predict what the text is about.

□ Read the first two sentences and add more to your prediction.

Prior Knowledge
□ a lot
□ some
□ none

	O	I	S	A	Rp	Rv
The Civil War						
1 During the early and mid-1800s, there was much talk in the United States						
2 about slavery. Most of the northern states had outlawed slavery. However, in the						
3 South, slaves were considered important to the plantation owners who grew cotton						
4 and tobacco. The slavery issue was not settled until Abraham Lincoln was elected						
5 president in 1860.						
6 Until 1861 all the states had worked together as the United States.						
7 However, in 1861, leaders in the southern states believed that states had the right						
8 to leave, or secede from, the United States. The leaders in the northern and western						
9 states believed that no state had the right to secede. This difference in beliefs was						

The text is continued on the next page.

Cueing Systems

Miscue	L I N E #	Grapho-phonically Similar I M F (word level)	Syntactically Acceptable Unacceptable (sentence level)	Semantic Change in Meaning (CM) No Change in Meaning (NCM) (sentence level)

The cueing system grid is continued on the next page.

FORM SS

FORM SS

	O	I	S	A	Rp	Rv
1 0	one cause of the Civil War.					
1 1	The states that seceded from the Union were states that used slaves. Those					
1 2	states formed a group called the Confederate States of America, or simply, the					
1 3	Confederacy. When the Civil War began in 1861, there were eleven southern states					
1 4	in the Confederacy.					
1 5	The Civil War was very difficult because Americans were fighting					
1 6	Americans. In some cases brothers fought on opposing sides. After four long years					
1 7	of fighting, the South surrendered in April of 1865.					

TOTALS   Number of miscues _____   Number of self-corrections _____

Fluency: Does the Reader . . .

☐ read smoothly, accurately, in meaningful phrases?
☐ read word-by-word, choppy, plodding?
☐ use pitch, stress, and intonation to convey meaning of the text?
☐ repeat words and phrases because s/he is monitoring the meaning (self-correcting)?
☐ repeat words and phrases because s/he is trying to sound out words?
☐ use punctuation to divide the text into units of meaning?   ☐ ignore the punctuation?

Rating Scale: Circle One
4 = fluent reading / good pace   2 = choppy, plodding reading / slow pace
3 = fairly fluent / reasonable pace   1 = clearly labored, disfluent reading / very slow pace

Cueing Systems

	Miscue	Grapho-phonically Similar I M F (word level)	Syntactically Acceptable Unacceptable (sentence level)	Semantic Change in Meaning (CM) No Change in Meaning (NCM) (sentence level)
L I N E #				

Summary

☐ Most, ☐ few, ☐ no   miscues were graphophonically similar to the word in the passage.

☐ Most, ☐ few, ☐ no   miscues were syntactically matched.

☐ Most, ☐ few, ☐ no   miscues maintained the author's meaning.

☐ The self-corrections demonstrate that the reader monitors the meaning.

Form SS, Level 5

Retelling

Note: Indicate any probing with a "P"			
Expository Elements	All	Some	None
Description			
Collection			
Causation			
Problem / Solution			
Comparison			
Reader's Thumbnail Summary:			

Retelling Summary: ☐ many details, logical order ☐ some details, some order ☐ few details, disorder

Comprehension Questions and Possible Answers

___ (RIF) 1. Where does this text take place? (United States)

___ (PIT) 2. Why were slaves considered important to the South? (the plantation owners grew cotton and tobacco and needed workers to harvest the crops)

___ (RIF) 3. Who was president during the 1860s? (Abraham Lincoln)

___ (CAR) 4. What do you know about the phrase *no state had the right to secede?* (no state had the right to leave the United States of America) What does the phrase *no state had the right to secede* have to do with this text? (the leaders of the northern and western states believed that no state could leave the United States of America, but the southern states did secede)

___ (RIF) 5. What happened when the southern states decided to secede? (the Civil War began)

___ (RIF) 6. What were the southern states called during the Civil War? (Confederate States of America; the Confederacy)

___ (RIF) 7. How long did the Civil War last? (about four years)

___ (EAS) 8. In your opinion was the Civil War uniquely difficult? You think this because . . . (yes, it said Americans were fighting Americans; sometimes brothers fought on opposite sides)

Reader Text Relationship (RTR)　From the Text ☐ adequate ☐ not adequate　From Head to Text ☐ adequate ☐ not adequate

Scoring Guide Summary

WORD RECOGNITION
Independent......2
Instructional......9-10
Frustration......19+

COMPREHENSION
Independent......0-1
Instructional......2
Frustration......4+

Emotional Status:

Form SS, Level 5

FORM SS

Cueing Systems

L I N E #	Miscue	Grapho-phonically Similar I M F (word level)	Syntactically Acceptable Unacceptable (sentence level)	Semantic Change in Meaning (CM) No Change in Meaning (NCM) (sentence level)

The cueing system grid is continued on the next page.

FORM SS, LEVEL 6   Reader's Passages page 59

Prior Knowledge/Prediction

☐ Read the title and predict what the text is about.

Prior Knowledge

☐ a lot
☐ some
☐ none

☐ Read the first two sentences and add more to your prediction.

	O	I	S	A	Rp	Rv
How the Industrial Revolution Changed the Textile Industry						
1 In the late 1700s in the United States, the Industrial Revolution was						
2 making rapid changes in the way people lived. One of history's stories of how						
3 lives changed was told in the growth of the textile industry. Textile is woven or						
4 knitted cloth.						
5 For hundreds of years before the Industrial Revolution, farm families had						
6 spun yarn or thread and then woven the cloth. This was done in their homes. It						
7 was one way they could earn extra money. Oftentimes, a whole family would						
8 help to make the cloth. Merchants who wanted cloth to sell in their shops						
9 supplied a family with the raw goods like wool or cotton.						

The text is continued on the next page.

Cueing Systems

LINE #	Miscue	Grapho-phonically Similar I M F (word level)	Syntactically Acceptable Unacceptable (sentence level)	Semantic Change in Meaning (CM) No Change in Meaning (NCM) (sentence level)

Summary

- ☐ Most, ☐ few, ☐ no   miscues were graphophonically similar to the word in the passage.
- ☐ Most, ☐ few, ☐ no   miscues were syntactically matched.
- ☐ Most, ☐ few, ☐ no   miscues maintained the author's meaning.
- ☐ The self-corrections demonstrate that the reader monitors the meaning.

	O	I	S	A	Rp	Rv
1 0	In 1733, an Englishman named John Kay invented the flying shuttle,					
1 1	which helped weavers work more quickly. In 1764, James Hargreaves invented					
1 2	the spinning jenny. His invention could produce eight threads at once instead					
1 3	of only one. Finally, a power loom was invented.					
1 4	Soon the new machines became so big and cost so much that a family					
1 5	could not afford them. Also, they needed to be located near some kind of power					
1 6	source. Buildings called factories were built near fast-moving streams. Instead					
1 7	of spinning cloth in the farm homes, workers had to leave their homes. They					
1 8	traveled to the factories and worked long hours away from home.					

TOTALS

Number of miscues _____ Number of self-corrections _____

Fluency: Does the Reader . . .

- ☐ read smoothly, accurately, in meaningful phrases?
- ☐ read word-by-word, choppy, plodding?
- ☐ use pitch, stress, and intonation to convey meaning of the text?
- ☐ repeat words and phrases because s/he is monitoring the meaning (self-correcting)?
- ☐ repeat words and phrases because s/he is trying to sound out words?
- ☐ use punctuation to divide the text into units of meaning?   ☐ ignore the punctuation?

Rating Scale: Circle One

4 = fluent reading / good pace   2 = choppy, plodding reading / slow pace

3 = fairly fluent / reasonable pace   1 = clearly labored, disfluent reading / very slow pace

FORM SS

Retelling

Note: Indicate any probing with a "P"

Expository Elements	All	Some	None
Description			
Collection			
Causation			
Problem / Solution			
Comparison			

Reader's Thumbnail Summary:

Retelling Summary: ☐ many details, logical order ☐ some details, some order ☐ few details, disorder

Comprehension Questions and Possible Answers

____ (RIF) 1. Where does this text take place?   (United States)

____ (CAR) 2. What do you know about the phrase *spun yarn and thread?*   (yarn is a thick, twisted strand of many threads of wool, cotton, etc.; thread is a thin strand of cotton or flax; yarn and thread were made, spun on a spinning wheel) What does the phrase *spun yarn and thread* have to do with this text?   (it said farm families spun yarn or thread)

____ (RIF) 3. Why did farm families spin yarn and weave cloth in their homes?   (they wanted to make extra money)

____ (CAR) 4. What do you know about the phrase *raw goods?*   (the material used to make thread or yarn such as wool, cotton, flax, silk, etc.)   What does the phrase *raw goods* have to do with this text?   (it said that merchants supplied a family with the raw goods)

____ (PIT) 5. Why did the invention of the spinning jenny speed up the production of thread?   (it could produce eight threads at once rather than one)

____ (PIT) 6. Why did the power loom need to be located near a power source?   (it was so big that it needed a great source of power to run it)

____ (RIF) 7. What power source was used?   (a fast-moving stream)

____ (EAS) 8. In your opinion, were the lives of the farm families improved by the invention of textile machines? You think this because . . .   (no, they lost a means to earn extra money; they had to leave home to go to work)   (yes, they could get better cloth at cheaper prices)

Reader Text Relationship (RTR)   From the Text ☐ adequate ☐ not adequate   From Head to Text ☐ adequate ☐ not adequate

Scoring Guide Summary

WORD RECOGNITION
Independent 2
Instructional 10-11
Frustration .... 21+

COMPREHENSION
Independent 0-1
Instructional 2
Frustration .... 4+

Emotional Status:

Form SS, Level 6

FORM SS, LEVEL 7 Reader's Passages page 60

Prior Knowledge/Prediction

☐ Read the title and predict what the text is about.

☐ Read the first two sentences and add more to your prediction.

Prior Knowledge

☐ a lot
☐ some
☐ none

	The Birth of Public Education and Leisure Time	O	I	S	A	Rp	Rv
1	In the 1870s, some states turned their attention to public education. They passed						
2	compulsory attendance laws. These laws required that children attend school						
3	for a certain part of the year. By 1900, thirty states had passed such laws.						
4	More people turned their attention to higher education during the late 1800s.						
5	One of the reasons for this was the Morrill Act, passed in 1862. Under this act, states						
6	were given public lands to set up state colleges of engineering, teacher training, and						
7	agriculture. Meanwhile, the total number of colleges grew from about 500 in 1870 to						
8	nearly 1,000 in 1900. During these years, educational opportunities increased for both						
9	women and blacks. By 1900, nearly 100,000 women were attending college. Also,						
10	blacks had founded over thirty colleges, mostly in the South. Over 2,000 black students						

The text is continued on the next page.

Cueing Systems

LINE #	Miscue	Grapho-phonically Similar I M F (word level)	Syntactically Acceptable Unacceptable (sentence level)	Semantic Change in Meaning (CM) No Change in Meaning (NCM) (sentence level)

The cueing system grid is continued on the next page.

Cueing Systems

	Miscue	Grapho-phonically Similar I M F (word level)	Syntactically Acceptable Unacceptable (sentence level)	Semantic Change in Meaning (CM) No Change in Meaning (NCM) (sentence level)
L I N E #				

Summary

☐ Most, ☐ few, ☐ no   miscues were graphophonically similar to the word in the passage.

☐ Most, ☐ few, ☐ no   miscues were syntactically matched.

☐ Most, ☐ few, ☐ no   miscues maintained the author's meaning.

☐ The self-corrections demonstrate that the reader monitors the meaning.

Form SS, Level 7

	O	I	S	A	Rp	Rv
1 1	had graduated from these colleges.					
1 2	The growing interest in education was matched by a growing amount of time					
1 3	spent at leisure. Greater use of labor-saving machines both at work and at home made					
1 4	it possible for people to have more free time. This free time was spent in a number of					
1 5	ways. Americans spent a great deal of time at sports. The most popular spectator					
1 6	sport was baseball. In 1869, the first professional team, the Cincinnati Red Stockings,					
1 7	was formed. In 1876, teams from eight cities formed the National League, and in 1900,					
1 8	the American League was set up. The first World Series, between the Boston Red Sox					
1 9	and the Pittsburgh Pirates, was played in 1903.					
2 0	Football was nearly as popular a spectator sport as baseball. It had first been					
2 1	played between teams of students from the same college. Then in 1869, the first					
2 2	intercollegiate (involving two or more colleges) game took place between Princeton					
2 3	and Rutgers.					

TOTALS

Number of miscues _____   Number of self-corrections _____

Fluency: Does the Reader . . .

☐ read smoothly, accurately, in meaningful phrases?

☐ read word-by-word, choppy, plodding?

☐ use pitch, stress, and intonation to convey meaning of the text?

☐ repeat words and phrases because s/he is monitoring the meaning (self-correcting)?

☐ repeat words and phrases because s/he is trying to sound out words?

☐ use punctuation to divide the text into units of meaning?   ☐ ignore the punctuation?

Rating Scale: Circle One

4 = fluent reading / good pace   2 = choppy, plodding reading / slow pace

3 = fairly fluent / reasonable pace   1 = clearly labored, disfluent reading / very slow pace

Retelling

Note: Indicate any probing with a "P"

Expository Elements	All	Some	None
Description			
Collection			
Causation			
Problem / Solution			
Comparison			
Reader's Thumbnail Summary:			

Retelling Summary: ☐ many details, logical order ☐ some details, some order ☐ few details, disorder

Comprehension Questions and Possible Answers

_____ (RIF) 1. Where does this text take place?　(United States)

_____ (CAR) 2. What do you know about the phrase **compulsory attendance laws?**　(a law states that someone has to, is forced to, or is required to be present somewhere)　What does the phrase **compulsory attendance laws** have to do with this text? (it said that some states passed a law that required children to be present at school for a certain part of the year)

_____ (RIF) 3. In 1862, why did more people turn their attention toward higher education?　(the Morrill Act was passed)

_____ (PIT) 4. Why was the Morrill Act such a boost to higher education?　(states were given public lands to set up colleges of engineering, teacher training, and agriculture; the total number of colleges grew from 500 in 1870 to 1,000 by 1900)

_____ (EAS) 5. In your opinion, what impact did the Morrill Act have on equal rigrts?　You think this because . . .　(it was an early catalyst for establishing equal rights; it said that educational opportunities for women and blacks increased)

_____ (CAR) 6. What do you know about the phrase **time spent at leisure?**　(time a person has for recreation, time not spent working)　What does the phrase **time spent at leisure** have to do with this text?　(it said the growing interest in education was matched by a growing amount of time spent at leisure)

_____ (RIF) 7. Why did people have more leisure time?　(greater use of labor-saving machines at work and at home)

_____ (RIF) 8. In the late 1800s, what was the most popular sport?　(baseball)

Reader Text Relationship (RTR)　　From the Text　☐ adequate ☐ not adequate　　From Head to Text　☐ adequate ☐ not adequate

Scoring Guide Summary

WORD RECOGNITION

Independent......... 3
Instructional ... 14-15
Frustration .... 29+

COMPREHENSION

Independent...... 0-1
Instructional 2
Frustration .... 4+

Emotional Status:

Form SS, Level 7

FORM SS

Cueing Systems

Miscue	Grapho-phonically Similar I M F (word level)	Syntactically Acceptable Unacceptable (sentence level)	Semantic Change in Meaning (CM) No Change in Meaning (NCM) (sentence level)
L I N E #			

The cueing system grid is continued on the next page.

FORM SS, LEVEL 8   Reader's Passages page 61

Prior Knowledge/Prediction
☐ Read the title and predict what the text is about.

Prior Knowledge
☐ a lot
☐ some
☐ none

☐ Read the first two sentences and add more to your prediction.

	O	I	S	A	Rp	Rv

The Vietnam War

1   In 1955, American advisers had been sent to South Vietnam to train the

2   army. Both Presidents Eisenhower and Kennedy sent more advisers, support

3   troops, and military supplies between 1956 and 1962.

4   By the time Lyndon Johnson became president, a group of South Vietnamese

5   Communists, called the Viet Cong, were well established in South Vietnam. They

6   fought as guerrillas—bands who make war by harassment and sabotage. The Viet

7   Cong were getting help from North Vietnam.

8   In August 1964, after an attack by North Vietnamese gunboats on American

9   warships in the Gulf of Tonkin, President Johnson asked Congress to allow him to

10 take steps to prevent future attacks. Congress replied by passing the Tonkin Gulf

11 Resolution. It allowed the President, as Commander in Chief, to use any measure

12 necessary to halt an attack on American forces, stop North Vietnamese aggression,

13 and aid any SEATO member who asked for help defending its freedom.

14 In February 1965, Viet Cong attacks killed several Americans. This led

The text is continued on the next page.

Cueing Systems

Miscue	Graphophonically Similar I M F (word level)	Syntactically Acceptable Unacceptable (sentence level)	Semantic Change in Meaning (CM) No Change in Meaning (NCM) (sentence level)
L I N E #			

Summary

□ Most, □ few, □ no   miscues were graphophonically similar to the word in the passage.

□ Most, □ few, □ no   miscues were syntactically matched.

□ Most, □ few, □ no   miscues maintained the author's meaning.

□ The self-corrections demonstrate that the reader monitors the meaning.

Form SS, Level 8

	O	I	S	A	Rp	Rv
15	President Johnson to order the bombing of North Vietnam. The President also sent					
16	the first combat troops to South Vietnam. By the end of 1968, there were more than					
17	500,000 American soldiers there. The war was costing the United States about $25					
18	billion a year.					
19	Public opinion was divided over the Vietnam War. Many people felt that the					
20	war was necessary to stop communism. Others felt that it was a civil war that should					
21	be settled by the Vietnamese. Still others felt that the money spent on the war could					
22	be put to better use at home. These divisions were seen in Congress, which was					
23	divided between the "hawks"—those who favored greater military effort—and the					
24	"doves"—those who wanted the war effort lessened.					

TOTALS

Number of miscues _____   Number of self-corrections _____

Fluency: Does the Reader . . .

□ read smoothly, accurately, in meaningful phrases?

□ read word-by-word, choppy, plodding?

□ use pitch, stress, and intonation to convey meaning of the text?

□ repeat words and phrases because s/he is monitoring the meaning (self-correcting)?

□ repeat words and phrases because s/he is trying to sound out words?

□ use punctuation to divide the text into units of meaning?   □ ignore the punctuation?

Rating Scale: Circle One

4 = fluent reading / good pace   2 = choppy, plodding reading / slow pace
3 = fairly fluent / reasonable pace   1 = clearly labored, disfluent reading / very slow pace

FORM SS

Retelling

Note: Indicate any probing with a "P"

Expository Elements	All	Some	None
Description			
Collection			
Causation			
Problem / Solution			
Comparison			
Reader's Thumbnail Summary:			

Retelling Summary: □ many details, logical order □ some details, some order □ few details, disorder

Comprehension Questions and Possible Answers

____(RIF) 1. Where does this text take place? (United States/South Vietnam)

____(RIF) 2. In 1955, why were American advisers sent to South Vietnam? (they went to train the South Vietnamese army)

____(PIT) 3. Who were the Viet Cong? (a group of South Vietnamese communists who were well established in South Vietnam)

____(CAR) 4. What do you know about the phrase *made war by harassment and sabotage?* (to fight by disturbing or irritating; constantly damaging property to keep things from operating smoothly) What does the phrase *made war by harassment and sabotage* have to do with this text? (it said the Viet Cong made war in South Vietnam by harassment and sabotage)

____(PIT) 5. In 1965, why did President Johnson ask Congress to allow him to strengthen U.S. military power in South Vietnam? (because North Vietnamese gunboats had attacked American warships in the Gulf of Tonkin and he wanted to prevent future attacks)

____(EAS) 6. In your opinion, should President Johnson have ordered the bombing of North Vietnam? You think this because . . . (yes, Viet Cong attacks had killed many Americans and more lives could have been lost) (no, we should have brought the Americans home because it was a civil war)

____(RIF) 7. By the end of 1968 how many American soldiers were in South Vietnam? (500,000)

____(PIT) 8. What was the difference between the hawks and the doves? (the hawks were Americans who favored a greater military effort in Vietnam; the doves wanted the war effort lessened)

Reader Text Relationship (RTR)   From the Text □ adequate □ not adequate   From Head to Text □ adequate □ not adequate

Scoring Guide Summary

WORD RECOGNITION
Independent 3
Instructional 14-15
Frustration .... 29+

COMPREHENSION
Independent 0-1
Instructional 2
Frustration .... 4+

Emotional Status:

Form SS, Level 8

FORM SS, LEVEL 9   Reader's Passages page 62

Prior Knowledge/Prediction

☐ Read the title and predict what the text is about.

Prior Knowledge
☐ a lot
☐ some
☐ none

☐ Read the first two sentences and add more to your prediction.

Knowing the American Economy

		D	I	S	A	Rp	Rv
1	In recent years, the American economy has been changing. It has been						
2	growing steadily. The gross national product (GNP), the value of all goods and						
3	services produced in one year, rose. In 1950, the GNP was $286 billion. In 1984, it						
4	was $3.6 trillion. This growth, aided by new technology, has affected the labor force						
5	and farming. Nevertheless, there are problems with the economy that need to be						
6	corrected. One thing that has helped change the American economy is technology—						
7	application of ideas, methods, and tools to the production of goods. Technology has						
8	helped Americans make more goods with less work. It has also helped Americans						
9	raise their standard of living, and it has given them more leisure time.						
10	One example of the new technology is automation, the making of products						
11	by machines that are controlled electronically. For example, machines can be used to						
12	weld parts of cars together and to print newspapers. Machines that are run by only						
13	one or two people can roll and shape steel. However, automation eliminates the						
14	need for certain jobs. This means fewer jobs and more people out of work.						

The text is continued on the next page.

Cueing Systems

Miscue		Grapho-phonically Similar I M F (word level)	Syntactically Acceptable Unacceptable (sentence level)	Semantic Change in Meaning (CM) No Change in Meaning (NCM) (sentence level)
L I N E #				

The cueing system grid is continued on the next page.

FORM SS

Cueing Systems

		Grapho-phonically Similar I M F (word level)	Syntactically Acceptable Unacceptable (sentence level)	Semantic Change in Meaning (CM) No Change in Meaning (NCM) (sentence level)
Miscue				
L I N E #				

Summary

☐ Most, ☐ few, ☐ no — miscues were graphophonically similar to the word in the passage.

☐ Most, ☐ few, ☐ no — miscues were syntactically matched.

☐ Most, ☐ few, ☐ no — miscues maintained the author's meaning.

☐ The self-corrections demonstrate that the reader monitors the meaning.

Form SS, Level 9

	O	I	S	A	Rp	Rv
1 5	Another example of the new technology is computerization. Computers					
1 6	were first developed in the 1950s, but they were large and expensive. During the					
1 7	1960s, scientists replaced bulky tubes with small transistors, and computers became					
1 8	smaller and less expensive. They were used by banks, hospitals, and businesses to					
1 9	store and file vast amounts of information. In the 1970s, computers became even					
2 0	smaller when they were powered by microchips, tiny chips of silicon smaller than a					
2 1	postage stamp. Soon, doctors, lawyers, housewives, students, and others were able					
2 2	to buy their own computers. Now, many schools and colleges require their students					
2 3	to own a personal computer.					
2 4	Problems with foreign trade affect the economy. Over time, the United					
2 5	States has imported more resources, such as oil, along with a growing number of					
2 6	manufactured goods. Cars, radios, cameras, and hundreds of other items made in					
2 7	other countries are sold to Americans every year. So much has been sold that the					
2 8	United States has a poor balance of trade.					

TOTALS

Number of miscues _____ Number of self-corrections _____

Fluency: Does the Reader . . .

☐ read smoothly, accurately, in meaningful phrases?

☐ read word-by-word, choppy, plodding?

☐ use pitch, stress, and intonation to convey meaning of the text?

☐ repeat words and phrases because s/he is monitoring the meaning (self-correcting)?

☐ repeat words and phrases because s/he is trying to sound out words?

☐ use punctuation to divide the text into units of meaning?   ☐ ignore the punctuation?

Rating Scale: Circle One
4 = fluent reading / good pace   2 = choppy, plodding reading / slow pace
3 = fairly fluent / reasonable pace   1 = clearly labored, disfluent reading / very slow pace

Expository Elements	All	Some	None
Description			
Collection			
Causation			
Problem / Solution			
Comparison			

Reader's Thumbnail Summary:

Scoring Guide Summary

WORD RECOGNITION
Independent 3-4
Instructional 17-18
Frustration ...... 35+

COMPREHENSION
Independent 0-1
Instructional 2
Frustration ...... 4+

Emotional Status:

Form SS, Level 9

Retelling

Retelling Summary: ☐ many details, logical order ☐ some details, some order ☐ few details, disorder

Comprehension Questions and Possible Answers

(RIF) 1. Where does this text take place? (United States)

(CAR) 2. What do you know about the phrase **gross national product (GNP)?** (it is a measure of our nation's wealth) What does the phrase **gross national product (GNP)** have to do with this text? (it said the value of all goods and services produced in one year rose)

(PIT) 3. How has modern technology affected Americans? (technology has helped Americans make more goods with less work; it has raised their standard of living and given them more leisure time)

(CAR) 4. What do you know about the word **automation?** (if a machine is automated, it is self-moving and self-regulating) What does the word **automation** have to do with this text? (it said that one example of new technology is automation, the making of products by machines that are controlled electronically)

(EAS) 5. In your opinion, has automation affected our economy for better cr for worse? You think this because . . . (for better, because automated technology has helped Americans make more goods for less work) (for worse, because it eliminates the need for certain jobs)

(RIF) 6. When were computers first developed? (in the 1950s)

(PIT) 7. Why did the invention of the microchip have such a dramatic effect on the economy? (many people, doctors, lawyers, homemakers, students, and others were able to buy computers)

(PIT) 8. Why does the United States have such a poor balance of trade? (so many products from other countries are sold each year in America)

Reader Text Relationship (RTR)   From the Text ☐ adequate ☐ not adequate   From Head to Text ☐ adequate ☐ not adequate

FORM SS

SECTION V

Development and Validation of the ARI

DEVELOPMENT AND VALIDATION OF THE *ARI* ———————————

Considerable effort has been devoted to establishing the content validity of the *ARI*. From the first edition through this edition, data has been collected and field studies conducted. This section provides information concerning the development of the passages, readability data for the narrative passages, vocabulary diversity scores for narrative and expository passages, and the field-testing information gathered from working with elementary students, middle school students, and teachers.

The development of the first edition of the *Analytical Reading Inventory* took place over a two-year period and included writing, field testing, computer analyses, and several revisions of the 30 original passages. With the inclusion of expository passages in the fourth edition, the same procedures were followed. During the preparation of the sixth edition, students and teachers from Lynwood Elementary and West Newton Elementary schools in Decatur Township, Indianapolis, Indiana, and Central Elementary School in Lebanon, Indiana, participated in field testing the newly developed format for the Teacher Record, the redefined comprehension questions, and the newly written passages. The new material created for the seventh edition was field tested with preservice teachers at the University of Indianapolis and in-service teachers in Albuquerque, New Mexico, and Lebanon, Indiana.

Matching *ARI* Assessment Components to National Standards and Indicators

This eighth edition matches each *ARI* assessment component to NCTE/IRA standards that describe reading competency. More definitively, Indiana and other state standards/indicators lists and the standards compendium compiled by Mid-continental Research for Education and Learning (McREL) were used as resources. An assessment component is one essential element of a comprehensive assessment session. The data from all 10 *ARI* components constitute a reader's multidimensional profile because each component represents a comprehensive analysis of the standards and indicators that describe reading competency.

Passage Content: Narrative and Expository

The *ARI* includes originally written narrative passages that are motivational and nonsexist in nature. Therefore, time was spent learning about the reading interests of students at various grade levels. Such sources as *Children and Books* (Sutherland & Arbuthnot, 1972), *The New York Times Report on Teenage Reading Tastes and Habits* (Freiberger, 1973), *Reading Interests of Children and Young Adults* (Kujoth, 1970), *Reading Children's Books and Our Pluralistic Society* (Tanyzer & Karl, 1972), *Through the Eyes of a Child, An Introduction to Children's Literature* (Norton, 2003), *Children's Literature, Briefly* (Jacobs & Tunnell, 2000), and *Teaching Children to Read: From Basals to Books* (Reutzel & Cooter, 2004) provided information that influenced the content and style of the passages in the *ARI* from the first edition through the seventh edition.

The situations described in the passages involve actions and events that engage children's feelings so that the reader can empathize with the principal character. The topics were carefully selected to appeal to both boys and girls, and the content was written to be grade-level appropriate.

Consistency across all forms is an essential factor to maintain the integrity of the assessment instrument; therefore, with a passage level, the same content topic occurs across the three narrative forms. For example, all three passages at the passage Level 6 are written about famous African American scientists or inventors. This consistency enables the examiner to change forms when determined necessary.

Although the narrative passages were not written with a controlled vocabulary, careful selection of words was a factor taken into consideration. In the first edition word selection was guided in some cases by the graded word lists contained in *Basic Elementary Reading Vocabularies* (Harris & Jacobson, 1972). In the sixth and seventh editions, word selection was governed by a computer analysis of the number of difficult words found on the Dale-Chall list (Micro Power and Light, 1995a).

The expository passages reflect the style of writing that students encounter in science and social studies texts. The science passages at passage Levels 4 through 9 are from various science textbooks published by Merrill Publishing Company. Passages 4 through 6 are from *Accent on Science* (Sund et al., 1985); passages 7 and 8 from *Principles of Science* (Heimler, 1986); and passage 9 is from *Merrill General Science* (Moyer & Bishop, 1986). Passage Levels 1, 2, and 3 were originally written and represent topics that are included in the Merrill primary texts.

The social studies passages were selected from various social studies textbooks. Passage Levels 7 through 9 were selected from *America Is* (Drewery & O'Connor, 1987), published by Merrill Publishing Company. Passage Levels 1 through 6 were originally written and represent topics that are included in published social studies textbooks.

Because the passages, narrative and expository, were intended for assessment rather than instruction, the selection of each passage was based on a list of considerations that correlate with the function of the assessment. These considerations include the following:

- A passage must be short with cohesive, captivating, meaningful content.
- From primer passage to passage Level 9, the passages should increase in difficulty. The length of the passage, the concept load, the density of ideas, and the use of polysyllabic words are significant factors affecting the readability of a text.
- The content of each passage must be contextually descriptive, without reliance on illustrations.
- All originally written passages must reflect the style of writing, the topics, and the vocabulary found in narrative and expository texts.

Readability and Vocabulary Diversity Results

Passage level validation was established through the use of readability formulas and vocabulary diversity scores. The readability formula scores provided grade level readability estimates for each passage. The vocabulary diversity scores (type-token ratios) provided specific information about the vocabulary diversity and syntactic complexity of the language used in each passage. The formulas and ratio were used to ensure that the passages within a form progressively increased in difficulty and that the passages across Forms A, B, and C were comparable.

The revised Spache formula (Micro Power and Light, 1995a) was used to calculate the readability estimates for Passage Levels Primer through 3. The Powers formula (Micro Power and Light, 1995a) was used for Passage Levels 4 through 6, and the Flesch (Micro Power and Light, 1995a) for Passage Levels 7 through 9. The results are summarized in Table 1.

> The term *passage level* refers to the assigned level of difficulty of a passage.
>
> The term *reading level* refers to the reader's level of ability with a given passage: independent, instructional, frustration, or listening.

TABLE 1 Readability Formula Results

Level	Form A	Spache	Powers	Flesch	Form B	Spache	Powers	Flesch	Form C	Spache	Powers	Flesch
PP	The Lost Candy	1.2			Winning the Game	1.1			The Runaway Dog	1.1		
P	Pat Hides Out	1.8			Growing Up	1.6			Too Many Animals	1.6		
1	The Crowded Car	2.0			The Surprise Party	1.9			The Show-Off	1.8		
2	The Baseball Star	2.1			The Soccer Game	2.5			The Busy Road	2.0		
3	Exploring a Cave	2.9			The Baseball Card	3.0			Belonging to the Club	3.2		
4	Crossing the River		4.7		The Small Pony		4.6		The Beloved Horse		4.5	
5	The Bicycle Race		4.9		A Woman Jockey		4.8		A Woman Race Car Driver		5.3	
6	Remembering a Surgeon		5.6		The First Gas Mask		5.7		Open Heart Surgery		6.0	
7	Turning Himself In			7.8	Dating a Loner			7.0	Broken Friendship			7.6
8	Adjusting to a New School			8.3	First Day of High School Jitters			8.2	The Science Project			8.3
9	The Crystal Clear Lake			9.9	Restoring Pigeon Creek			9.9	The Urban Garden			9.6

The results of a readability formula can provide an easy-to-use device for estimating the relative difficulty of a text, yet it should be kept in mind that a formula score is only an estimate. Conceptual difficulty and background knowledge are other factors of text difficulty that a formula does not assess (Leu & Kinzer, 2003). In some instances, the use of a readability formula to rate the difficulty of a passage can provide limited if not misleading data. For example, because a readability formula generally assumes that more syllables imply greater difficulty, use of a formula would consider the word *America* more difficult than *atom*. The polysyllabic word *America* would cause the passage readability score to increase, when actually a reader's background and concept knowledge could cause the passage to be easily readable.

In addition to using a readability formula to demonstrate the difficulty of the passages, a Vocabulary Diversity Score (Micro Power and Light, 1995b) was calculated for each passage. Vocabulary diversity refers to the extent to which the words differ within a text. For example, a 100-word passage written with 100 different words is more diverse than a 100-word passage written with only 20 different words. The factors used to compute a vocabulary diversity score are the total number of words and the number of different words. The technical term for this score is *type-token ratio.* Because the passages varied in length, a corrected type-token ratio was calculated. The number of different words was divided by the total of the square root of two times the total number of words. The Vocabulary Diversity Scores are summarized in Tables 2 and 3.

The data presented in Tables 2 and 3 provide the following quantitative information about the narrative and expository passages:

- Within each form (A, B, C, S, SS), there is a progression of increasing difficulty demonstrated by one or both factors.
- Within each form there is an increase in the total number of words from one passage to the next (except Form A, passage levels 3 and 4).

Level	Form A			Form B			Form C		
	Number of Total Words	Number of Different Words	Vocabulary Diversity	Number of Total Words	Number of Different Words	Vocabulary Diversity	Number of Total Words	Number of Different Words	Vocabulary Diversity
PPrimer	28	22	2.889	27	19	2.586	28	19	2.539
Primer	52	28	2.746	53	29	2.817	55	32	3.051
Level 1	79	42	3.341	79	61	4.853	76	51	4.137
Level 2	118	71	4.622	116	69	4.523	122	83	5.403
Level 3	146	88	5.150	147	95	5.541	149	86	4.982
Level 4	145	94	5.520	153	98	5.602	152	101	5.793
Level 5	170	114	6.183	181	114	5.992	193	107	5.446
Level 6	188	122	6.292	189	118	6.069	190	118	6.053
Level 7	259	147	6.459	236	149	6.855	261	145	5.910
Level 8	298	198	8.114	304	181	7.358	285	173	7.238
Level 9	342	209	7.99	347	206	7.820	343	199	7.609

■ **TABLE 3** *ARI* Vocabulary Diversity Scores Expository Passages

Level	Form S Science			Form SS Social Studies		
	Number of Total Words	Number of Different Words	Vocabulary Diversity	Number of Total Words	Number of Different Words	Vocabulary Diversity
Level 1	83	45	3.488	80	38	3.015
Level 2	121	57	3.653	130	80	4.968
Level 3	140	61	3.653	156	90	5.084
Level 4	173	102	5.483	172	96	5.189
Level 5	200	108	5.400	190	95	5.016
Level 6	218	106	5.096	206	139	6.847
Level 7	282	122	5.148	290	142	5.916
Level 8	288	134	5.583	288	158	6.583
Level 9	352	164	6.189	349	184	6.964

■ Within each form there is a consistent increase in the number of different words; therefore, with only a few exceptions, an increase in the vocabulary diversity is demonstrated.

■ Finally, looking from Forms A, B, and C (then from S and SS), the number of total words, the number of different words, and the vocabulary diversity scores are within a reasonable range of variation, demonstrating consistency from one form to the next.

When one combines the quantitative data presented in Tables 2 and 3 with the qualitative considerations such as conceptual difficulty and background knowledge, the passage levels assigned to the narrative and expository passages are valid. It should be kept in mind that the actual measure of difficulty of any text is related to the concept load and the reader's background knowledge as well as the quantitative information. A more authentic means to determine if the passage level is appropriately assigned is to have it read by readers for whom it is intended; therefore, extensive field testing with elementary and middle school students was undertaken.

Field Testing

A description of all the steps that led to the field testing of the narrative passages with students is difficult because, at various stages in the development of the inventory, some portions were partially tested and revised prior to the field testing. For example, if doubt arose concerning the content or the wording of a specific passage, it was tried out on school-age children. A similar procedure was used with the comprehension questions. Often the advice of classroom teachers and reading specialists was solicited when a particularly troublesome problem arose.

Finally, the *ARI* needed field testing by individuals unassociated with its development. This testing was accomplished by having approximately 80 advanced undergraduate students (in their second course on reading instruction) use it to assess the reading strategies of approximately 200 students in grades two through eight. The users of the inventory were asked to pay particular attention to (1) the appropriateness of the directions for its use, (2) the motivational appeal of the respective passages, (3) any ambiguities in the passages or the questions, and (4) the extent to which the comprehension questions were passage dependent.

Results of the field testing showed the major problem to be with the comprehension questions, and many were subsequently revised. Field testing also indicated that some passages were too difficult, and these were rewritten at an easier reading level. Finally, the passages and the questions were sent to Merrill Publishing for editing, and then the final readability checks and computer analyses of the texts were conducted.

During the preparation of the fourth edition of the *ARI*, some field testing was done related to the differences between narrative and expository text. Eighty-six students in grades two through eight (Orchard School in Indianapolis, Indiana) participated in the study. The purpose of the study was to find out from among three *ARI* passages—narrative, science, or social studies — which passage the students felt was most difficult to comprehend and the reasons for the difficulty. For a full explanation of this study refer to Section II, "Acquiring Background Knowledge," pages 11–13.

The material written for the eighth edition was field tested with undergraduate students at the University of Indianapolis, Indianapolis, Indiana, and with in-service teachers in Lebanon, Indiana, and Albuquerque, New Mexico. As a result of this testing, revisions were made to Section II and several reader's passages. In its final form the eighth edition offers copy-ready lesson plans for university professors and staff developers.

Illustrations at Preprimer, Primer, and Level 1

A study was done to find out if illustrations included with the preprimer and primer passages influenced results of the assessment. Twenty-five end-of-year first graders from one urban school and one rural school participated in this study. Teachers were asked to include students of all reading abilities, independent to frustration. According to their teachers' final reports, the following numbers of students read first grade material at the various levels: the independent to definite instructional level = 6 students; the definite instructional to high transitional level = 11; the low transitional to frustration level = 8.

Based on the reading level information from the teachers, students at the independent level or high definite instructional level read passages without illustrations. Students at the transitional level read a mix of passages with and without illustrations. Students at the frustration level read passages with illustrations. The format for administering the passages was followed according to *ARI* instructions: reading the title (aiding words if necessary); making a prediction and accessing prior knowledge; reading the passage; retelling; and responding to comprehension questions. The results were:

- Students at the independent or high definite instructional level read passages without the support of illustrations. They demonstrated word recognition and comprehension at the independent or definite instructional levels.
- Students at the barely definite instructional level and the high transitional level read some passages without illustrations and some with illustrations. If the reader was strategic and focused on making meaning rather than on just pronouncing words, the comprehension of the passage was adequate with or without illustrations.
- Students at the lower transitional level read the passages without illustrations with some miscues, with partially correct retellings, and with some comprehension questions correctly answered. The same results occurred when they read the passages with illustrations.
- Students at the frustration level read only passages with illustrations. In some instances the students looked to the illustrations as a means of pronouncing an unknown word. Thus, the illustration did support word recognition for students at the frustration level. However, the use of illustrations did not affect comprehension; in many cases, the retellings included background information rather than facts from the text. When asked comprehension questions, readers often answered, "I don't know."

Conclusions About Illustrations

The *ARI* is not designed to assess the reader's ability to access information from picture clues. Rather, the *ARI* is designed to assess a reader's ability to process text, including the ability to make a logical prediction and access prior knowledge, to pronounce words, and to comprehend.

After reading the title, independently or with aiding, the reader is asked to make a prediction and access prior knowledge. Then, after reading the first two sentences, the reader is asked to apply the same skills. If a reader applies these skills, the illustration has little to no impact upon the results. On the other hand, if the reader relies upon picture clues rather than strategically thinking while processing the text, the illustrations at the preprimer or primer level may affect word recognition, but fail to adequately influence the reader's comprehension. This finding matches the *rule of thumb* established for passages preprimer and beyond (Section II, Two Instructional Levels Chart, pages 44–47). The rule of thumb is that if the word recognition totals and the comprehension totals do not indicate the same reading level, the comprehension data (question error count, retelling, and fluency) determines the student's accurate reading level for that passage.

The results of the study established that the prime function of an *ARI* illustration is to serve as a means for making a friendly connection to the text. Based on this notion, the decision was made to use illustrations for the preprimer, primer, and level 1 *ARI* passages, and each illustration reveals only information contained in the title and the first two sentences. Darren Wall, a second-third grade teacher at Fishback Creek Public Academy, Pike Township Schools in Indianapolis, Indiana, is the illustrator.

Inter-Scorer Reliability Study

In March 2003, nine reading teachers at Metropolitan School District (MSD) of Pike Township, Indianapolis, Indiana, participated in an inter-scorer reliability study conducted by Jenny Stapp. The participating teachers were responsible for collecting and reporting assessment data for all of the district's elementary schools. Previous to this study, the teachers had participated in a three-day professional development workshop with Mary Lynn Woods that focused upon training the teachers how to use the *ARI*.

This study was conducted to determine inter-scorer reliability—the degree of consistency among the Pike teachers' scores when using the *ARI* to assess students. It was important for the district to establish inter-scorer reliability for several reasons:

1. If there is consistency in examiners' scores, it is possible to confidently compare data from different schools within the district.

2. If there is consistency in examiners' scores, reading teachers can have confidence in the data for children who transfer between schools within the district.

3. If there is inconsistency, there may be a need for further discussion and professional development.

To determine inter-scorer consistency the teachers listened to *ARI* passages read by students on CD 2, tracks 8-11, featuring readers at three of the reading levels—independent, instructional, and frustration. As teachers listened, each completed the corresponding Examiner's Record passages. The four areas of documentation analyzed were:

1. total miscue count—good consistency with small variation related to categorizing some miscues

2. fluency rating—some variation (for example, the more fluent a reader, the more consistency; the less fluent reader, the more variation between the 2 and 3 rating); however, none of the variations affected the overall determination of reading level

3. comprehension questions—some variation in the way teachers gave half or zero credit for a response; the variations did not affect the overall determination of reading level

4. overall reading level—great consistency and accuracy

The Pike teachers met to discuss the results of the study. Mary Lynn Woods attended the meeting and the information on comprehension questions located in Section II, Learning How to Use the *ARI*, was reviewed and clarified. Teachers felt that additional staff development was needed to help them distinguish the subtleties in reader cognition (RTR). The descriptions for fluency rating scale were discussed, and as a result revisions were made for the *ARI* eighth edition.

SECTION VI

Appendix

Component 3

**Prior Knowledge/
Prediction Analysis**

• Page 22.

Directions

1. In the Prior Knowledge/Prediction box at the top of the passage, the rating scale serves as a way to rank the amount of a reader's prior knowledge. If the student reads the title and the first two sentences of the text, he or she can advantageously gather information—using it to access background knowledge which will support a more logical prediction. As the student reads further into the passage, the background knowledge will support word recognition and comprehension.

3. Patrick was using his background knowledge to attempt the pronunciation of the words, but soon began to struggle with a mismatch between what his head was telling him and what his eyes were seeing on the page. He grew stressed and frustrated because he knew he wasn't succeeding.

4. When a reader accesses background knowledge and uses it to predict both the meaning and the pronunciation of the text, he is in a more advantageous position than when he focuses solely upon the pronunciation of the words. The ability to access prior knowledge is an essential skill to comprehending a text. The *ARI* assesses the reader's ability to access prior knowledge before and during reading the text. On a standardized or any other silent reading assessment, no one would ever find out whether the reader was able to apply this essential skill.

Directions

Component 4

**Oral Reading Miscue
Analysis**

• Page 23.

2.

Reader #1: "The Surprise Party"

"Hurry," / *She* called to all her sisters and brothers. "Hide the balloons and then everybody hide. Don't make / a sound or say a word. Dad will be coming home soon."

When Mr. Brown came into the house, he didn't see his children. All was still, so he didn't / hear anything. Then he / heard his children laughing, singing, and calling, "Surprise!" He saw many blue, green, and red balloons flying in the air. A big smile grew on his face.

Reader #2: "The First Gas Mask"

The explosion was ~~horrible~~ *terrible* that (tragic) day in/Cleveland, Ohio, in 1916. Thirty-two (men) were trapped in a tunnel 250 feet below Lake Erie, *ake SC* and *on* (no) one could enter the smoke-filled atmosphere *at atom at*. "Someone *Some SC* get Garrett Morgan to help!" ~~shouted~~ *yelled* a man. "Morgan's breathing/device *br breath SC* is the only thing that can help (to) rescue the survivors!"

Garrett Morgan and his brother quickly (volunteered) (to) assist *assisted*. "My breathing device will save those victims' lives," Morgan announced *said* with confidence. "I invented it so firemen <u>can breathe</u> when they enter a burning house filled with suffocating *suff suffica SC* gases. We tested my device in an air-tight tent that was filled with/(the) (foulest,) ~~thickest~~ *thick* smoke. A man put (my) diver's helmet-(like) device with ~~long~~ *many* breathing tubes running to the floor over his head, went into the tent, *and* stayed twenty minutes, and *he* emerged unharmed!"

Then, Morgan and *^* his brother ~~placed~~ *played* the/devices over their heads *^* and rushed into the death-trap tunnel. One by one they carried each man to *out* (the) (surface.) Although not every life was spared *saved*, it was Morgan's/invention, the first gas mask, that saved lives that day and in (the) years to come.

Directions

2. Most examiners would predict Caitlin's reading level as independent. The telltale qualities in her voice are meaningful phrasing, appropriate pitch, stress, intonation, and effective use of punctuation.

3.   a. reads smoothly in meaningful phrases
      b. uses pitch, stress, intonation to convey meaning
      c. repeats words to self-correct
      d. uses punctuation to divide text into meaningful units

4. 4 = fluent reading/good pace

5. After listening to Amanda read, most examiners would predict her reading level to be independent. After hearing her highly accurate retelling, it is clear that the level is independent. Amanda's repetitions served as self-corrections. The intonation of most sentences and phrases tell us that she comprehends ("Strike two, screamed the man!").

Component 6

Retelling Analysis

• Pages 27 and 28.

1. Well, this is a story about a
dog, and the boy yells to his
dog, "Look out, you're gonna
get hit!"
The dog runs across a busy
road,
and he gets hit anyway.
The boy feels real scared! He
starts to cry.
If he can get help fast it will
be okay.
Then, he runs home to tell
his mom and dad.
If they hurry up, they can save the dog.

Story Elements	All	Some	None
Main Character(s)	✓		
Time and Place	✓		
Problem	✓		
Plot Details in Sequence	✓		
Turning Point	✓		
Resolution	✓		
Reader's Thumbnail Summary: *A dog gets hit on a busy road.*			

The quality of this retelling is excellent. Yes, you should agree that the examiner marked the correct Retelling Summary as: ☐ many details, logical order.

Yes, the elements are logically ordered.

Jenny used some of author's words and style of language.

The Reader's Thumbnail Summary statement is adequate (states the problem).

2. It's about a pony. Jody
is really worried
about her pony. It's sick.
The barn door shook.
She was really tired.

P: Can you tell more?
SR: That night Jody stayed
with her horse.
She took a blanket to
the barn.

P: Can you tell more?
SR: No.

Note: Indicate any probing with a "P"

Story Elements	All	Some	None
Main Character(s)	✓		
Time and Place		✓	
Problem		✓	
Plot Details in Sequence			✓
Turning Point			✓
Resolution			✓
Reader's Thumbnail Summary: *A sick pony.*			

The quality of this retelling is poor. Yes, you should agree that the examiner marked the correct "Retelling Summary"—☐ few details, disorder. No, elements are disordered.

Jenny used little of the author's words or style of language.

The Reader's Thumbnail Summary is barely adequate (states problem in a phrase, not a sentence, and matches the quality of the poor retelling).

3. Busy
   a. in complete, well-structured sentences
   b. mimics the author's choice of words
   c. mimics the author's style of language
   d. all story elements in logical and proper sequence

Beloved
   a. simple sentences, some phrases
   b. few of author's word choices
   c. little of author's style of language
   d. some elements, few plot details, little logical or proper sequence

Component 7

Comprehension Question/Reader Text Relationship Analysis

• Page 30.

Directions

1.   Who are the two main characters in this story?   Res: *Pat and his mom*
RIF; retells literal facts;   from text

2.   Where is Pat sitting?   Res: *by the tree*   RIF;   retells literal facts;
from text

3.   What is Pat's problem? Res: *he does not want to work*
PIT;   connect a problem with the cause;   mostly from the text
Explanation: Even in a primer passage, information can be implied.
Here the reader must connect two pieces of information and infer there is a problem.

4.   What do you know about the word *work*? What does the word *work* have to do with this story?   Res: *work is a chore like doing dishes; his mom wanted Pat to do some work*
CAR;   accesses prior knowledge, uses context and author's intended meaning to comprehend; from head to text

5.   What did Pat decide to do about this problem?   Res: *hide by a tree*
PIT;   connects two facts at literal level, cause and effect;   from the text

6.   Where did Pat hide and why?   Res: *by the big tree, so his mom can't find him*
PIT;   connect two literal facts;   from the text
Res: *the big tree is large enough to hide him so mom won't find him*
PIT;   connects two facts, infers information, deducts;   from head to text

7.   Do you think Pat's mom will find him? You think this because . . .
Res: *Yes, she might know because he often hides by the tree.*
EAS;   evaluates, substantiates response with an inference;   from head to text
Res: *No, she might not see him because the tree is too big.*
EAS;   evaluates, substantiates response with an inference;   from head to text

Component 8

Cueing Systems Analysis

• Page 32.

1.

L I N E #	Miscue	Graphophonically Similar I M F (word level)	Syntactically Acceptable Unacceptable (sentence level)	Semantic Change in Meaning (CM) No Change in Meaning (NCM) (sentence level)
	wert	IF	U	CM
	want	IF	A	CM
	they	I	A	CM
	breath	IM	U	CM
	much		U	CM
	straight	I	U	CM
	large		A	NCM
	laughed		A	NCM

Cueing Systems (table title)

2. The reader's self-corrections indicate that she is monitoring the meaning of the text. Cognitively the reader is matching what she sees with her in-head prior knowledge.

Component 9

Q & Q Analysis Developing a Reader's Multidimensional Profile

• Page 34 (2–4).
• Page 43 (11).

Level	Word Rec.	Comp.
Ind.	99–100%	90–100%
Instr.	95–99%	75–89%
Frust.	90–below	50%–below
List.	N/A	75%

Directions

2. You found out that qualitative factors identify the significance of a particular miscue. For example, a miscue can be significant, but if it does not affect comprehension, it may not be critical. Additionally, qualitative factors refer to those reading behaviors that are observed as a student orally reads. A reader's self-corrections are important bits of information because they indicate that the reader is focusing on the meaning of the text.

3. Quantitative data reflects the number of miscues occurring in a given passage and the number of comprehension errors. The number of errors is translated into a percentage. Quantitative data alone does not represent a reader's total ability.

4. Both types of data are essential when generating a reader's multidimensional profile. An examiner must learn how to record, analyze, synthesize, and summarize both types of data.

Five Readers' Qualitative Summary Chart

QUALITATIVE FACTORS ↓	Reader #1: Freddie Independent Level	Reader #2: Kala Independent Level	Reader #3: Patrick Instructional Level	Reader #4: Andrew Frustration Level	Reader #5: Abi Listening Level
PRIOR KNOWLEDGE	☐ a lot ☑ some ☐ none	☑ a lot ☐ some ☐ none	☐ a lot ☑ some ☐ none	☐ a lot ☑ some ☐ none	☐ a lot ☑ some ☐ none
PREDICTION	☑ logical ☑ uses context and adds more info. ☑ complete sentence	☑ logical ☑ uses context and adds more info. ☑ complete sentence	☐ logical ☐? uses context and adds more info. ☑ complete sentence	☐ logical ☐ uses context and adds more info. ☐ complete sentence _no_	☑ logical ☐? uses context and adds more info. ☑ complete sentence
CUEING SYSTEMS (Miscue Analysis) *Most miscues are . . .*	☐ graphophonically similar ☐ a syntactic match ☐ maintain author's meaning (sem.) ☑ self-corrections for meaning	☐ graphophonically similar ☐ a syntactic match ☐ maintain author's meaning (sem.) ☑ self-corrections for meaning	☑ graphophonically similar ☐ a syntactic match ☐ maintain author's meaning (sem.) _no_ ☐ self-corrections for meaning _some_	☑ graphophonically similar ☐ a syntactic match ☐ maintain author's meaning (sem.) ☐ self-corrections for meaning _no_	☐ graphophonically similar ☐ a syntactic match ☐ maintain author's meaning (sem.) ☐ self-corrections for meaning _N/A_
FLUENCY	☐ fluent ☑ fairly fluent ☐ choppy ☐ disfluent Rating = *3*	☑ fluent ☐ fairly fluent ☐ choppy ☐ disfluent Rating = *4*	☐ fluent ☐ fairly fluent ☑ choppy ☐ disfluent Rating = *2*	☐ fluent ☐ fairly fluent ☐ choppy ☑ disfluent Rating = *1*	☐ fluent _N/A_ ☐ fairly fluent ☐ choppy ☐ disfluent Rating =
RETELLING	☑ all story elements ☐ some story ele. ☐ few story ele. ☑ organized ☐ disorganized ☑ well-constructed sentences; author's style and words	☑ all story elements ☐ some story ele. ☐ few story ele. ☑ organized ☐ disorganized ☑ well-constructed sentences; author's style and words	☐ all story elements ☑ some story ele. ☐ few story ele. ☑ organized ☐ disorganized ☐ well-constructed _no_ sentences; author's style and words	☐ all story elements ☐ some story ele. ☑ few story ele. ☐ organized ☑ disorganized ☐ well-constructed _no_ sentences; author's style and words	☐ all story elements ☑ some story ele. ☐ few story ele. ☑ organized ☐ disorganized ☐ well-constructed _no_ sentences; author's style and words
SUMMARY STATEMENT	☑ adequate ☐ scanty	☑ adequate ☐ scanty	☐ adequate ☑ scanty	☐ adequate ☑ scanty	☐ adequate ☑ scanty
COMPREHENSION QUESTIONS RTR	☑ RTR from text adequate ☑ RTR from head to text adequate ☑ well-constructed sentences; matches author's vocab.	☑ RTR from text adequate ☑ RTR from head to text adequate ☑ well-constructed sentences; matches author's vocab.	☑ RTR from text adequate ☐ RTR from head _no_ to text adequate ☐ well-constructed sentences; matches author's vocab. _no_	☐ RTR from text adequate _no_ ☐ RTR from head _no_ to text adequate ☐ well-constructed sentences; matches author's vocab. _no_	☑ RTR from text adequate ☐ RTR from head _no_ to text adequate ☐ well-constructed sentences; matches author's vocab. _no_
EMOTIONAL STATUS	☑ relaxed/confident ☐ some stress ☐ high stress	☑ relaxed/confident ☐ some stress ☐ high stress	☐ relaxed/confident ☑ some stress ☐ high stress	☐ relaxed/confident ☐ some stress ☑ high stress	☐ relaxed/confident ☐ some stress ☑ high stress

In summary, at the independent level a reader demonstrates solid control over each factor. A reader feels confident and successful. At the instructional level control can be mixed; however, all too often when problems occur, most of the factors are affected. At the frustration level a reader loses control of all factors, and frustration shows up in the reader's emotional status. After studying this loss of control from independent to frustration, you can see why it is important to select appropriately leveled reading material for reading instruction.

Directions

Taking a Closer Look at the Scoring Guide Summary
Two Instructional Levels

15. Based upon the quantitative data included in the Scoring Guide Summary and the Qualitative Factors information, you should have determined the following:

> Form C: Level 1 Independent
> Form C: Level 2 Definite Instructional
> Form C: Level 3 Transitional Instructional
> Form C: Level 4 Frustration

17. A rule of thumb . . .
If the number of miscues exceeds the assigned number at the instructional level, but the comprehension question score, backed up by an excellent retelling, is clearly instructional—the level is determined from the comprehension information. The comprehension score tells if the reader is monitoring the meaning. If the reader is not monitoring the meaning, he or she is just calling words.

Directions

Talking Through the Data

5. Talk-Through for Case Study—Form C, Level 3, "Belonging to the Club"

Prior Knowledge/Prediction
Jenny had some prior knowledge (her mom belonged to a club). She made a logical prediction and after reading the first two sentences, she added more to her prediction.

Word Recognition
Oral Miscues # Miscues = 13 # Self-Corrections = 5 Cueing Systems
Jenny made 6 substitutions. Graphophonically she is noticing the initial letters of the words. All substitutions were syntactically acceptable, but semantically they changed the meaning. Jenny omitted 5 words, and made 1 insertion. Even though she has background knowledge, I wonder why she did not apply that knowledge to improve the word recognition and support comprehension.

Fluency
There was more word-by-word reading than at Level 2. Some repetitions were made because she was self-correcting. She used punctuation to divide text into meaningful units most of the time. The fluency improved toward the end of the passage. Rating = 3

Retelling/Summary
Her retelling contained some details, but was not thorough. She had most story elements represented in her retelling, but without complete details. The summary statement was adequate. It was difficult to assess the comparability of language to the author's because her retelling was so short.

Comprehension Questions

3½ wrong out of 8

The lack of details in her retelling showed up in comprehension question responses. Correct responses were mostly from the text—from head to text responses were not adequate. Many responses were in phrases.

Emotional Status

She was less confident than at Level 2. She seemed hurried, as if she read fast, her reading would improve.

6.

Component	NOTES Level 2 "The Busy Road"	NOTES Level 3 "Belonging to the Club"
Prior Knowledge/ Prediction	*some, useful prediction*	*some; useful prediction, but didn't use it much for word recognition and comprehension*

Word Recognition
   Oral Miscues
   Cueing Systems
	miscues = 6; 4 SC
	mostly substitutions; mostly CM
		miscues = 13 5 SC
		mostly substitutions; but more omissions and insertions; miscues mostly CM

Fluency	*Rating = 4*	*Rating = 3*
Retelling Summary Statement	*many details; logical order;* *in language of author*	*some details; some order; mostly in own language*
Comprehension Q.	*errors = 0 RTR = adequate*	*errors = 3½ RTR = almost inadequate used phrases*
Emotional Status	*confident*	*less confident, more stress*

Summary Statement

When the material gets harder, Jenny's reading deteriorates both quantitatively and qualitatively. One reason is that she fails to apply prior knowledge to recognize words and comprehend. As the number of miscues increases, the self-corrections decrease.

REFERENCES

References for Research and Instruction

ALLINGTON, R. C. (2001). *What really matters for struggling readers: Designing research-based programs.* Boston: Allyn & Bacon.

ANDERSON, W. W. (1977, December). Focus on measurement and evaluation—Commercial reading inventories: A comparative review. *Reading World,* 99–104.

ARMBRUSTER, B., LEHR, F., & OSBORN, J. (2001). *Put reading first: The research building blocks for teaching children to read, kindergarten through grade 3.* Rockville, MD: The Partnership for Reading: National Institute for Literacy, The National Institute of Child Health and Human Development, and the U.S. Department of Education.

BARR, R., & SADOW, M. (2004). *Reading diagnosis for teachers.* Boston: Allyn & Bacon.

BEERS, K. (2003). *When kids can't read, what teachers can do. A guide for teachers 6–12.* Portsmouth, NH: Heinemann.

BELDIN, H. O. (1970). Informal reading testing: Historical review and review of the research. W. Durr (Ed.), *Reading difficulties: Diagnosis, correction, and remediation.* Newark, DE: International Reading Association.

BIXBY, M., CRENSHAW, S., CROWLEY, P., GILLES, C., HENRICHS, M., PYLE, D., & WATERS, F. (1983). *Strategies that make sense: Invitations to literacy for secondary students.* Columbia, MO: Mid-Missouri TAWL.

BLACHOWICZ, C., & FISHER, P. (2002). *Teaching vocabulary in all classrooms* (2nd ed.). Upper Saddle River, NJ: Merrill/Prentice Hall.

BROZO, W. G., & SIMPSON, M. L. (2003). *Readers, teachers, learners: Expanding literacy in the secondary schools* (4th ed.). Upper Saddle River, NJ: Merrill/Prentice Hall.

CECIL, N. L. (1999). *Striking a balance: Positive practices for early literacy.* Scottsdale, AZ: Holcomb Hathaway.

CECIL, N. L., & GIPE, J. (2003). *Literacy in the intermediate grades: Best practices for a comprehensive program.* Scottsdale, AZ: Holcomb Hathaway.

COLLINS-CHEEK, M., & CHEEK, E. H. (1993). *Diagnostic-prescriptive reading instruction* (4th ed.). Dubuque, IA: Wm. C. Brown.

EHRI, L. C., NUNES, S. R., WILLOWS, D. M., SCHUSTER, B. V., YAGHOUB-ZADEH, Z., & SHANAHAN, T. (2001). Phonemic awareness instruction helps children learn to read: Evidence from the National Reading Panel's meta-analysis. *Reading Research Quarterly* (July/August/September), *36*, 250–287.

EKWALL, E. E. (1976a, April). Informal Reading Inventories: The instructional level. *The Reading Teacher, 29,* 662–665.

EKWALL, E. E. (1976b). *Diagnosis and remediation of the disabled reader.* Boston: Allyn & Bacon.

EKWALL, E. E., & SHANKER, J. L. (1993). *Diagnosis and remediation of the disabled reader* (3rd ed.). Needham Heights, MA: Allyn & Bacon.

FREIBERGER, R. (1973). *The New York Times report on teenage reading habits.* New York: New York Times Company Survey.

GAMBRELL, L., PFEIFFER, W., & WILSON, R. (1985). The effects of retelling upon reading comprehension and recall of text information. *Journal of Educational Research, 78,* 216–220.

GILLET, J. W., & TEMPLE, C. (2003). *Understanding reading problems* (6th ed.). Boston: Allyn & Bacon.

GIPE, J. P. (2005). *Multiple paths to literacy: Corrective reading techniques for the classroom teacher.* Upper Saddle River, NJ: Merrill/Prentice Hall.

GOODMAN, K. S. (ED.). (1973). *Miscue analysis: Application to reading instruction.* Urbana, IL: ERIC Clearinghouse on Reading and Communication Skills, National Council of Teachers of English.

GOODMAN, Y., & BURKE, C. (1976). *Reading miscue inventory manual: A procedure for diagnosis and evaluation.* New York: Macmillan.

HARRIS, A. J. (1976). Some new developments in readability. In J. E. Merritt (Ed.), *New horizons in reading.* Newark, DE: International Reading Association.

HARRIS, A. J., & JACOBSON, M. D. (1972). *Basic elementary reading vocabularies: The first R series.* New York: MacMillan.

HARVEY, S., & GOUDVIS, A. (2000). *Strategies that work: Teaching comprehension to enhance understanding.* Portland, ME: Stenhouse Publishers.

HASBROUCK, J. E., & TINDAL, G. (1992). Curriculum-based oral reading fluency norms for students in grades 2 through 5. *Teaching Exceptional Children, 24*(3), 41–44.

HEILMAN, A. W., BLAIR, T. R., & RUPLEY, W. H. (1998). *Principles and practices of teaching reading* (9th ed.). Upper Saddle River, NJ: Merrill/Prentice Hall.

HEILMAN, A. W., BLAIR, T. R., & RUPLEY, W. H. (2002). *Principles and practices of teaching reading* (10th ed.). Upper Saddle River, NJ: Merrill/Prentice Hall.

JACOBS, J. S., & TUNNELL, M. O. (2000). *Children's literature, briefly.* Upper Saddle River, NJ: Merrill/Prentice Hall.

JOHNS, JERRY L. (2001). *Basic reading inventory* (8th ed.). Dubuque, IA: Kendall/Hunt Publishing.

JOHNSON, M. S., & KRESS, R. A. (1965). *Informal reading inventories*. Newark, DE: International Reading Association.

KEENE, E. O., & ZIMMERMANN, S. (1997). *Mosaic of thought, teaching comprehension in a reader's workshop*. Portsmouth, NH: Heinemann.

KUJOTH, J. S. (1970). *Reading interests of children and young adults*. Metuchen, NJ: Scarecrow.

LESLIE, L., & CALDWELL, J. (2005). *Qualitative reading inventory—4*(4th ed.). Boston: Allyn & Bacon.

LEU, D. J., & KINZER, C. K. (2003). *Effective reading instruction K–8* (5th ed.). Upper Saddle River, NJ: Merrill/Prentice Hall.

MANZO, A., MANZO, U. C., & MCKENNA, M. C. (1995). *Informal reading-thinking inventory*. Fort Worth, TX: Harcourt Brace College Publisher.

MAY, F. B. (2006). *Reading as communication* (7th ed.). Upper Saddle River, NJ: Merrill/Prentice Hall.

MCCORMICK, S. (2003). *Instructing students who have literacy problems* (4th ed.). Upper Saddle River, NJ: Merrill/Prentice Hall.

MCGEE, L. M., & RICHGELLS, D. J. (1985, April). Teaching expository text structure to elementary students. *The Reading Teacher, 38,* 739–748.

MCLAUGHLIN, M., & ALLEN, M. B. (2002). *Guided comprehension, a teaching model for grades 3–8*. Newark, DE: International Reading Association.

MEYER, B. J. F., & FREEDLE, R. O. (1984). Effects of discourse type of recall. *American Educational Research Journal, 21,* 121–143.

MEYER, B. J. F., & RICE, G. E. (1984). The structure of text. In P. D. Pearson *Handbook of reading research*. New York: Longman.

MICRO POWER & LIGHT. (1995a). *Readability calculations*. Dallas, TX: Author.

MICRO POWER & LIGHT. (1995b). *Vocabulary assessor*. Dallas, TX: Author.

MORROW, L. M. (1988). Retelling stories as a diagnostic tool. In S. M. Glazer, *New trends and procedures* (pp. 128–149). Newark, DE: International Reading Association.

NATIONAL READING PANEL. (2000). *Report of the national reading panel: Reports of the subgroups*. Rockville, MD: National Institute of Child Health and Human Development Clearinghouse.

NESSEL, D. E. (1987). The new face of comprehension instruction: A close look at questions. *The Reading Teacher, 40,* 604–606.

NORTON, D. E. (2003). *Through the eyes of a child: An introduction to children's literature* (6th ed.). Upper Saddle River, NJ: Merrill/Prentice Hall.

PAPPAS, C. C. (1993). Is narrative "primary"? Some insights from kindergartners' pretend reading of stories and information books. *Journal of Reading Behavior, 25*(1), 97–129. Chicago: National Reading Conference.

PICCOLO, J. A. (1987, May). Expository text structure: Teaching and learning strategies. *The Reading Teacher, 40,* 838–847.

PIKULSKI, J. A. (1974, November). A critical review: Informal reading inventories. *The Reading Teacher, 28,* 141–151.

POWELL, W. R. (1970). Reappraising the criteria for interpreting informal reading inventories. In D. DeBour (Ed.), *Reading diagnosis and evaluation*. Newark, DE: International Reading Association.

POWELL, W. R., & DUNKELD, C. G. (1971, October). Validity of the IRI reading levels. *Elementary English, 48,* 637–642.

RAPHAEL, T. E. (1982). Teaching children question-answering strategies. *The Reading Teacher, 36,* 186–191.

RAPHAEL, T. E. (1986). Teaching question-answer relationships, revisited. *The Reading Teacher, 39,* 516–522.

Rasiniski, T., & Padak, N. (2004). *Holistic reading strategies: Teaching children who find reading difficult* (3rd ed.). Upper Saddle River, NJ: Merrill/Prentice Hall.

Reutzel, D. R., & Cooter, R. B. (2004). *Teaching children to read: From basals to books* (4th ed.). Upper Saddle River, NJ: Merrill/Prentice Hall.

Robb, L. (1995). *Reading strategies that work: Teaching your students to become better readers.* New York: Scholastic Professional Books.

Robb, L. (2000). *Teaching reading in the middle school.* New York: Scholastic Professional Books.

Robb, L. (2004). *Teaching reading, social studies, science, and math.* New York: Scholastic Professional Books.

Searfoss, L. W., & Readence, J. E. (2001). *Helping children learn to read: Creating a classroom literacy environment* (4th ed.). Boston: Allyn & Bacon.

Shanker, J. (2003). *Locating and correcting reading difficulties* (8th ed.). Upper Saddle River, NJ: Merrill/Prentice Hall.

Short, K. G., Harste, J. C., & Burke, C. (1995). *Creating classrooms for authors and inquirers.* Portsmouth, NH: Heinemann.

Short, K. G., & Pierce, K. M. (1990). *Talking about books: Creating literate communities.* Portsmouth, NH: Heinemann.

Spache, G. D. (1981). *Diagnosing and correcting reading disabilities* (2nd ed.). Boston: Allyn & Bacon.

Sutherland, Z., & Arbuthnot, M. H. (1972). *Children and books* (9th ed.). New York: Longman.

Tanyzer, H., & Karl, J. (1972). *Reading children's books and our pluralistic society.* Newark, DE: International Reading Association.

Tompkins, G. E. (2003). *Literacy for the 21st century: A balanced approach* (3rd ed.). Upper Saddle River, NJ: Merrill/Prentice Hall.

Tovani, C. (2000). *I read it, but I don't get it, comprehension strategies for adolescent readers.* Portland, MA: Stenhouse.

Tuinman, J. J. (1971, February). Asking reading-dependent questions. *Journal of Reading, 14,* 289–292, 336.

Vacca, R. T., & Vacca, J. L. (2004). *Content area reading: Literacy and learning across the curriculum* (8th ed.). Boston: Allyn & Bacon.

Valmont, W. J. (1972, March). Creating questions for informal reading inventories. *The Reading Teacher, 25,* 509–512.

Vygotsky, L. (1978). *Mind and society.* Cambridge, MA: Harvard University Press.

Walker, B. J. (2004). *Diagnostic teaching of reading: Techniques for instruction and assessment* (5th ed.). Upper Saddle River, NJ: Merrill/Prentice Hall.

Zutell, J. (1988). Developing a procedure for assessing oral reading fluency establishing validity and reliability. Reprinted in: Walker, B. J. (1996). *Diagnostic teaching of reading: techniques for instruction and assessment* (3rd ed.). Upper Saddle River, NJ: Merrill/Prentice Hall (1996).

References for Web Sites
Standards for English Language Arts

Indiana's Academic Standards, http://www.doe.state.in.us/standards/grade_te.html

Mid-continent Research for Education and Learning, http://www.mcrel.org/compendium/

National Council of Teachers of English, http://www.ncte.org/about/over/standards/110846.htm

References for Content of Narrative and Expository Passages

ABRAMOWITZ, L. H., & ABRAMOWITZ, J. (1981). *The United States: People and leaders.* Cleveland, OH: Modern Curriculum Press.

ANDERSON, J., & ANCONA, G. (1993). *Earth keepers.* New York: Harcourt Brace.

BORSTEIN, L. (1975, July 31). Woman drag racer after speed record. *Christian Science Monitor, Midwestern Edition.*

BURNFORD, S. (1961). *The incredible journey.* Boston: Little, Brown.

CONE, M., & WHEELWRIGHT, S. (1992). *Come back, salmon: How a group of dedicated kids adopted Pigeon Creek and brought it back to life.* San Francisco: Sierra Club Books for Children.

DREWERY, H. N., & O'CONNOR, T. H. (1987). *America is.* Woodland, CA: Glencoe/McGraw-Hill.

GENTRY, J. (1973, January). How one town solves pollution and saves water. *The PlainTruth: A Magazine of Understanding,* 30–35.

HABER, L. (1970). *Black pioneers of science and invention.* New York: Harcourt Brace Jovanovich.

HEIMLER, C. H. (1986). *Principles of science.* Woodland Hills, CA: Glencoe/McGraw-Hill Publishing.

HENRY, M. (1972). *Justin Morgan had a horse.* New York: Rand McNally.

HINTON, S. E. (1969). *The outsiders.* New York: Viking Press.

MCKAY, R. (1969). *Dave's song.* New York: Meredith Press.

MOYER, R. H., & BISHOP, J. E. (1986). *Merrill general science.* Woodland, CA: Glencoe/McGraw-Hill.

SMITH, R. (1974). *The Lincoln library of sports champions,* Vol. 12 (pp. 32–35). Columbus, OH: Sports Resources.

Sportswomanlike conduct. (1974, June 3). *Newsweek,* 50–55.

SUND, R. B., ADAMS, D. K., HACKETT, J. K., & MOYER, R. H. (1985). *Accent on science.* New York, NY: McGraw-Hill.